NAZI SABOTEURS
on the BAYOU

by

STEVEN BURGAUER

NAZI SABOTEURS
on the BAYOU

© Steven Burgauer 2016

Battleground Press
Oxford, Florida

FOR FURTHER INFORMATION:

steven.burgauer@gmail.com
http://sites.google.com/site/stevenburgauer/

ISBN 978-0692808122 (sc)
ISBN 978-1370981212 (e)

"God, will I ever be able to expunge that wretched monster from my memory?"

PFC Robert DeGise, writing seventy years after the Battle of Iwo Jima, and without whose help this book might never have been written.

"I have been in the Marine Corps now forty years as an officer, and I say that I have never taken part in maneuvers where I thought we were landing in any craft superior to the Higgins Eureka boat."

U.S. Marine Corps General E.P Moses, September 13, 1942, on the occasion of presenting to Andrew Jackson Higgins the Army-Navy "E," the highest award for production excellence that the armed services could bestow upon a private company. Higgins was applauded by the military for taking ten thousand untrained workers and turning them into some of the finest boat builders in the world. The pennant was hoisted to the top of the flagstaff by soldiers of the Amphibian Command, many of whom were enrolled as students at the Higgins Boat Operators School.

Author's Note —

Despite repeated requests under the Freedom of Information Act, the United States Department of Defense and the Central Intelligence Agency continue to claim that none of what follows actually happened . . .

THURSDAY
JULY 30, 1942
2 a.m.

French Quarter, New Orleans

"Quick, empty de man's pockets."

The speaker was a woman, Kentucky Rose, a colored prostitute working out of Lulu White's once-beautiful whorehouse on Basin Street in New Orleans.

"We cain't be seen doin' this," said the man helping her. Hector was a light-skinned black man. Lulu White, founder of the brothel, was his mother, now dead.

"Come on now, hurry," Kentucky Rose said, her chest heaving with anxiety.

Hector quickly crossed himself in the manner of a Catholic. "Man dies in a woman's bed. How dat not be bad *juju*?"

Kentucky Rose instinctively reached for her *gris-gris* charm. The voodoo queen who sold it to her said the amulet would help protect her from evil spirits.

"See whether he gots any money on him," she said, stroking the amulet. "Bad *juju* or not, we gots to d'spose of de body. We gots to move de corpse 'fore it starts to smell, 'fore anyone notices his cracker white ass be missin' and come lookin' for him."

"Dis peckerwood be big. Moving him ain't gonna be no easy thing, no which way."

"Damn it, Hector. Pull off his shirt an' pants. Vest too. Drag him by de arms 'cross de room. Stuff his hairy white ass into dat footlocker 'side my closet."

Hector rolled the big man onto his left side, slid one fat arm out of his shirt and vest, no easy task. The vest was snug and close-fitting around the dead man's chest and torso. It was threadbare and had surely seen better days. Four silver buttons ran down the front of the garment, where once there had been five. The four remaining buttons were all badly tarnished.

"Who dis peckerwood be anyways?" Hector took hold of the white man's hand, slipped a large ornate ring off his fourth finger and slid it into his pants pocket.

"I don't take no names an' 'dresses, you know dat."

"Spill it, Rose. Who de hell he be?"

"Some old German. De man was half-drunk when he gots here. Could barely get de ugly thing up. Mumbled somethin' about beings aristocracy."

"What be air-oh-stock-krissy?"

"I don't know. A duke or earl or some business like dat. Now get dat button-down vest off him already."

Hector did as he was told, then leaned down to unzip the big man's pants.

"Thar be somethin' in his pocket," he said.

"Probably some dosh. Pocket de dough and let's get a move-on."

"Not money, I don't think. It be sewn into de lining of his vest."

"A letter from home perhaps. I 'member now. Cracker said he was a baron. Baron von Brock, or some business like dat."

Hector pulled out his pocketknife and sliced open the lining of the big man's vest. A slender book fell out of the lining and onto the floor.

"Told you weren't no money."

"Must be important, though. Why else sew de soddy thing into de lining?"

"We never gonna be able to stuff this big boy into dat tiny footlocker of yorn, Rose. We needs a steamer trunk or somethin' even bigger. And evens if we do manage to stuff this lard butt in there, de two of us cain't possibly haul dat footlocker down dem stairs and out into the alley with his fat ass rolled up inside."

By now, Kentucky Rose had the small book in her hand and was trying to read its pages. But reading was not a strong point with her. She never finished grammar school.

"You had any book learnin'?" she asked.

"Same as you, prob'ly less."

"Well take a look-see at dis. This be no language I never seen."

Hector grabbed the book from Rose's hand and looked closely at its contents. He shook his head. "This not English. Ain't no French Creole neither."

"What den?"

"You said he be a Heinie Kraut. Maybe dis here writin' be German."

"So you sayin' dis could be some silly German novel or cookbook or somethin'. A family Bible?"

"I don't think so. Look at 'dese drawings. Maps and such." Hector opened the book to a crude map that looked much like nearby Lake Pontchartrain and the city of New Orleans with some landmarks marked on it.

"Maybe this be one of dem travel guidebooks," Kentucky Rose offered. "Negroes gots dem so dey kin travel 'round de country safely. *Negro Green Book*, or some business like dat. Petunia dun tol' me 'bout it. Plus white folk gots dem books too. *N'Orleans City Guide*. Lady Belle gots a copy hidden 'way somewhere. Signed by de mayor, it is. Said he gave it to her. In exchange for favors, I reckon. Belle said it be written by some newspaper people back afore de war. I seen it once. Big old thing. Colorful cover. Confed'rit soldier on a fancy horse, some business like dat. Maybe dat be what dis be, some sorta travel guidebook for Heinie Krauts. He may have used it to find his way here, to our place. We be listed in de *Blue Book*."

Hector shook his head. "This not be like no *Blue Book* I ever seen." He looked more closely at the map. "De brothel not be marked on here. But de Eureka Tugboat Comp'ny is. Dat be Master Higgins shop. I worked there as a boy, same as mon Pappy. Naval station be marked on here too."

"So what you saying? Dis big fat dead guy be some sorta German spy?"

"Well, there be a war on, you know dat, right? Pearl's Harbor was attacked last December. We bin helping de Frogs and de Limeys for quite a spell now. Gov'nor 'a Lou'sana say de Germans and we now be mort-all enemies."

"What would this peckerwood be doing here, at Lulu's Mahog'ny Hall? Why would he give a fig 'bout dem Higgins boats? Dem boats be used in de bayou for runnin' rum, not fer rowin' 'cross the 'lantic."

"I think we oughts to give dis here book to Nico," Hector said, fingering the large ornate ring in his pocket.

"Our Nico? Nico Carolla?"

"Who else? Carolla mob own dis here brothel. They owns all de brothels dis side of town. Carlos took over dis one after Momma died."

"But what if'n dis dead Heinie be a friend of Nico's? What if'ns he were a fren'a Nico's gramps, Silver Dollar Sam? What den? Nico gonna be royally pissed. Carolla family might blame me for de man's death," Kentucky Rose said, anxious again. "Don't you never forget. Nico's brother be a lawman, a sheriff or marshal or some business like dat."

"If'n de two rilly be brothers."

"What you sayin'?" Kentucky Rose asked. "O'course dey be brothers."

"Some say Nico be a bastard child, dat he an' Earl Ray not even be related."

"Don't you never let Nico hear you talk dat way. Call de man a bastard an' he gonna cut out your tongue, if'n he don't kill you first."

"My lips be sealed. Even so, if Nico and Earl Ray are brothers, dey cain't be dat close. Earl Ray don't even use Carolla as a last name no more. Goes by Mackerel now, Earl Ray Mackerel. Dem boys say he be raised by foster parents after his momma passed. De street people now calls him de Big Fish."

"But Earl Ray still be de law. He gonna put me in de klink for sure. He gonna think I killed dis here peckerwood. I gots nothin' to prove diff'rent."

"Don't matter," Hector said. "We dump de body in Pontch'train. But we gives de book to Nico. He gonna know what to do with it."

"If'n you say so. He be comin' 'round here in de morning, same as always. Takes his mornin' walk in City Park reg'lar as clock's work, den shows up here 'bout eight o'clock to collect de previous day's take an' pay de girls. Every day de same."

"Good. Dat be jus' six hours from now. We gives it to him den."

THURSDAY
JULY 30, 1942
7:45 a.m.

Bayou La Croix, Mississippi (northeast of New Orleans)

"My man missed his window. I never got his call."

The speaker was Sebastian Grimm, a young captain in the Waffen-SS, a branch of the German Army under the direct authority of *Reichsführer* Heinrich Himmler. Grimm's youth and freckled complexion sometimes led others to underestimate his abilities. But that would be a mistake. When circumstances dictated, Grimm could be as tough and mean and ruthless as any highly-trained infantryman. Otherwise, he maintained a veneer of cool detachment.

The sun was barely up. But even at this early hour, the still morning air hung heavy with the sounds of buzzing insects and the cruel weight of oppressive humidity. It was the end of July and, aside from August, no month was hotter or more unpleasant in the Deep South. Sebastian Grimm was sweating profusely from every pore. The heat and humidity were simply overwhelming.

Captain Grimm fanned himself slowly with an improvised hand fan. He had fashioned it from a large, slightly rounded piece of tree bark he found earlier this morning on the grounds of the rented bayou house.

Grimm could not fathom such heat, not in the early morning, not at any point of any day. Such conditions were unknown in Germany, indeed anywhere in northern Europe. *What he wouldn't have given for a simple electric fan.* Not that it would have done him any good in this disgusting backwater hovel. Electricity had not yet arrived in this desolate and ugly corner of the world, an unanticipated source of discomfort to both men as they tried to cope with the heat.

The second man in the room was a senior German diplomat newly arrived at this location. His name was Günter Kesselring. The car he drove was an unusually nice one for these parts, a Custom Super Eight Packard purchased for his use by a loyal industrialist in Baton Rouge.

After passing through several hands to hide its provenance, the Packard was delivered to Kesselring the day before yesterday by Rudyard Pfingsten, a leading citizen of a predominantly German community located just west of the city of New Orleans. Pfingsten had warned him that to keep its monthly fuel ration allotment the Packard would soon have to be registered with the state's newly organized motor vehicle department. With the advent of war, car manufacture had ceased in the United States five months ago. Now only doctors and clergymen were permitted to purchase new automobiles still held in inventory by dealers.

The senior man began to pace anxiously, his treasured meerschaum pipe in hand. It was unlit and not yet stuffed with smoking tobacco.

In short order, Kesselring came to stand beside Grimm in the backwash of the bark fan as Grimm moved it to and fro. He slowly air-dried the beads of sweat from his hands in the moving air.

"Why don't you give me that fan so I can cool myself?" Kesselring suddenly demanded.

"Go find your own piece of bark, you lazy fool."

"*Unverschämt schwein.* Impertinent bastard."

The windows of the small bayou house were wide open. But inviting in the outside air did not improve matters. The intensity of heat inside the house and the level of humidity remained unchanged.

The stagnant air was drenching hot and dripping wet. Being soaked in sweat was becoming an everpresent state for these men. *And the smells?* Oh, my. The banks of the nearby bayou were slathered in mud, hot sticky yellow mud. When the afternoon rains came, as they did nearly every day this time of year, fish got washed onto the banks and soon became hopelessly entangled in the overgrowth. Then, when the high waters receded, the dead fish rotted in the blazing sun.

The heat was oppressive, the air heavy and thick with humidity and alive with the sounds of bullfrogs and flying insects. Cypress trees ringed the house, each draped in a curtain of Spanish Moss, each a home to unseen animals at night.

"I do not like this place," Kesselring said.

"Nor do I," Grimm replied. "It was not my choice. Pfingsten made the arrangements before I even arrived."

"Can we agree never to meet here in this place again?"

"Yes. Before our next meeting, I will find someplace better. Maybe a place with electricity and running water."

Kesselring looked nervously at his pocket watch, studied the carved bowl of his smoking pipe, then said, "Your man Heinrich. Has he ever missed his window before?"

"Günter, please. We are in America now. In this country we speak English. In this country, Heinrich Brock goes by the name Henry," the younger man said.

What Sebastian Grimm lacked in authority he made up for in arrogance. He both feared and loathed Günter Kesselring, and with good reason on both counts. The older man had no business being here in the United States. In fact, he would never have been in the United States at all, if not for the influence of his father, General Field Marshal Albert Kesselring.

"Fine," Kesselring said, contemplating the empty smoking pipe. "Then let me rephrase. Has your man Henry ever missed his window before?"

"Yes, once before. But on that occasion, he checked in with us by radio about two hours later. He had been mixing it up with a colored woman in a local whorehouse and lost track of time. Or at least that is what he said when Pfingsten and I interrogated him afterwards. It never happened again until today."

"How long has your man Henry been out of touch?"

The older man stuffed his meerschaum pipe with aromatic tobacco and proceeded to light the contents of the bowl with a wooden match. He loved this pipe. It had been a gift from his father, the Field Marshal. Now, pipe in mouth, Günter Kesselring looked the part of the senior diplomat that he actually was. It was illegal for him to be in this country. The United States and Nazi Germany had broken off diplomatic relations at the outbreak of the war.

"Henry has been dark for three days now."

"*Was ist die bedeutung von* 'dark'?"

"It means silent or out-of-touch."

"Oh, yes, I see. Dark. Good word," Kesselring said. "We must notify Oberst Richter that your man has gone dark, as you say."

"English, please."

"As if the Americans would not line us up against a wall and shoot us dead if we got caught."

The younger man frowned and pawed through a metal strongbox filled with manila file folders marked TOP SECRET in German. He found the one he wanted and pulled it out.

"Fine. English it is," Kesselring said. "We must notify Colonel Richter at Waffen-SS Headquarters of the delay. Oberst Richter insists on regular updates, you know that. This Higgins business has become a big issue with Himmler and with Göring. Our orders come from the highest levels. Göring believes these landing boats could win the war for the Americans. We must interrupt their production at all cost."

"I am well aware of our orders, Herr Kesselring. *Stören und Zerstören.* Disrupt and Destroy. Those are our orders, and sabotage is our mission. It is the mission of all our teams. *Stören und Zerstören.*"

"How dare you use that arrogant tone with me."

"My tone has nothing at all to do with it, Kesselring. Do as you must. If you feel the need to contact Colonel Richter, then by all means please do so. I cannot stop you, nor will I try. But I am under orders of my own. The job Himmler has given me is quite different from your own. I need to find my man, Henry Brock."

"And where will you look for him?" Günter Kesselring puffed on his pipe. Circles of smoke billowed skyward. He pulled out his metal pipe tool and gently tamped down the thatch of burning tobacco in the bowl.

Captain Grimm looked on with uncharacteristic envy. A fine meerschaum pipe, rich in color from years of use, was an unmistakable symbol of status.

Meerschaum was a soft and relatively rare mineral. It was sometimes found floating in the waters of the Black Sea. Easy to carve, much prized by pipe smokers for its porosity, valuable on account of its relative scarcity.

Meerschaum hardened upon exposure to solar heat or when dried in a warm room. In the hands of a skilled craftsman, a rough block of meerschaum could be bored out to fashion the bowl for an exquisite smoking pipe, then the exterior of the bowl carved with sharp tools to render the likeness of a sea captain, perhaps, or the face and bosom of a beautiful woman.

Kesselring found deep satisfaction in Grimm's envious look. To know that he possessed something another man coveted made Kesselring feel powerful.

In its natural state, the soft mineral resembled sea-foam, hence the German origin for its name. "Foam of the sea."

Meerschaum. The porous nature of the material drew moisture and tobacco tar into the stone, allowing a man a dry, cool, and flavorful smoke. Over time, as a meerschaum pipe was smoked, it would gradually change color. Older meerschaums would turn incremental shades of yellow, orange, red, and amber beginning with the base and moving up. The bowl of Kesselring's meerschaum pipe was nearly fire-red from years of use.

"Where in the city will you look for him?" Kesselring repeated his earlier question.

Grimm put aside his envy. "Ever since Henry Brock was a young man, he has made it a habit to frequent whorehouses or else get sex on the street."

"*Bordsteinschwalben?*"

"Crudely put. But yes. Curbside swallow. It is in his file. He did so regularly in France during the Great War. Then, after the war, when he settled in New Jersey, he was known to frequent the red-light district in Atlantic City. It is what led to his divorce. Following his divorce, he moved here, to New Orleans, a city known for its *hurenhaus*. There is an area of the city where brothels were once legal and prostitution is still tolerated. The locals call it Storyville. Along Basin Street, just east of the French Quarter."

"Yes, I have read of it in this book of yours," the diplomat said, motioning to the fat volume on the table.

"It has been useful, that book," Grimm said. "The *New Orleans City Guide*. It was supplied to me as part of my training package. Five hundred pages. Every detail there is to know about the city. Churches. Restaurants. Museums. Dance halls. Street cars. Everything. That Jew-lover Roosevelt hired thousands of out-of-work authors and university professors to write these city guides to many American cities."

"Yes, yes. It was in my briefing packet as well. Mahogany Hall. House of whores. *Das Hurenhaus*. Basin Street is quite famous for such establishments. Mahogany Hall even more so. I have seen the fancy brochures these scum, these *abschaum der Erde* hand around. The *Blue Book*. They are filled with pictures that advertise their exotic women and the crude services these women perform. All photographed by that Jew Bellocq."

"I must object, dear sir. E.J. Bellocq is no Jew. The man is French Creole, and quite talented with a camera."

"Jew? Creole? What is the difference? They are all mutts."

"E.J. Bellocq is no mutt," the younger man protested. "He is white and comes from a wealthy family. John Ernest Joseph

Bellocq. That is his full name. His brother is a Jesuit priest. Bellocq has assembled an amazing collection of photographs. Landmarks. Sailing ships. Machinery. Also a collection of high quality nudes. Women from the Storyville area. That place — Mahogany Hall — has quite the history. One of a handful of high-end brothels on Basin Street. At one time it was run by Lulu White. But no longer. Now the Sicilian mob has seized control of it, along with several other brothels. But in its day, Mahogany Hall was known as a sumptuous Octoroon Parlor. It reportedly cost forty thousand dollars to build — an unimaginable sum at the time. It housed forty women."

"You sound like you are in love, Sebastian. What do you plan to do? Go door to door looking for our lost whoremonger?"

"Yes, if I have to. Every last whorehouse in the city is listed in the *Blue Book*, even the cribs. But there is a man I am familiar with who might be able to help me track down Brock. A policeman."

"*Polizist?*"

"Yes, a police officer, one with ties to the Sicilian mob. Goes by the name of Earl Ray Mackerel."

"I prefer we not bring the Gestapo into this, certainly not a brown shirt with sticky fingers." Günter Kesselring's tone was filled with derision.

"I really don't think the man's fingers are sticky. Anyway, this is America. These sorts of men are police, not Gestapo. There may be no other way."

"Let me see Brock's file," Günter Kesselring ordered, pointing to the file folder in Grimm's hand. It was stamped top-secret in red letters: STRENG GEHEIM.

"If you insist." Waffen-SS Captain Sebastian Grimm handed the other man a manila folder that was labeled:

Baron Heinrich von Brockdorff

"Ah, yes. The Baron," Kesselring said, paging through the contents of the file.

"Is that on the level?"

"Is what on the level?"

"The barony."

"Oh, yes. Our man Brock is the genuine article. Or at least he once was. Baron Heinrich von Brockdorff. Veteran of the Great War. Outcast from the German noble family of the same name.

Father tossed him out of the family for consorting with a Jewess. Now a naturalized American citizen. In the States, he goes by the name of Henry Brock. With the loss of his nobility, Henry has become an enemy of the ancient barony system."

"Which is what makes the man a natural ally of The Führer."

"Yes. That is precisely how and why we recruited him," Günter Kesselring said. "That plus the promise of a handsome reward."

"According to his dossier, Henry had several children by that same Jewess," Grimm said. "He has one grandson that we know of. Russell Brock. An American serviceman now serving in the Pacific. A United States Marine."

The diplomat shook his head in disgust. "The Japanese should never have attacked Pearl Harbor. This was unexpected and inconvenient. The attack forced Hitler's hand. Under the Tripartite Pact, Germany promised help if Japan was attacked. But Germany had no such obligation should Japan be the aggressor."

"So why did The Führer go before the Reichstag last December and declare war on the United States, when he did not have to? It was one of the last times the Reichstag met. Why bring the Americans into the war, when it was not necessary? It seems a mistake to me," Grimm said.

"You dare question The Führer?"

"Not in so many words, but yes. Everyone knows that von Ribbentrop advised against a declaration of war against the Americans."

Kesselring sucked pensively on his pipe. "Yes, I know von Ribbentrop well. German Foreign Minister Joachim von Ribbentrop. He had tried to make the case to The Führer that the addition of another antagonist, the United States, would overwhelm the German war effort. But The Führer thought otherwise. By then, the U.S. Navy was already attacking German U-boats in the water. Plus, The Führer despised President Roosevelt for his repeated verbal attacks on Nazi ideology. Hitler continues to believe that once Japan has defeated the Americans that Japan will turn west and help Germany defeat the Russians."

"*Wunschdenken.* Wishful thinking. *Ein wunschtraum.* A pipe dream. Can we trust the slant-eyed heathens to honor the agreement, the Pact?"

"No, we cannot." Kesselring shook his head. "I was there that day, in the Reichstag, the day of Hitler's speech. Göring sat in his usual spot. December 11, 1941. Hitler addressed the Reichstag to defend the declaration of war against the United States. He said the failure of Roosevelt's New Deal was the real cause of the war. He said that with the support of American plutocrats and the Jews that Roosevelt has attempted to cover-up the collapse of his economic agenda. Roosevelt incites war, Hitler said, then Roosevelt falsifies the causes and wraps himself odiously in a cloak of Christian hypocrisy that slowly but surely leads the world to war. Hitler's very words. When he was done, the Reichstag leapt to its feet in thunderous applause."

"Hitler wouldn't have it any other way."

"Derision for The Führer?"

"Maybe just a little," Grimm admitted. "You know what the people say, don't you?"

"No, what do the people say?"

"The people sometimes call the Reichstag the *teuerste Gesangsverein Deutschlands.*"

Kesselring chuckled, then caught himself. "The most expensive singing club in Germany?"

"Yes, due to the frequent singing of the national anthem during sessions."

"Captain Grimm, you best keep that seditious thought to yourself, yes?"

"Yes, of course. We are all agreed. The Fatherland will prevail; it must prevail. Our job here in the United States is to help ensure the Fatherland's inevitable victory. Now that America has entered the war, Henry Brock is an integral part of that plan."

"This man who fucks Jews and sleeps *mit huren?* Such a man is an integral part of our plan?"

"We fight the war with the soldiers we are given, Herr Kesselring. It is not necessary that we like them, only that we can work with them. What I must do now is to find him, Brock. Brock himself must take personal delivery of the explosives."

"What sort of explosives?" Kesselring asked.

"RDX."

Kesselring answered with a blank stare.

"Yes, I have forgotten. You have no training. You are not a soldier. RDX. Hexogen. A form of explosive that can be molded by hand. Individually wrapped satchels of *plastiksprengstoff.* The explosives necessary to carry out the demolition will be arriving onshore shortly. They are to be delivered to a location not far from here. We have no choice now but to see this thing through to the end."

"And I must radio headquarters. You have a wireless, yes?"

"Open that closet door. The wireless is inside." Sebastian Grimm pointed across the front room of the rented bayou house.

"Yes, and I will also need the code phrase for the day."

"Let me pull out the book. Ah, yes . . . here it is . . . three words . . . BEAUT KRAUT EGO. You must transmit the three code words in precisely that order. And while you're at it, don't forget to put that *von Brockdorff* file back in the box along with the rest of them."

"I suppose we will need to take the strongbox along with us in the boot of the Packard when we leave."

"Not boot," Grimm corrected. "Trunk. An American car has a trunk with a lid in the rear, not a boot."

Kesselring grunted his disapproval at having been once again corrected by this lesser man. Like so many Germans attached to the diplomatic corps, Kesselring had learned his English in Great Britain between the wars, not in America. Certain everyday British words like "boot" would sound strange to an American ear.

"In the trunk then, you impertinent weasel," he said.

Grimm ignored the other man's slur. "Yes, in the trunk. But after you have finished with the wireless, we simply must find a safer place than the trunk of an American automobile to secure our box of secret files."

**THURSDAY
JULY 30, 1942
7:58 a.m.**

"Little Palermo," French Quarter, New Orleans

Nico Carolla was built like a tank, wide at the shoulders, solid through the middle, with strong arms and thick legs. He would win no beauty contests, not with that scar running down his left cheek.

Nor was Nico Carolla a man to be taken lightly. When Nico Carolla gave an order, he expected it to be obeyed down to the last detail. Sometimes he had to enforce his will with the small pistol he carried with him in his pocket, a .25 caliber *Bernardelli* semi-automatic. Most times, a stern order and a fierce look would suffice.

"I am not at all happy with this week's receipts."

Those were the first words out of Nico Carolla's mouth after he entered the brothel and took a seat at the table in the back room. Nico's personal bodyguard, Luca, stood at his side. Before them stood Hector, hands in his pockets and slouching. Lady Belle, the madam, would join them shortly.

"I am not happy with this week's receipts," Nico said again. "Nor those of the week before. I am warning you, Hector. I better not find that someone in this house has had his hand in the till. Hands with sticky fingers can be easily removed. We take them off at the wrist with a hack saw."

Hector stiffened at the threat. Nico's penchant for violence was legend. The entire Carolla family had the same violent reputation. Sylvestro, Nico's grandfather, shot and killed a federal narcotics agent during an undercover drug bust ten years ago. It bought him two years behind bars. Nico's father died in a gunfight.

"No, Nico," the smaller black man said nervously. "No one be robbing you. I promise. Mah hand not been in no till, not now, not never." Hector's eyes darted rapidly between Nico and Nico's bodyguard. Luca was often the source of whatever pain Nico dished out.

"Well, I can see that your hand has been somewhere, Hector. *Che cazzo?* How did you come to have that fancy ring you are wearing? You pinch it off someone?"

Hector's face turned white, at least as white as any black man's face could turn. It worried him when Nico started using funny-sounding words he didn't understand. "Well . . . I . . . well you see . . . "

"Hector, I do not enjoy being lied to. Especially not by some Negro. I have cut off a man's hand for less. I have cut off his zibb just to make a point."

"I likes both mah hands — and mah zibb. I ain't stealing from you, Nico. Nots from you. Nots from your family. Nots from anyone. Your father paid mah moms a fair price for de place. No skimming goin' on here, not by me, not by anyones else. Receipts are down 'cause de law be squeezing all the houses. City be wantin' every last one of dem closed."

"Yeah, people like my brother Earl Ray want it both ways. American police are different from the Carabinieri back home. But once a fascist, always a fascist."

"I knows you told me once before. But where be home again?"

"Monreale."

"Dat be in Alabama?"

"Monreale. It is a village in Sicily. Near Palermo. On the north coast of the island."

Nico found such discussions boring and tedious. He had an agile mind which easily outshone the light of the dim bulbs he had to work with each day. When Hector answered his explanation with a blank stare, Nico just sighed. "Sicily. It is a large island off the coast of Italy. In the south of Europe."

"At least you knows from where you come. Most us colored folk don't even knows from where our family come."

"All Negroes the same. Came to the Americas as slaves from Africa. My people don't knuckle under so easily. *Madre di Dio.* Mother of God. A Sicilian man would never allow himself to be captured and sold into slavery. A Sicilian man would rather die first."

"Abraham Lincoln freed de slaves. I be a free man. I belongs to no one."

"Free in name only," Nico observed. Luca, still standing beside him, smirked and nodded his head. He wore a shoulder holster beneath his arm. It bulged with the weight of a revolver, a Colt .38 Special.

"All men be slaves in some way, Mistah Carolla. Even important men like your own self."

"You a philosopher now?"

"Just sayin' . . . "

"Negroes not like Sicilians, Hector. We were hunted by the Fascists in the old country. Here in America the *famigghia* have had to muscle their way into every one of our businesses. The Matranga family was the first to settle in this area. Carlos and Antonio. They adopted American names. Charles and Tony. The two brothers set up shop here in New Orleans more than a generation ago. Ulysses S. Grant was still President at the time. The brothers Matranga opened a saloon and a brothel."

"But you be Mafia, not no simple tenant farmer."

"*Merda*. You calling me a criminal?"

"I call you no such thing, Nico. But people talk. They say you be in organized crime."

Nico laughed. "Crime is many things, Hector. But organized, it is not. Back in the day, the two Matranga brothers had running feuds with all the other Sicilian families."

"The Provenzano family? I heard tell 'bout a big fight. I think mah moms told me. There was a fight. Down by the docks."

"You must separate the corn from the cob, Hector. Even Davy Crockett has a legend, and some of it is true."

"But your legend actually be true. We all hears things 'round here, things de families be into. Extortion. Bootlegging. Labor rackets. Dat be how Matranga brothers did business. They collected tribute from Dago laborers. Also from slow-minded dockworkers. Also from the rival Provenzano crime family."

"Now that is a word I do not like."

"What word?" Hector asked fearfully.

"Dago. I do not ever want to hear that dirty word come out of your mouth again. *Capiche?* Never again."

"Yes, sir." Hector nodded slowly as Nico continued with his story.

"The part about the Provenzanos may be true," Nico said. "At one time the Provenzano family held nearly total control over commercial fruit shipments coming into port from South America. Carlos and Antonio began to move in on Provenzano fruit-loading operations. They threatened the Provenzanos with violence. Killed a few of them. Eventually, the Provenzanos withdrew and gave the

Matrangas a cut of the waterfront rackets. Later, the Provenzanos pushed back. By the late 1880s, the two families had gone to war over the grocery and produce businesses. Each side employed large numbers of Sicilian *Mafiosi* from their native Monreale. The war was large enough to draw the attention of outsiders, including the local *polizia*. Before long, the police chief of New Orleans got involved. His name was Hennessy, David Hennessy."

"Dat be one story mah moms never told me. Mah dads neither. Mon Pappy worked for Master Higgins back in de day, he did. I was just a boy. In dem days, the boat plant on City Park Av'nue next to the Trades School was much smaller than tis today. Mon Pappy worked on the loading dock. I play'd in the fact'ry yard. I watched him whilst he worked. Mon Pappy and dis other fella took plywood planks off de railcar. Drilled holes in the planks. Bolted dem to dese crossbeams. Fastened dem together to makes seats and floors of dem older Higgins boats. First the *Wonder* boat; later the *Eureka* boat. When dey were assembled, dem boys would put the finished boats on a railcar and bring dem over to Bayou St. John where they would drops dem in de bayou, get dem wet and drive dem out onto Lake Pontch'train."

"You done interrupting me, boy?" Nico asked impatiently. "Where is Lady Belle anyway? She should have been here by now."

"You want I should go look for her, Boss?" Luca asked, eager to be helpful.

"Yes, do that. I have better things to do with my time than stand here and yack with this colored boy all day."

Hector took no offense. "Why not tells me de rest'a your story whiles we waits fer Belle?"

Yes, yes. Now where was I? Oh, yes, Police Chief Hennessy. It was late summer. The year was 1890. Hennessy began investigating the two warring organizations, the Matrangas and the Provenzanos. But the man's investigation did not last long. Hennessy was shot dead one night, killed while walking home alone. This is how those sorts of problems had always been dealt with in the old country. Any government official stupid enough to get in the way of the Sicilian Mafia ended up dead, usually face-down in a roadside ditch." Nico used his index finger to figuratively slit his own throat.

Nico Carolla continued. "But America at the turn of the century was different from Sicily. The murder of Police Chief Hennessey created a huge backlash from the city. Charles and several members of the Matranga family were arrested. They were put in front of a judge, put on trial and later acquitted. Hung jury every last one of them."

"Dat probably be when all de trouble started."

"You are not wrong about that, Hector. The judge's decision to release the Matranga gang members drew strong protests from the locals. They were outraged by the outcome of the case. It amounted to jury tampering in the face of overwhelming evidence. A lynch mob stormed the jail. They hanged nearly a dozen Matranga members still waiting to stand trial. The backlash affected *Mafiosi* across the country. The crime families met and soon agreed. The Hennessey lynchings led the American Mafia to adopt a hard and fast rule. Policemen and other law enforcement officials were off-limits, not to be harmed."

Nico continued. "Charles Matranga himself was able to skip town and escape the vigilante lynchings. Later, when Charles returned to New Orleans, he resumed his position as head of the New Orleans crime family. He eventually forced the Provenzanos out. Matranga would then rule over the New Orleans underworld until shortly after Prohibition. That is when he turned over leadership of the syndicate to my grandfather, Sylvestro, in the early 1920s. Most people know my grandfather by a different name. Silver Dollar Sam. *Nonno* is still alive, still helps run things. My father Michael was one of three children *Nonno* had with my grandmother Caterina. She is dead now, God rest her soul."

"No no?"

"*Nonno*. Means grandfather in Italian."

Nico pushed back from the table and got to his feet. He strolled into the front room. It was lavishly furnished, but in a garish, almost barbaric manner. Gaudy tapestries. Heavy drapes. Ivory curios. Leopard skin rugs. Cut-glass candelabra.

"Now I am done talking, Hector. History lesson is over for today, done and complete. Get me a drink. Get me the cashbox. Hand over last night's receipts and tell me what this is all about."

Hector handed Nico the cashbox as well as the dead German's belongings. Then he cleared his throat to speak.

"Kentucky Rose pinched this here book off a john middle 'a' de night last night."

"Kentucky Rose? The young octoroon?"

"She don't like dat word. But yes. Dat be her."

"Spare the whore's feelings, of course." Nico laughed. "One black grandparent; no other black ancestors. I don't know any other word besides octoroon. Mulatto?"

"No, dat be a child with one Negro parent, one white parent," Hector said.

"Ah, mulatto. Yes. Like a mule. What you get when you cross a horse with a donkey. We have a parallel word in Italian. Arab traders have a similar word — *muwallad* — a person of mixed ancestry."

"Yes, dat be Kentucky Rose. A person of mixed ancestry. A quadroon be de child of a mulatto and a white. Dat makes dem one-fourth Negro. A *griffe* be de child of a mulatto and a Negro. They gots three-fourths Negro blood. Dat is what I am, a *griffe*. But, like I said, Rose pinched dis here book off a john earlier today, last night really."

"*Che minchia?* That girl brings in a lot of business to the house. I can't have her stealing from the men. She will give the house a bad reputation. Men may begin to go elsewhere. Maybe Rose needs to be punished. Maybe you do as well. You stole that ring didn't you?"

"Please don't punish Rose. She didn't do nothin' wrong."

"But you said she nicked this book off a john."

"I lied."

"*Che cazzo!* What the fuck? What would possess you to do such a thing, Hector? And why hand the stolen thing to me?"

"Nico, please. 'Fore you get upset. Take a look at what I be giving you."

Nico Carolla slowly turned the pages of the book. His eyes widened as he tried to comprehend its contents. Luca looked over his shoulder.

Hector asked. "You understand any dis stuff? I haven't had much schooling mah-self."

"I am Sicilian, Hector. Not German."

"Dat be what this be? German? I thought de wops and de Heinie Krauts were allies. In the war, I mean."

"Strange bedfellows more like. Plus, the Carolla family are not wops. Nasty word, that. Wine gone flat. That is how Sicilians translate the word. Back in the old country, it derives from slang — *guappo* — which means thug, one who struts about. It is how the arrogant men of Naples greet one another on the street. Sicilian men are not like that. We know our place. And we certainly are not in league with the Nazis. They are fascists, like Mussolini. Bad for business. We want no part of those people."

Nico continued to turn the pages. He stopped at one of the hand-drawn maps and studied it more closely. "What is this? Directions to some buried treasure? This looks like City Park."

"I cain't say," Hector said quietly. "Why not give it to yor brother? Earl Ray may be the only one here'bouts with detailed maps of de parish."

"He will want to know who you robbed to get your hands on this book. Besides, we have operations at some of these spots marked on the map."

"Bad *juju*. De john died in Rose's bed," Hector said flatly. "Me and Rose, we took dat book off de dead man's body. It be sewn into de lining of de man's shirt vest."

"Is that so? *Che cazzo?* What the fuck did you do with the body?"

"Still upstairs," Hector said sheepishly. He pointed.

"How long has it been up there? A corpse starts to stink after a few hours."

"Ain't been long. Middle of de night dis mornin'. But me and Rose had no ways to move the body. You have a truck. Maybe Luca, plus one or two of your strongbacks can get de body downstairs, out de backdoor and into de truck."

"You got it all figured out, don't you Hector? What to do with the body, what to do with the book. How about that fancy ring?"

"Due respect, Boss Man. But I wouldn't be standin' here askin' for your help if'n I had it all figured out."

"Well we cannot dump the body here, not in the river and not in Pontchartrain. We will have to cart the remains across the state line into Mississippi, then dump the body in Bay St. Louis. At least that will place the corpse in someone else's jurisdiction."

"Thankya Boss."

"Don't thank me yet. You and Rose have to sew this book back into the lining of the dead man's vest. Whatever is written on the pages of this book, I want no part of it. *Madre di Dio*. Let the book be discovered by someone else when they recover the body."

"You sure 'bout dat?"

"As sure as I am ever going to be."

"And what abouts de ring?" Hector asked.

"Keep it for all I care," Nico said as Luca walked back into the room with Lady Belle trailing behind. "But don't be surprised if someone doesn't come looking for it before long. That ring is no trinket. It is worth something to someone. Now put it in gear, as you people say. Both of you!"

THURSDAY
JULY 30, 1942
8:03 a.m.

Lake Pontchartrain, New Orleans

"You fool! You're doing it all wrong!" Andrew Higgins boomed. He was the military's foremost boat builder. "Don't cut the engine as you approach the shore. Gun the damn thing!" The trainees were practicing boat maneuvers out on the choppy waters of Lake Pontchartrain. An early morning storm was brewing in the distance.

"But sir, the Coast Guard taught us to always throttle back in shallow water or on approach to a pier."

The coxswain was a young man, one of nearly two dozen onboard the landing craft, each no more than twenty years of age. To a man, every last one of them had enlisted in the Coast Guard and were now enrolled in the Higgins Boat Operators School. The school had been organized the summer before at the request of Marine Corps General Holland Smith. Nevertheless, Higgins paid all of the school's operating costs.

"I don't give a fuck what the Coast Guard taught you, boy. You were taught wrong!" Higgins boomed again, more red-faced than before. "And the same goes for the rest of you Coasties. This is a Higgins boat, not some damn, second-rate Yankee skiff. A Higgins boat is not like other boats. It is made to be run up on a riverbank or over a bar or onto a rocky beach. Gun it, I tell you, or we will surely run aground and get stuck but good!"

Andrew Higgins was in a foul mood. He had only yesterday returned from Washington, D.C., where he testified before several congressional committees. He told them in no uncertain terms how disgusted he was with the Navy's recent cancellation of the multi-million-dollar Liberty boat contract. That contract had been extended to him only sixty days before. The adverse decision had cost him oodles of money and set his business plan back by months, if not years.

Higgins growled. "Step aside, boy, and let me take the wheel."

Higgins pushed the young Coastie roughly aside and throttled the boat up to full speed. The bow fairly leapt out of the water as he charged the concrete banks of Lake Pontchartrain at top speed, nearly 20 knots. The boat's Gray Marine diesel engine was basically indestructible, if a bit noisy and messy. But, like a sawed-off shotgun, it was hard to argue with the engine's effectiveness.

"Jesus H. Christ, we are all going to die," the young man exclaimed as he fell back against the gunwale.

"Rubbish! We are going to learn how to drive a Higgins landing boat. Hell, the Brits have been driving these things without problem since before we Yanks got in the war. If the Limeys can learn to do it properly, so can you pirates."

Andrew Jackson Higgins was not a man to be trifled with. Rough-cut and brusque. Hot-tempered and outspoken. Foul-mouthed and brilliant, with a wild imagination. The man had been trained in the school of hard knocks. He knew everything there was to know about building and sailing small boats, and he expected these men to learn the basics as well as he — small boat handling and navigation; use of compass; position finding; essentials of celestial navigation; signaling; emergency boat and engine repair.

The motor was running full bore, now, as they closed uncomfortably fast on the concrete shore. He shouted over the roar of the engine.

"Your average man is a chickenshit. His every instinct tells him to cut his speed when a boat runs aground on a sandbar. But this craft operates full throttle. And it continues to do so until it clears the bar. Even when troops are jumping from the boat on the beach, the engines continue to run wide open. It's counter-intuitive, I know. But that is why you boys are here — to learn how to do it the right way, which is to say the Higgins way."

The young man nodded his head, as if he agreed. But he held tight to the gunwale expecting to be thrown from the boat at any moment. The other trainees onboard the LCVP were doing the same.

"Believe me," Higgins said. "The boat can take it. Thick planking. Strong frame. Heavy keel and skeg."

Without flinching, Higgins ran the *Eureka* boat straight up on the concrete bulwarks of the shore. The boat creaked a bit but held together fine.

"See?" Higgins said as the boat ground to a halt on the step-type concrete seawall of Lake Pontchartrain. "That wasn't so bad, was it?"

The young Coastie, mostly white-faced, looked over the side of the boat. Most of the length of the boat was clean out of the water. All he saw beneath the hull was concrete. He was properly impressed.

But Higgins was nonplussed. He had done this maneuver a thousand times before, always with the same result: the boat came away undamaged.

"What now?" the Coast Guard recruit asked. "How do we get out of here? I mean, are we stuck for good? Do all of us have to get out of the boat here and push?"

"No, not at all," Higgins said. "But now it's your turn. Take the wheel. Slam her into reverse. She'll back her own self right off the seawall, sweet as you please."

"Seriously?"

"Seriously." Andrew Higgins was a man of extreme confidence.

The engine controls were a single lever combination throttle and gear, binnacle mount system. The young man grasped the controls gingerly and slammed the throttle hammer into reverse. Instantly the boat jerked backward and, much to his surprise slid easily back into the water. He swung the wheel hard to port as Higgins directed and pushed the boat back out into deeper water.

Though the hour was early, the bugs were already out in full force. Another hot summer's day was getting underway in New Orleans. It was one of the many pleasures of driving a fast boat — the bugs couldn't keep up; they didn't bother a man much when the boat was in motion.

"Now run the boat up to the seaplane ramp at Shushan Airport. It is that way. At this speed, it should take you no more than five minutes to get there." Higgins pointed. "The airport is near Pontchartrain Beach. Adjacent to Industrial Canal. That is where I will be getting out. When you get there, run the boat full speed right up the seaplane ramp. Don't hesitate. Just do it."

Higgins turned now to speak with Captain Richard McDerby. Mac, as McDerby liked to be called, was chief instructor at the Higgins Boat School. Since the school opened a year ago, Mac had already trained more than two thousand servicemen from various branches of the military to pilot and crew various classes of Higgins boats. Mac didn't like it when Higgins interfered with his class, but Mac was a patient man. Higgins was his idol, so he didn't say much.

"Mac, this is what these boys need to know. This is why I set up this school. This is why I pay for its operation out of my own pocket. Rip these boys a new one, if you have to. But teach 'em how to drive our fucking boats. And run them through the obstacle course after you drop me off. That will wake them up and get their attention."

McDerby smiled. The run with the boat through the obstacle course was always a hoot. Bounding over logs as much as three feet in diameter, over fifty-gallon drums floating in the water, across two sandbars, through a thick cluster of water hyacinth, and then up the concrete boat ramp at high speed.

When, two minutes later they had reached the seaplane ramp at Pontchartrain Beach and the coxswain had driven the boat up the ramp, Higgins jumped from the boat and said his goodbyes.

"See you later, Mac, back at the plant."

"Sure you'll be okay?"

"Hell yes. It isn't much of a walk from here to the electric streetcar line. I'll jump on the Spanish Fort Line, switch to the Canal Streetcar Line, then ride back downtown. My sons will be waiting for me. Thanks for the ride!" And then he was off, digging in his pocket for the 7-cent fare.

As Higgins walked the short distance to the streetcar stop, his nose hairs twitched. He could smell the sudden electricity in the air. A storm was moving into the bayou from out in the Gulf of Mexico. It made him remember. He harkened back to his early days as a lumberman in Natchez. It was the first business he owned.

Higgins stood that day, twenty years ago, under the roof of the portico of their small home and winced under the weight of the hot, humid, heavy air. Angele was pregnant with their first child, Edmond. A rumble of thunder rolled into the bay from the Gulf of Mexico only a dozen miles away. He lifted his eyes to the horizon and saw the menacing bank of dark storm clouds make their approach.

This one is going to be bad, he thought. Higgins knew it instinctively. The fury of a gulf coast squall was nearly unmatched on the planet. Violent, straight-line winds. Torrential rainfalls. A sudden down-rush of cold air. Torturous, gale-strength cloudbursts. Fierce twisting winds. Saltwater spray pushed miles inland.

A gulf coast bayou was little more than a series of ugly thumbs of water poking into the land in a hundred ways and in a hundred places. No spot of land was ever dry, only less wet than other spots. Houses had to be built on stilts, sometimes wood, sometimes stacks of cinder blocks, sometimes metal posts badly rusted. Storms could charge onshore with surprising speed and leave behind destruction, a storm surge and a devastating amount of rainwater.

The plant vegetation of the bayou was immune to the onslaught. But, human structures were feeble irrelevancies in the face of a tropical storm. The landscape regenerated itself. Uprooted trees regrew. Rivers changed course. Animals found new shelter. Fish washed ashore, rotted in place, became added fertilizer to an already rich soil.

The wind would rise; the leaves would quiver, shiny side up; the deer would take cover; smaller mammals would scurry away. The bayou was blanketed by a bottomland hardwood forest. The dominant plant species was the bald cypress tree. It grew in wet, marshy areas, which meant pretty much everywhere in the region. The cypress tree's most striking feature was its "knees" — woody, often gnarly protrusions from a tree's root system. The knees projected above the surrounding ground or water.

The trees grew tall. The knees provided the tree with stability and structural support. Sometimes the roots formed a buttressed base, a strong intertwined root system that allowed the tree to resist extremely strong winds, even of hurricane strength.

Higgins felt the first drops of rain on his face. He hurried now to the streetcar stop, where there would be a bit of cover. The drenching downpour would start soon enough.

FRIDAY
JULY 31, 1942
6 a.m.

Fiji, South Pacific

PFC Russell Brock put aside his entrenching tool, brushed the sand from his hair, and settled into his foxhole.

"Would make a nice vacation spot," his foxhole mate muttered. PFC Leonard Woods was a solid lad. Not terribly bright. But not a complainer either. The two men had been together in the same unit since boot camp at Parris Island, South Carolina. After boot, they were both transferred to Camp Lejeune, North Carolina, for light machine-gun training. Then on to Camp Pendleton, California, where they waited for a Liberty ship to transport them to Hilo, Hawaii, their last stop before being dropped here in the South Pacific.

"Yes, a lovely vacation spot," PFC Russell Brock replied. "Except that there is a full-scale war on." The sand they had just worked was thick and granular, like that found on countless island beaches in the Pacific.

"Yes. Except for that," PFC Leonard Woods replied. The two men were hunkered down in the shadow of what appeared to be an ancient volcanic peak. All the islands in this part of the world were the same: coral reefs, volcanic peaks, and birds in numbers too great to count.

"You two Jarheads done already?"

Brock and Woods jumped to their feet. The question came from Gunnery Sergeant Forrester, one of the few seasoned Marines on the beach. All across the beachhead, Marines were busy digging foxholes. This was to be a day of practice. Not everyone was taking it seriously.

"Does it pass muster, Gunny?" Private Brock asked in a hopeful tone, trying to stand at attention.

"At ease, Marine. Yes, your fucking little muddy foxhole passes muster. Deepest one I seen all morning. Now excuse me while I go kick some Semper Fi butt further down the beach. These other Jarheads in your squad need to follow your example.

They need to dig their mud holes deeper. Otherwise, they're going to get their asses shot off when we execute an actual beach assault."

Gunnery Sergeant Forrester walked away, working his way down the beach, screaming at the other Marines. "This ain't no Sunday picnic, you know. Didn't they teach you boys nothing in basic?"

Sergeant Forrester's voice grew less shrill as he drew further away. "Listen up, you nuggets. We will all be in battle soon enough. Time to forget about your mommas and your girlfriends. You are part of a Marine Infantry Division, not a woman's sewing circle. Throw your backs into it already. Dig, damn it! Deeper!"

Private Brock breathed a sigh of relief. He was one of the younger Marines on the beach, and one of the smaller ones. He felt he had to work harder than the other men in his Company.

Brock peered around him. Blue, tumbling waves to his rear. Hard-crusted beach beneath his feet. Craggy volcanic cliffs in the foreground. Basalt. Hardened lava fields. Volcanic peaks. *Nice vacation spot indeed.*

"I gotta take a crap," Brock said. The feeling had come on suddenly.

"So go take a crap." Woods pointed up the beach to a small outcropping.

"Not supposed to leave our foxhole," Brock said.

"You ain't taking no crap here," Woods replied. "We just got done digging this fucking hole. I ain't bedding down for the night beside a steaming pile of your shit. No way, not happening."

"Don't want to take a dump," Brock muttered. "Have to take a dump. You got any paper?"

"Damn you anyway, Brock. All I gots is a *Time* magazine from a few weeks back. Can you even read?"

"You know that I can. Anyway, what's it to you? I'm wiping my ass, not studying for a history exam."

"Well, if you're gonna wipe your ass with a page from my magazine, perhaps you ought to read it first."

Private Brock took the magazine, stole out of the foxhole and moved to a nearby patch of kunai grass to do his business. Here on the island of Fiji, the tall, kunai grass grew everywhere. The name of the plant varied from island to island — kunai grass, cogon grass, Japanese bloodgrass. But its uses were the same everywhere, regardless of what the locals called it. Thatch for their roofs, reed for weaving baskets and mats, starch-filled roots that could be cooked and eaten.

Brock squatted, tore a page from the *Time* magazine, read it quickly while he did his business. The war correspondent was reporting from London about the progress of the war in Europe. The London Blitz had failed to bring England to its knees as Hitler hoped, and the potency of RAF fighters had increased sharply. More and more of the aerial combat had moved out into the North Sea and away from the island of Great Britain. Pilots who bailed out or were shot down were dying in the cold waters of the English Channel or North Sea.

The article Russell Brock read was sheer propaganda. It described how the Germans were bringing their fliers back to life after having been shot down over the English Channel.

The flier, still numb from his frigid dip in the water, was stripped naked and wrapped tightly in a blanket with a nude and buxom gypsy lass, chest-to-breasts as it were. After several hours of cuddling, nearly all of the fliers who underwent this difficult therapy recovered enough strength to resume their brave attacks against the Allies, especially over the channel.

Whatever the future held for those buxom, gypsy girls was unclear. The article continued on the next page, which was missing. But Private Brock guessed the German airmen were enthralled with such an innovative, non-invasive therapy. Then again, maybe it proved to be invasive after all.

As Brock wiped his rear end, he wondered whether those girls would ever be recognized for their contributions to the war effort. Then he heard Sergeant Forrester approaching and knew potty time was up.

Brock rolled up the magazine, jerked up his jungle fatigues, and snuck back into his beach foxhole alongside PFC Woods.

"Took you long enough," Woods said.

"I am a slow reader."

"Where'd you grow up, Brock?"

"New Jersey."

"Me, too. Ocean City."

"Weehawken. Just across the Hudson from Hell's Kitchen. Midtown."

"Rough neighborhood."

"Rough childhood."

"Why'd you join up?" Woods asked.

"Why so many fucking questions all of a sudden?" Brock answered.

"Pretty soon this war is going to get quite real for the both of us. Just want to know who the fuck I am sharing a foxhole with," Woods said. "Me? I'm named for a distant cousin. Everyone thinks I'm named for Army Major General Wood. He was Chief of Staff of the United States Army. But that is Wood, no 's'. My name is Woods. My great-great grandfather was an ordained pastor. Congregational Church. West Newbury, Massachusetts. Founded the Temperance Society, among other things. Guess my pappy had great hopes for me. Didn't want me to join the Corps. Thought I ought to join the Ministry. Okay, Brock, that's my story. Now it's your turn. Tell me the truth. Why'd you join up?"

"To kill Japs."

"Everybody says that. Why'd you really join up?"

PFC Russell Brock hesitated. "Because I hated my mother. We had a toxic relationship."

"I can't believe what you're saying to me, man. No one hates their mother. And what the hell does toxic mean anyway?"

"A story for another day, perhaps," Brock replied.

"We got plenty of time to kill. The Sarge is still dealing with the slowpokes."

"Okay. But only if you promise not to laugh."

"I ain't promising nothing. Spill."

Brock cleared his throat and took a deep breath. "Where do I begin?"

"Start by telling me something you have never told anyone else."

Brock nodded, looked around, kept his voice low. "My mother divorced my father six months after they were married."

"That ain't much of a scandal."

"No? Then how 'bout this? I was born three months later."

"Ah, now we are getting somewhere."

"I never knew my father. In my memory, he never once came to visit. I always wondered why. My aunt, who I was close to, said my mother was the reason. She said that when I was a baby, my mother threatened to toss me out the window if my father were to ever come by. We lived on the fifth floor at the time. Plus, we moved more times than I can count when I was a little boy. My mother was like a gypsy, constantly changing jobs. She said she had problems getting along with her coworkers."

"Geez, Brock. Sounds like your mother was the one with the problems, not you."

"My mother was a nomad, a gypsy really. Her parents were nomads too. I barely knew my grandfather. My mother's mother came from Bohemia."

"Is that in upstate New York?"

"No, that is in Europe. A province in Czechoslovakia, I think. But you are right about one thing. There is a city by that name on Long Island, where a lot of Czechs actually do live. Mom's family came from the Old Country. Interesting story. My mom has a cousin name of Lazaar. He enlisted in the Navy before Pearl. When we last heard from him, he was stationed in the Philippines. But no one has heard from him since the Japs invaded Manila and our fleet was forced to withdraw to Java. Then came the Bataan Death March. Now everyone assumes Cousin Lazaar is dead."

"Maybe he was captured and is now a POW."

"If he isn't dead, he might wish that he were."

"How can you possibly say that about a man?"

"War Department says the Nips cannot afford to feed and house prisoners of war, not like the Nazis do in Germany. Those the Japs do keep alive become slave laborers in their factories and fields and die soon anyway. But this is the strange part. I heard my grandmother once say that Lazaar might have some Jewish blood running through his veins. Maybe my mother was part Jewish. Sometimes I wonder. Would that make me a Jew too? All I really know about the Jewish people is that the neighborhood kids always made fun of them, sometimes threw rocks."

"Brock, my friend, the gypsy Jew. Now there is one for the record books."

"A pox on your house if you say anything about this to anyone else."

"DILLIGAF. My lips are sealed. Tribes of Abraham are okay by me. Plenty of them live in New Jersey where I grew up. They were never any trouble."

"DILLIGAF?" Brock asked.

"Do I Look Like I Give A Fuck?" Woods answered.

"Something you picked up in boot?"

"Nah. Heard it yesterday, for the first time."

Brock nodded and continued his story. "About the time I was in the fifth grade, we lived for nearly a year in an apartment building away from the rest of the family. I sold newspapers after school. One winter day I sold only one paper and returned home to the apartment nearly empty-handed for my trouble. My mother was furious. She ordered me to go back out on the street and not to come back until I had sold the lot of them. I did as I was told. That is what boys of that age did, obeyed their mother. I didn't get back to the apartment until about nine p.m., well past my usual bedtime. She screamed at me for coming home so late."

"Sounds like something from the pen of Charles Dickens, *David Copperfield* or something. Did you get all your newspapers sold?"

"Oh, yes. Like I said, my mother was compulsive and irrational, short on logic, long on street smarts."

Private Brock paused and choked back a wave of emotion. "Not long after that, my mother told me she was sending me to a military school about thirty miles away from home. The Freehold Military Academy. At the time, I was devastated. Nowadays I chalk it up to the woman's itchy feet and thighs. With me out of the way she would be free to do her thing, be a gypsy, never have to take responsibility."

"Perhaps all she had on her mind was sex."

"That thought had occurred to me as well. No one likes to admit that their mothers think with their snatch. But it's true. Her boyfriend at the time lived downstairs from us in the same apartment building. Either way, at the age of eleven, off I went."

"Geez, Brock. Your mother sent you away from home at age eleven? No wonder you can't stand her."

"Yes, perhaps hate was too strong a word. But it was hard for me. I was desperately lonely. The first week away I felt terribly homesick. I sobbed and fought with my roommate for hours. But, by the morning of the second day, my tantrum was over. I never again shed a tear of homesickness. Fact is, I soon had much larger ordeals to face. Hazing was in vogue and it could be quite brutal, with wire coat-hangers and everything. I was only eleven and I had no support from you know who. So I had to suck it up.

"Somehow or other, I made it through that year. But then, that summer, my mother transferred me again, this time to a second military school, one even further from home, in Virginia, three hundred miles away."

"I am surprised you didn't find your way to West Point or Annapolis. You would be a commissioned officer by now instead of a grunt, ordering Marines to dig foxholes instead of digging them your own self."

"Me? An officer? I hardly had the credentials to get into one of those places. Front Royal was difficult enough."

"Strange name."

"Front Royal, Virginia.   Home to the Randolph-Macon Military Academy. Desolate place. During the Beaver Wars, years before America was even a country, the area around Front Royal was annexed by the Iroquois as part of their hunting grounds, trespassers keep out. Later, in the mid-1700s, the Iroquois sold their entire claim east of the Alleghenies to the Virginia Colony. This was the Treaty of Lancaster."

"How the hell do you know all this crap?"

"Knowing the school's history was mandatory for a new cadet. Before the French and Indian Wars, Front Royal was known as Helltown. This was on account of the many livestock wranglers and boatmen who worked the Shenandoah River Valley and came into town looking for alcohol."

"But why the name Front Royal?" Private Woods asked. "Why such a strange name for a place?"

"When I was a rat plebe, I heard no less than three different stories to explain away the name. The stories may all be bogus, for all I know. But I will tell you the version I think is true. Back in the early decades of European settlement, the French trappers referred to the area east of the mountains as *le front royal*, the British frontier.   In British English, *le front royal* would have translated roughly as the Royal Frontier, which to them it definitely was.   The British Crown had made a land grant of the Ohio Territory to the colonials, a land grant that French trappers and settlers and explorers would almost certainly have been aware of and probably respected. After 1763, when King George III set the so-called Proclamation Line, the British themselves likely called the area Front Royal. The Proclamation Line ran along the spine of the Allegheny Mountains. Colonists were not to cross west of that line, as it was meant to separate the settled portions of the colonies from territory reserved by the Crown for Indians in the interior of the continent. This was the Front Royal."

"Whatever you say, Mr. Textbook." Woods laughed.

"It ain't funny. My family doesn't come from money. I was completely out of my element in that place. The Randolph-Macon Academy was an elitist school. My mother knew it right along. She must have wondered how a Brock of uncertain pedigree would fit in with a southern elite consisting of Carters and Taylors and Yardleys. Plus, she had done the unthinkable. In her gypsy way she had aroused suspicions in the Cadet Corps that I was a bastard son. Then, anticipating questions about my heritage, she advised me to say that my name was Dutch, which was, in those days, more acceptable to my new surroundings than German."

Russell continued. "I was there at the academy for six years, practically until the day I enlisted in the Corps. I came to love that place, miss it even now. But in all that time she visited me only twice, both times with her boyfriend. I would be lying if I didn't say I was often lonely."

Brock became wistful. "Between terms, I had my summers free. I have to tell you. There was this one summer, two years back. I was fifteen at the time. The four of us lived together in my grandparents' house in New Jersey, my aunt, my uncle, my mother and myself. Our relationships were so twisted and confused, Dr. Freud would have had a field day. My aunt and my mother were like two polecats, each waiting to pounce on the other. My uncle was a cold, distant man. He was totally dominated by my aunt, and he resented her for it. I was a master at wasting my time. All I did with my free time was go to the beach. It was only a mile from the house."

"Beach? What beach? Where did your grandparents live?"

"In your hometown. Ocean City. By then, my grandparents were separated. Grandfather Heinrich had moved to New Orleans. I think he had a gambling problem."

"Small world. You and I were practically neighbors growing up."

"I didn't grow up there. Just that one summer. Mowing the lawn, sitting on the beach, hunting for frogs, strolling on the boardwalk. It stretched for miles. I can still smell the saltwater taffy. It wafted into this place where I collected money for a game called Fascination."

"Sure, I know the game," Woods said. "A bit like skeeball, only you compete against other players for time, like in Bingo. When I was a boy, there were Fascination parlors all up and down the boardwalk."

The two men quietly thought back to those simpler times, Ocean City, the boardwalk, the pastime called Fascination. The playing board was inclined. It had holes in it like a Bingo card. A player sat at one end of the table and rolled hard rubber balls onto the board. When a ball dropped through one of the holes, it lit up a corresponding circle on the screen in front of the player at the far end of the table. The idea was to get five lights in a row before any of the other players could. The hole in the center was free, also like on a Bingo card. The five lights could be diagonal or along any row or column.

"Yep, that is the game," Brock said. "I made eighteen dollars a week that summer; worked six hours a night, five or six nights a week, six p.m. to midnight. During the day, I rode my bicycle a lot. In the evenings, when I wasn't working, my aunt, uncle, and I would play blackjack, sometimes poker with deuces wild. When my mother came home from work in the evening, she would storm into the house, give us all a hostile look, and go straight to her bedroom. That's when I figured it out. My mother was jealous of any attention I paid my aunt. Two weeks later I found out why.

"It was a hot summer evening, a Sunday in mid-July. I know it was a Sunday, because the Sunday paper always had the funny pages with them. My uncle was playing cards that night at some gin joint down the street. My mother was out on another one of her dates. My aunt and I were in the house alone.

"About eight p.m. my aunt went upstairs. She took the newspaper and the funny pages along with her upstairs. I was downstairs listening to Jack Benny on the radio. I heard the shower run. Then my aunt called for me to come upstairs and put on my pajamas. I did. When I entered her bedroom, she had the papers all spread out on the bed with the funny pages on top. She was drunk. I could smell the alcohol on her. She said it was for her hay fever and laughed.

"As I entered the room, she gently patted the empty side of the bed next to her in a come-hither manner and told me to hop in. I thought — *Oh, what the hell* — and jumped in bed with her. Things went forward from there."

"You fucked your aunt?"

"More like she fucked me."

"Put it anyway you like, Brock. That is about the most fucked-up story anyone ever told me. FUBAR, and then some, if you ask me."

Brock was about to argue when they heard the boom of Gunnery Sergeant Forrester's voice.

"Okay, Marines. Out of your foxholes. Into the boats. We need to practice launching these Higgins boats from the shore."

"Again?"

"Until we get it right, Semper Fi. Muscles Are Required, Intelligence Not Essential."

"Don't know what that means."

"First letter from each word. Muscles Are Required, Intelligence Not Essential. Spells MARINE. We practice this 'til we get it right. Here in the South Pacific, 1st Marine Division is supposed to be the sharp point of the spear. We cannot afford to fuck this thing up. When the order is given, 1st Division will be first in. You need to know how to start up these engines, how not to tip over one of these boats by standing on the gunwales, how to raise and lower the ramps, and how to not get your butts shot off while doing it. We practice with the boats in shallow water first. Then tomorrow or the next day at the latest, we take them out into deep water for the real thing. Those Coast Guard boys over yonder will be driving them." He pointed. "They've already received two weeks of intensive boat training at the Higgins School."

"What the hell is a gunnel?" Woods asked quietly, pronouncing the word *gunwale* the way Sergeant Forrester had just said it. "Sarge told us not to stand on the gunnel."

Brock answered just as quietly. "Spelled gunwale — G,U,N,W,A,L,E. But pronounced gunnel. Don't ask me why. It is the side of the boat, the top edge of the side of the boat. I think in the olden days it actually did mean *gun wall*, the upper ridge of the deck against which a man laid his guns."

"Geez, here we go again with Mr. Textbook. That story sounds made-up. Besides, these boats are a bad joke," Private Woods said under his breath, as the squad scrambled over the gunwales and into the wooden boat.

"Not true," Brock said. "I have seen boats like this before. One time when I visited my grandfather down in New Orleans. They are parked everywhere along the bayou. Locals call them *Eureka* boats, though I'm not sure why."

"What in dickens do the locals use a flimsy plywood boat like this for?"

"Shallow lakes and bogs. The boats haven't much draft. A man can run one right up on shore, no problem at all. Then he can push it back out into the water without damaging the bottom of the boat or the screw."

Woods harrumphed. "So the Corps has recruited these things as landing craft, have they?"

"Would seem so," Russell answered, settling in. The men sat shoulder to shoulder on short benches or kneeled on the bare wood bottom.

"And they are letting Coast Guard rummies drive them instead of our regular Navy boys?"

"I'm told these Coast Guard boys know how to run small boats like they're nobody's business," Brock said. "They learned how to drive them running lifeboat drills off the Jersey coast. You must have seen them hauling half-dead kids out of the water come summertime."

Private Woods nodded. He had witnessed such near-drownings in his youth.

"Okay, Marines," Forrester barked suddenly. "Listen up. Captain Whittaker wants to have a word."

Woods whispered to his friend. "It is going to be a long war."

"Just figured that out, did you?" Brock whispered back. "Semper Fi."

FRIDAY
JULY 31, 1942
2 p.m.

City Park Avenue, New Orleans

"We are going to need more boats."

The speaker was Vice Admiral James Carmichael, thick eyebrows, short cropped hair. Under his arm he clutched an official looking briefcase. Of the two naval officers in the workroom office of Andrew Jackson Higgins, Carmichael was the more senior. But a happy man, he was not.

Vice Admiral James Carmichael was sweating profusely. It was mid-afternoon, the end of July, in New Orleans, a place where heat and humidity were standard fare.

A swarm of gnats had gathered around Carmichael's nose and eyes. No sooner would he brush them away with his hand, than they would regroup somewhere else equally annoying — around his ear lobes, the side of his mouth, on his forehead. *It was maddening!* Even the overhead fans didn't help.

Vice Admiral James Carmichael was dressed only in his short-sleeved Navy service uniform. But in this heat it made no difference how a man was dressed — everything turned to sweat. Bayou humidity was about as debilitating as it got anywhere in the continental United States. Carmichael had grown up in the mountains of western Pennsylvania, where summertime temperatures rarely rose above eighty degrees.

"How many more boats?" Andrew J. Higgins asked. He was long ago acclimated to the sub-tropical climate of New Orleans, loved it in fact. He had grown up in the dry environs of Omaha, Nebraska. This wonderful place was everything Nebraska was not.

Andrew Higgins did not sweat, not like other men his size. He was neither slender nor fat, but solidly built. Anyone who knew Andrew Higgins knew him to be single-minded and tough as nails. As a young man, Higgins had been expelled for brawling while attending a Jesuit-run preparatory high school. Then he went on to become a 1st Lieutenant in the Nebraska Army National Guard, before joining the Infantry and later becoming an Army Engineer. While in the Guard, he gained his first experience with boatbuilding and with moving troops on the water. The insights came during militia maneuvers on the Platte River. Later, boatbuilding would become his life's work, as the clutter in his workspace office attested.

Now, as Higgins waited for the Vice Admiral from the U.S. Navy's War Department to answer his question, he signaled to both his chief engineer and senior architect to come join the meeting. Moments later, the entire design team crowded in. George Huet, a naval architect, formally trained, with a logical and scientific mind. Graham Haddock, an engineer's engineer, who worked for Huet. Higgins' oldest son Edmond, the mechanical genius of the family. Plus, two of his senior draftsmen.

Graham Haddock was no stranger to this office. He had the ability to go to a jobsite, oversee the work, and then, when an unforeseen problem arose, go to a drawing board and figure out a solution. He and Huet and the other engineers often lived nights at their drafting tables, arguing, fighting, working toward an answer. Their boss, Andrew Higgins, was a man who could quickly grasp an idea, translate it into a practical design, and then have his workers construct a prototype while others were still pondering the problem.

But now, as they all gathered in Higgins' office, the big room felt suddenly crowded. Vice Admiral Carmichael had not yet answered Higgins' question about the number of boats the Navy needed. Finally, the other officer in the room did.

Marine Colonel Peter Morgan. Thin, tall, solidly built. A man with intelligent eyes, a sharp temper, and a penchant for getting things done on time and by the book. Morgan squared up his shoulders and cleared his voice to speak.

"How many more boats, you ask? More than you can possibly imagine. Hundreds. Perhaps thousands."

A wry smile crept over Andrew Higgins' face. *Success at last*, he thought. *Success at last.* Higgins had not always been successful in business. His first venture, Higgins Lumber and Export Company, had foundered in the late 1920s, a victim of declining world trade, stiff competition, and the employment of tramp steamers to carry lumber cargoes. But the man was dogged and determined. He had been able to keep his earlier boatbuilding venture afloat. Now all that hard work was about to pay off.

Higgins turned to address his new partner, Preston Tucker, now vice president of the aviation division, who had also stepped into the meeting along with the engineers and draftsmen. Tucker was not well-liked by the others, who thought him a charlatan.

"What do you think, Tuck?"

"You cannot trust these government cardboard cutouts, Andrew. Get lots of money from them upfront. Lots."

Preston Tucker was a brilliant and tremendously inventive figure. He had done business with the Navy since before the war, when he gained the Navy's attention with his invention of a highly-mobile, power-operated gun turret.

The Tucker Turret, as it came to be called, was a breakthrough device. It was soon installed on every form of military hardware from Andrew Higgins' PT boats and landing craft to both the B-17 and B-29 bombers. Just four months ago, in March of 1942, Tucker sold Higgins his newly formed gun turret company.

After the acquisition, Preston Tucker relocated to New Orleans. Now he served as Higgins' vice president in charge of the Higgins-Tucker Aviation Division, a company that produced Tucker gun turrets, as well as armament and engines for Higgins' torpedo boats.

But there was friction between the two men. Both were strong-willed and they did not get along. Tucker was a fancy dresser and a fast-talker and Higgins did not like him. The partnership was destined not to work out.

By the following year Tucker would sever his relationship with Higgins. Regardless, his inventing days were far from over. After the war, he would go on to develop and become famous for the revolutionary 1948 Tucker Sedan, a project that became embroiled in litigation on account of its controversial financing technique.

"You make a good point, Tuck," Higgins said as he turned back to address the two men in uniform, Vice Admiral James Carmichael and Marine Colonel Peter Morgan. "Admiral, if my company is going to accept an order that large, we are going to need an advance. A big one."

"And we are going to need to make some design changes," the Vice Admiral replied as he passed the slender briefcase in his hand to Colonel Morgan.

"Such as?"

"Open it," Carmichael said.

Morgan nodded and dug into the case. "We have blueprints."

"Sketches, don't you mean?" Higgins harrumphed. "Or perhaps photographs? Only an engineer can draw a blueprint, and I have drawers full of them." Higgins pointed to a wooden cabinet with many narrow drawers on the far wall.

"An important distinction, to be sure." Like so many naval officers, the Vice Admiral was unaccustomed to dealing with an arrogant man who questioned his orders. Clearly, Higgins knew his business better than he did.

"Fancy colored paper and pretty lines don't make a boat float, Admiral. Guys like me and Haddock and Huet do. Guys with experience and moxie."

"No, Higgins. What makes a boat float is money. Now the Colonel and I are only going to ask you this question once. Are you willing to listen to what we have to say? Or do we take our checkbook and our drawings and go elsewhere?"

Higgins sported a wide grin. "After everything that has gone down between me and your Bureau of Ships; after Senator Truman has convened hearings to look into your shoddy practices; do you really still think that your threats will work with me? The Navy's Bureau of Ships doesn't know their asses from their elbows. They have been on the wrong side of this argument from the beginning. They want me to build an unsafe thirty-foot-long boat when every wet-test shows that the thirty-six-foot-long boat we designed is far superior. Every round of boat tests that the Navy has conducted has come out the same. The steel-ramp boat ought to be thirty-six feet long and Higgins Industries should be the one building it for you. Ask Leveau. C.W. Leveau. He works for you. The man is a topnotch naval architect. He said our test results were almost beyond comparison."

"Yes, I have read Leveau's report. I know what Marine Corps General Holland wants."

"Then what the fuck is wrong? Place the god damn order already!"

"It is not that simple, Higgins. There are other forces at work here."

"What other forces?"

"I am coming to that. The Truman Committee is due to make its report any day. In the meantime, take a look at these drawings and — as you say — photographs. Tell me what you think."

"You want to know what I think?"

The Admiral nodded. "These are working Jap models of their most advanced landing craft. The next generation of landing boats we need you to build for us will have to be larger than your original *Eureka* boats. They will have to be larger and they will have to be front-loading, preferably with a steel ramp. Some versions of the new boat will need to be large enough and have motors powerful enough to ferry a tank, maybe motorized artillery, half-tracks, that kind of thing."

"Way ahead of you, Admiral. My men have been busy." Higgins gestured with approval in the direction of his design team still in the room.

Higgins went over to a large drafting table at the opposite end of his large workroom office. It overlooked the factory floor. There were drawings and blueprints spread out everywhere, on the drafting table, on the floor, and on an adjoining countertop.

Each blueprint was numbered and signed with the date of the latest revision in the bottom right-hand corner, along with relevant drafting notes. These might include the scale of the drawing, the type of boat, boat registry numbers, government contract number, related material lists and construction details. Roll #111, dated June 24, 1942, was open and weighted down at the corners with four small blocks of wood. Roll #69, the latest revision not yet complete, was on the large drafting table next to it.

Higgins said, "Come see, Admiral. We have been working on exactly those upgrades. One of my people brought me those exact same photographs months ago. My boys and I have already built a working prototype. We have already run it through its paces. The boat performs flawlessly."

"You have already built a prototype? How is that even possible? How is it that you got hold of these photographs and drawings before our own intelligence services did?" The Admiral looked sideways at Colonel Morgan with questioning eyes, then approached the drafting table to scrutinize blueprint roll #69.

Higgins laughed. "I suppose you two blue water boys still believe in Santa Claus and the Easter Bunny as well? Everyone knows our intelligence services are a joke."

"Answer me, damn it! How the hell did you get hold of these photographs and drawings before the Navy did?"

"Keep your diapers on, Admiral. I have done business in the Philippines for years, going back to my first days in the lumber import business. This is a picture of a *Daihatsu* class landing craft. The Japanese have been using ramp-bowed landing craft like these since the Second Sino-Japanese War in 1937. I believe your very own Marine Corps Captain Victor Krulak took these pictures with a telephoto lens while he was in Shanghai. He showed them to me last summer after you folks filed his pictures away in some drawer and dismissed his ideas as being nutty. But they were a revelation to me. After seeing Krulak's pictures, I described the design to my chief engineer over the telephone. He built me a mock-up within weeks. We started testing a ramp-bowed version of the *Eureka* boat on Lake Pontchartrain last winter. It works great, though Tucker and I are still trying to work out machine-gun positions. The boat should operate easily with a crew of four."

"I was aware that you once did business in the Philippines. That much is in your file. But this Krulak connection is quite out of the ordinary. These matters are classified."

Andrew Higgins grew red in the face. "The Navy has a classified file on me?"

Vice Admiral James Carmichael became stern. "It is long past time you took this boatbuilding contract seriously, Higgins. General Eisenhower — the Supreme Allied Commander — is counting on you. Ike says you are the one man who can win the war for us. Ike has told Churchill and Admiral Nimitz that if Andrew Higgins had not designed and built the LCVP — the Landing Craft, Vehicle, Personnel — our troops would never be able to safely land on an open beach. We will soon see whether or not that claim is true."

"Eisenhower said that?" Andrew Higgins was taken aback.

Vice Admiral Carmichael nodded in the affirmative. "Even Hitler believes it to be true. He has spoken more than once to his staff of your heroic war efforts in ship production. He has bitterly dubbed you the New Noah, the man who built a lifeboat to save Western Civilization."

"Imagine that," Higgins said, puffing out his chest. "Me as Noah. My father would be so proud."

Vice Admiral Carmichael laid it on thick. "You were destined for this, Andrew. Every day of your adult life has been one long dress-rehearsal for this exact moment in time. We have it all down on paper, your history, paragraph by paragraph, line by line, down to the smallest detail."

"Is that what you have in that fucking file folder of yours? My life story? You think I am a security risk?"

This time, Colonel Morgan answered. "Higgins, every last one of us is a security risk. This whole place, in fact — all your operations — are one big security risk. This latest contract you are about to sign includes a provision that allows the Navy to place heightened security around every one of your facilities."

Andrew Higgins bristled with anger. "You fuck. I am a patriot. I talk practically every day with Marine Corps General Holland Smith. He commands the 1st Marine Brigade, Fleet Marine Force. The man trusts me implicitly."

Then Higgins turned to his assembled design team, Huet, Haddock, Tucker, and the others. "Outside, boys, all of you. Get the fuck out of my office this very minute. Me and the Admiral are about to have strong words and I'll not have you waste your valuable time being witness to a bloody fight." Higgins pointed to the office door and waited while George Huet, Graham Haddock, and the other men quietly filed out of the room. They knew better than to argue with the boss.

Then Higgins turned back to the two Navy men. "See that American flag hanging on the office wall behind me? I am a patriot. I love this country. What the hell do you have on me that says different?" By now Higgins was red-faced with anger and Vice Admiral James Carmichael was nearing the end of his patience.

"Well, let's see what I have." Vice Admiral James Carmichael opened Higgins' file and began to slowly read. "Left Omaha in 1906 at the age of 20. Went to work in the lumber business in Mobile, Alabama. Worked a variety of jobs in the lumber, shipping, and boatbuilding industries. After four years, became manager of a German-owned lumber import business in New Orleans . . . "

"Okay, okay, okay. So you have done your homework . . . "

"Formed his own import/export lumber company in 1922. Imported hardwood from the Philippines and Central America . . . "

"Don't forget west Africa," Higgins interrupted. "African coast is a good source of hardwood. See this desk? Solid as a rock. Built from that same African hardwood."

Vice Admiral Carmichael continued reading from the file. "Exported pine and bald cypress. Acquired a fleet of sailing ships to support his trading business; said to once have been the largest private fleet under American registry. Established his own shipyard to service this immense fleet. Built and repaired his own cargo ships, as well as the tugs and barges needed to support them. Then, in 1926, designed and built the first *Eureka* boat, a shallow-draft watercraft meant to be used by trappers and oil drillers in operations along the Gulf coast and lower Mississippi Basin. The boat featured a recessed propeller that was housed in a cylindrical tunnel beneath the boat. Though early versions suffered from cavitation, the boat could successfully be operated in shallow waters where flotsam and submerged obstacles would render more usual types of propellers useless."

Vice Admiral James Carmichael stopped and looked up from his paper. "Now here are several items which I left out of the official file."

"Oh? What items are those?"

"I think you know."

"No, I do not. Please spell it out for me, Admiral."

"If you insist."

Carmichael pulled out a slip of folded paper from his trousers pocket and held it up to the light. "Confidential sources we have interviewed state that your true intent when you designed the *Eureka* boat was to sell them to individuals and mob people so they might smuggle illegal liquor into the United States. Those same confidential sources state that your tale of selling *Eureka* boats to trappers and oil-drillers has mainly been a cover story for your illegal activities."

Vice Admiral James Carmichael re-folded the piece of paper. "Care to comment?"

Andrew Higgins said nothing.

"What will it be, Higgins? Back in my pocket? Or into your official file?"

"I would much rather you put that slip of paper back into your pocket and forgot about all those confidential sources."

"Are you sure? We also have this story in your unofficial file about an incident with the Texas State Troopers."

"That one is a lie!"

"We don't think so. Our sources are reliable. The story goes something like this: Last year, you needed bronze shafting for the landing craft you were building for the British. The materials were in short supply. Even so, you located supplies of the bronze shafting you needed in the oil fields of Texas. The stink of it is that the owner refused to sell you any of what you wanted and you were too damn impatient to go through channels. So you out and out stole the stuff."

"Well, I never . . . "

"You had some of your shadier workers remove the metal illegally from an oil well storage depot. Do not try denying it. We have the reports. Then, with the Texas police in hot pursuit, your people crossed the state line back into the friendly jurisdiction of the Louisiana State Troopers. Your workers apologized for what they called a mistake, and then they returned part of what they had stolen back to the rightful owner. But the rest was transported back to New Orleans under trooper escort, where you used it to complete work on an order of tank lighters. Is this something you want in your official file?"

"No, not really. In the end, though, everyone was happy and the customer got his order filled."

"Not everyone was happy. We certainly are not."

"Point taken," Higgins said. "I would rather you also put that slip of paper back into your pocket and not into my official file."

"So be it."

Vice Admiral Carmichael slipped the folded piece of paper back into his trousers and handed the closed folder back to Colonel Morgan. "But don't give me any more happy horseshit about you not being a security risk."

"Can we still do business together, you and me?"

"Of course we can. We have a war to win. The Marine Corps loves your boat. They will love it even more with the changes we are about to propose. From a troop-unloading-point-of-view, the operation of the ramp is still not ideal. But first things first. We simply must talk about improved plant security. We need to be certain that the people you employ in your assembly plants can be trusted."

"I have my own crew to see to security, thank you very much."

"What, those *Mafiosi* thugs I see strutting around the grounds?" Morgan said. "That just will not do. Once word of this new contract gets out, there will be reporters hanging about, maybe even the odd-duck Congressman or Senator. I understand that *Life* magazine wants to do a story on you."

Higgins shook his head. "The local syndicate controls much of the labor force in this backwater corner of the South. I have to work with these people, with the grandson especially, Nico Carolla. He is a good man, in his own way. I depend on the Carolla crime bosses and the labor unions to keep the peace."

"We do not see it that way," Vice Admiral James Carmichael said. "This man Carolla is trouble, pure and simple. Gambling, prostitution, labor rackets, the whole nine yards. The man's grandfather killed a federal agent ten years back. The old man spent two years in the federal pen for that crime, hardly enough. He was released in 1940. Then the courts ordered him deported back to Italy. But the war intervened. The deportation order was put on hold when Italy declared war on the United States."

Higgins shook his head. "Sorry, but none of this is news to me. Everyone knows about Silver Dollar Sam and his criminal past."

"Yes, they do. And that is why I have been instructed to post Marine guards here at the factory gates of the City Park Avenue plant and elsewhere around the Industrial Canal compound. Our men will be manning their posts 'round the clock until the war is over. Your boats are vital to the war effort, both the steel-ramp boats and the motor torpedo boats. People higher up the food chain than me are worried that enemy saboteurs may try to sneak into the country, perhaps disrupt the operations of your boatworks. All your people will have to undergo a basic background check."

Higgins became testy. "Is this my factory or yours?"

"I have only a limited number of choices here, Higgins. The Navy can award this newest contract to anyone we damn well please. There are people up around Groton and Newport News — important and connected people — who want this contract awarded to the boatworks up there. Or, if you prove particularly uncooperative, the War Department can simply commandeer your plant and you can watch Colonel Morgan and his men build your boats from *outside* the fence. There is a war on, a world war. It is being fought on three oceans and five continents. You get that, right? Truman Committee aside, it will be our way or no way. The first landings may well be within months. We simply must have those boats, lots of them."

"Months?"

"That information is top secret. Tell anyone and I will have you arrested and put in irons. The charge will be treason. You will be placed up against a concrete wall and shot."

"No worries. I can keep a secret."

"Can you? What about your mob connections? The Navy is quite uncomfortable with that. We want no scandals. We want no headlines."

"Actually, Silver Dollar Sam's family may be able to help our side with the war effort."

"How so?" Morgan asked.

"Even a bayou rat like me can read a map."

"Go on."

"We cannot beat the Krauts head on. That is my considered opinion as a former infantryman. The war to retake Europe begins in North Africa. That is where you will first need my boats. From North Africa, the front jumps to Italy, the weakest of the Axis Powers. But the entrance ramp into Italy is through Sicily, the Straits of Messina. By my reckoning, the Allies will have to land at Palermo. You will need intelligence on the ground. What better way to get it? The Carolla family comes from Monreale. Silver Dollar Sam was born less than two hundred yards from the Palermo city limits. He has trustworthy contacts on the island that the Allies can only dream of having."

"Maybe I underestimated you," Vice Admiral James Carmichael said, suddenly lost in deep thought. He was more than a little impressed with this man's grasp of strategy and tactics.

"Now this is where it gets interesting, Admiral. Tolerate the Sicilian mob families here in America. Help them even. When the time comes, they will hand you the keys to Sicily and thus to southern Italy. I do not see how we win the war without their help."

"Very perceptive, Mr. Higgins. Very perceptive."

"Now it is Mister Higgins, is it? What happened to that torpedo tube full of bravado you were packing earlier?"

"You make a compelling case. After we conclude our business here today, I will immediately pass your thoughts up the chain of command to General Eisenhower. You may have just made yourself indispensable."

"So Nico Carolla's men can stay?"

"For the moment, yes. But make no mistake. Ike will insist we position Marine Corps personnel at key chokepoints around the plant grounds. Colonel Morgan will see to it. The threat of sabotage is a large and ongoing risk. This is non-negotiable."

"Who should I be looking for?" Andrew Higgins asked. "These saboteurs. What do they look like? How would I pick out one of these buzzards from a crowd?"

"They will not be wearing a sign, if that is what you mean," Morgan said. "Some may speak English quite well. Others are likely leftovers from the first world war, the Great War."

"We are suddenly afraid of old men?"

"Dangerous old men. During the Great War, Germany very much wanted Mexico to come into the war on the side of the Kaiser and against the United States. I take it you have heard of the Zimmermann telegram? The Krauts sent people here, to the States, to help make that happen. Many of those people still make their homes here. They have embedded themselves deeply into our society . . . But their loyalties lie elsewhere."

"So now I have to be suspicious of anyone with a German accent or a Kraut-sounding last name?"

"Until we know more, that is as good a place to start as any."

"That doesn't narrow it down much. There are all kinds of Germans living in these parts. Plus who knows how many people hate the government on sheer principal."

"Nevertheless."

"Okay. I will throw up a fence around the entire area, from the bayou to the far west end of the property. But Admiral, I cannot possibly fence off the seawall. My people need access. Lumber and steel come in. Finished boats go out. Plus, there is a rail spur that comes into the facility from across the canal. I have to keep that access-way open at all times. On the other hand, we could set up call boxes near key buildings and increase patrols."

"Good thinking. That will have to do for now. Thank you, Higgins."

FRIDAY
JULY 31, 1942
11 p.m.

Bay St. Louis, Mississippi

The captain of the tiny vessel stood on the bow of his small boat and peered out into the murky waters ahead. He turned to his pilot Jaxon, a younger man who sat at the rear of the flat-bottomed skiff. Jaxon had his hand on the tiller of the Evinrude outboard motor. Two long rowing oars were stowed flat against the sidewall of the skiff beneath the gunwale on the port side. The men were towing a small rowboat behind the skiff on a length of weathered three-quarter-inch manila rope.

"These are treacherous waters to negotiate at night," the captain said, keeping his voice low. His name was Ernst Stengel. During the Great War, Stengel served as a Petty Officer onboard a Kaiser-class battleship in the Imperial German Navy. But that was twenty-five years ago, and his seafaring days were now mostly over.

For many men the Great War was a distant memory. But, for Ernst Stengel it was still front and center in his mind. To this day, Stengel harbored a special hatred for the Allied Powers, especially Great Britain.

As a young man, Stengel served aboard one of the battlewagons later interned at Scapa Flow, Scotland, after the close of World War I. The entire Imperial German Navy fleet of seventy-four ships was at anchor that day at the Royal Naval Base when the German Commander, Rear Admiral Ludwig von Reuter, ordered the magnificent fleet scuttled. Von Reuter's reasoning was simple. He was afraid that his entire fleet of mighty ships would be seized during the Armistice by his enemies and then divided amongst the allied powers, strengthening them and further weakening his beloved Germany. Adolf Hitler later used this insult against the German people to instill a sense of revenge against the victors of the Great War.

Stengel spoke again to his young pilot, Jaxon. "No running lights, no visible landmarks on shore to guide us, no moon overhead, cloudy skies. Bay of Saint Louis is hard to negotiate during the day; worse at night. I pray we don't get our boat caught up on a snag or a shoal in these dark, murky waters."

"Why the hell pick such a remote spot for a munitions drop?" Jaxon asked. He slipped the outboard motor into idle and instinctively began to tilt the motor shaft forward on the mounting bracket. Tilting the shaft forward in this fashion would serve to raise the propeller out of the water. It was a safety measure employed by small boat pilots when traveling through shallow waters where bits of debris might damage the motor or bend the propeller.

The captain continued to speak to his pilot in a low, even voice. "I guess the Waffen chose this spot for that very reason — because it is so remote. They didn't ask my opinion, and I had no say in the matter. The people who hired me selected the location. The man who contacted me, the man from the SS, all he asked me was whether or not I would be willing to make the drop. He made it seem as if I had no choice in the matter. Either I say yes, or else something bad would happen to me. So I said yes, I would do it. Then the man handed me an envelope stuffed with money and pointed out this location on a map."

"So how exactly is this supposed to work?" Jaxon asked, looking nervously about the shallow waters of the Bay.

"We take the dynamite. We place it beneath the seat of that rowboat we are towing behind us. We anchor the rowboat in shallow water. And we sail quietly away."

"Shit like this never turns out to be that simple," Jaxon said, hand still on the tiller. "Hell, this whole place is one big pool of shallow water."

The erstwhile captain grimly nodded. The Bay of Saint Louis — or, as some of the local people called it, St. Louis Bay — was a partially enclosed, shallow estuary of the Gulf of Mexico. It was perched along the southwestern coast of the State of Mississippi, northeast of the city of New Orleans.

The estuary received regular additions of freshwater from two blackwater rivers, both little more than swamps with a current. There was the Jourdan River on the west bank and the Wolf River on the east, plus any number of smaller streams. These murky waters were mixed in with saltwater from Mississippi Sound and the Mississippi Bight. The resulting stew was toxic. The air was acrid. During the hottest months of the year the place smelled like an open sewer. In time, the bay would come to be classified by the

EPA as an "impaired" waterway on account of the high fecal coliform levels.

"We have to get in much, much closer to shore than this," Ernst Stengel said. "We have to get well up into Cedar Bayou. It's just east of Grassy Point, which we just passed. We make the drop at the mouth of Cedar Bayou. I know the spot. Now angle the propeller back in the water, Jaxon. The depth here is just fine."

"I hope you know what the fuck you are doing."

"Trust me."

"That is the kind of trust that can get a man killed."

"No one is going to get killed here tonight, Jaxon," the captain said. He was crouching, now, near the pointed bow of the small, open, flat-bottomed, boat. A wooden skiff of this size could be powered by an outboard motor or — when the motor was stowed — oared like a rowboat.

The pilot continued in an anxious voice. "Ernst, are you absolutely certain these containers are watertight? Wet dynamite won't do anyone much good."

"It was given to me dry, and dry it remains."

"But dynamite has to be turned regularly. Dynamite sweats. That makes it unstable."

"The only thing unstable around here is you, Jaxon. I been turning these canisters regularly ever since they were given to me yesterday morning. So quit fussing, will you? Our bigger worry should be the rolls of detonation cord and the blasting caps. Those also need to stay dry. It may rain tonight, like it does most every night this time of year. Get a good downpour and that open rowboat may fill to overflowing with rainwater."

"Geez, this just keeps getting better and better," Jaxon complained.

"Quit bellyaching," Stengel ordered. "That stuff we're hauling isn't ordinary dynamite."

"I don't follow."

"Not sure I do either. The man who gave me this stuff said we Germans have the best chemical engineers in the world. He said every breakthrough in explosives was thanks to our chemists."

"So what the fuck we carrying?"

"The Americans call it Composition B. The Waffen-SS calls it W-Salt; other names too. It is a compound. 60 % RDX, 40 % TNT. Much more stable than dynamite. No chemical sweating to worry about. More the consistency of modeling clay."

"What the fuck is RDX?"

"Have not a clue. Some form of powerful bang-bang. That's all I know."

"Ernst, what the fuck are they going to use this stuff for anyway?"

"Do not know that either."

"What do you know?"

"I know that there is a payday in it for us. I also know that this stuff will help our side in the war effort."

"Our side, their side. Does it even matter? The war is ten thousand miles away. You and me are going to starve no matter which side wins."

"Shush!" Stengel said suddenly.

"You telling me to shut up?" Jaxon asked angrily.

"No. I am asking you. I hear something."

The two men fell into total silence. Ernst Stengel moved further back into the skiff, sat on the closest bench, pulled out his binoculars and stared into the darkness ahead.

"What do you see?" Jaxon asked quietly.

"I see a light," Stengel whispered back.

"No one should be out here this time of night."

"Probably some drunk jungle-bunny out fishing after dark."

"Ernst, we can't leave behind no witnesses, not to us delivering a boat full of explosives to some Nazi Krauts."

"No, we certainly cannot."

"Do we abort the mission? Or do we take out the light?"

"Hand me my hunting rifle, Jaxon. It's in my gun case beneath the second seat. Then bring us about real slow and quiet. We need to get ourselves between the jungle-bunny and the shoreline before he realizes what is afoot and bolts like a rabbit. Then we take out the jungle-bunny, along with the light."

Jaxon nodded his understanding and reached under the seat for the gun. He slowed the boat to a crawl.

Ernst whispered soft and low. "Bring us around and hand me some shells. Then cut the engine."

SATURDAY
AUGUST 1, 1942
7 a.m.

French Quarter, New Orleans

"Don't get me wrong," Nico said, raising himself up on one elbow from the mattress of the large, platform bed the two lay on. "I love my wife. Some days I even adore my children."

"I know that," Martina said, rearranging the silken bedcovers to better suit her. "What you and I have together is not love. It is convenience and diplomacy. I have no designs on your heart."

"Women always say that. Sometimes they even believe it to be true. The family can accept many things. But it is not at all open-minded about divorce. Girlfriends, yes. Divorce, no."

Martina got up from the bed, strode across the room. She was naked, a beautiful woman, with dark eyes and shimmering brown hair. Firm breasts, exquisite round bottom, delightful thighs.

Martina picked up her robe from over the back of the chair, where she left it. The robe was rose-colored, a perfect match to the rouge on her lips. Daylight peeked between the shades. She wrapped the robe around her silken shoulders but allowed her breasts to roam free. Enticing.

"I need a shower," she said, gliding gracefully toward the bathroom. The scent of soft perfume trailed behind her.

"Room enough in that shower for two?" he asked.

"A woman of means always showers alone. That is a rule you must never forget. There are no exceptions. I will happily share my bed with a man. But never my hot water."

Nico Carolla laughed, a pleasant easy laugh. "I can live with that."

Steam quickly filled the small bathroom as Martina Amerada ran herself a hot shower. This secret place where the two lovers shared their precious moments each week was a small apartment Nico maintained in the heart of the French Quarter, near the center of his operations. With the single exception of

Luca, no one knew about this place, not even *Nonno*. Nico preferred things stay that way.

"I like our regular get-togethers," Nico said through the curtain of the shower.

Martina stepped from the shower, now, skin glistening. Nico was instantly ready to have another go with her in bed.

"Put that thing away," she instructed, pointing to his erect penis. "Hand me that towel. Help me dry off. Then we talk business."

Nico pouted and handed her a bath towel. "This thing here is the only business I wish to discuss."

"First we talk business," she said. "Then you have my permission to bring that other thing back up again. Perhaps we can lay it out on the table, take the measure of your manhood there."

Nico laughed again, allowed her to dress. A few minutes later, they sat directly across from one another at the small kitchen table. A pot of coffee was brewing on the stove. His pistol was on the nightstand beside his pants.

"Cereal?" he asked.

"Fresh milk?"

"Check the icebox."

She opened the icebox. "Empty as usual."

"Dry cereal can often be tasty," he offered, pouring himself a bowl and sipping his morning coffee. "Use your imagination. Pretend the cereal is soaking in a bowl of cold milk."

"We talk business. Then you take me out for a real breakfast."

"You know that we cannot be seen on the street together, Martina."

"Then I suggest you talk fast. Sex makes me ravenous for food."

"Okay," Nico said. "To business. There may be a war on. But people have money to burn. Business in our part of town has been brisk. My operations are generating more cash than we can possibly bank safely here in the U.S. without inviting unwanted federal scrutiny. I need to send more couriers to you in Havana. More couriers, more money, more frequently."

"How much more frequently?" Martina asked, a worried look beading up on her face.

"Instead of twice a month, more like once or twice a week," Nico said, moving away from the table to continue dressing. "And the amounts will need to be larger, much larger."

"I don't know, Nico. The Cuban bank supervisors will get suspicious. That is so much cash for me to wash."

"What if I scramble the couriers? Use two or three different persons to keep the bank supervisors off-balance? Maybe once a month I give you a duffel to carry yourself? There is the twice weekly *Seatrain* ferry from New Orleans to the port of Havana and back again."

Martina Amerada shook her head vigorously. "No, not in this lifetime. Under no circumstances will I ever agree to personally carry any cash money for you. That is strictly non-negotiable, Nico. So you better get used to it."

"I can accept that. But what if I use multiple couriers, like we said?"

"Yes, I suppose that might work: some women, some men, perhaps the odd mulatto, maybe a Negro or two."

"No Negroes," he said sternly, retrieving his *Bernardelli* pistol from the nightstand and feeling its modest weight in his hand. "I don't trust them."

"Okay, no Negroes. But you will need people you can trust absolutely. Carrying large sums of cash between countries is inherently risky. People skim off the top, even good people. People steal. People get robbed."

"Rough crowd on the ferry?" Nico asked. "I have never been."

"Darn right it is a rough crowd. The SS *Seatrain New Orleans* is not your ordinary passenger ferry, not like the ones they run across the river several times a day here in the city," she said. "*Seatrain* is a railcar ferry owned and operated by the West India Fruit and Steamship Company."

"How many passengers on each run?"

"Not many. Your couriers will be hard to hide. The few regulars all know one another. Amenities onboard are few. Most of the passengers are crew, roughnecks who work either for the railroad or WIF. Railcars are loaded and unloaded by crane and cradle. Loud and dangerous work, though accidents are rare."

"The railroad business is a big, loud and complicated business," Nico said. "We run nearly everything down on the wharves. Freight from the U.S. can be routed to Cuban buyers, yet all the while remain in the same railcars and packaging as when they were first loaded at the point of origin."

"I have traveled alongside some of that cargo," Martina said. "Much of it is financed by banks in my country. Tobacco, rum, pineapples, sugar. Those products move by rail north. Manufactured goods, chemicals, steel products, machinery, temperate zone fruits. Those products move south by rail."

"Temperate zone fruits? What are those?"

"Fruits grown in the States. Apples, grapes, pears, that sort of thing."

"Yes, yes, and now laundered money as well," Nico said.

"On the northbound leg, I exit the rail ferry on the opposite side of the river at the Algiers terminal. Then I cross the river on the passenger ferry, and board the Canal Street streetcar which brings me up to you. When I return home to Havana, I cross the river on the Canal Street Ferry, exit at Bouny Street, and then board the *Seatrain* ferry. The rail connection at the other end is with the *Ferrocarriles Unidos de la Habana*, the United Railways of Havana."

"Do you need protection?" Nico asked with worry in his face. "A single woman traveling alone carrying all that money."

"Very touching. Is it the money you are worried about? Or is it me?"

"A little of both, I suppose. You have more than enough of your own risks to shoulder without me adding to your burdens."

"This is true. But you are paying me quite generously. Ten percent of the gross. That is my cut, and it is enough to cover my risks. But I never carry your money, only my own. Now may I please be allowed to find myself breakfast?"

Nico Carolla nodded, smiled, and sent Martina on her way.

Oh boy, life was good!

SATURDAY
AUGUST 1, 1942
2 p.m.

San Diego, California

PFC Stanley Whitehorse hesitated on the large, bottom step of the waiting school bus before boarding.

Aside from its color — olive-drab instead of yellow with black markings — it was an ordinary school bus, common to the times, the sort that could be seen on any city street. — Hinged double-door in front. Single exit door at rear. High side panels. Six square windows on each side. Twenty rows of bench seats within. The Marine base used this sort of school bus to transport men into and out of Camp Elliott.

"Hurry up, Stosh," the next soldier in line urged him. That's what they called him instead of his given name. Stosh.

The Marines were jostling for position in line, each lugging a heavy duffel. There were twenty-nine men in all. Save one or two that had been ordered to stay behind to train the next batch of code-talkers, the entire Marine platoon was now headed for the same unknown destination, somewhere in the South Pacific.

"Yeah, hurry up, Stosh," came the voice of another man further back in line. It was Stanley's friend, Chester Nez.

Whitehorse continued up the stairs of the bus, now, and heaved his duffel bag onto the pile at the back of the bus. He turned and quickly found a seat.

The air inside the bus was stifling. The bench seats were hard and uncomfortable. Whitehorse gave a quick tug and yanked down the two closest windows. It did not improve matters. There was hardly any air.

It had been twelve weeks since Stosh last sat in this bus, last sat in this very seat. That was the day he arrived here in Camp Elliott by bus from Arizona along with the other Navajo recruits. Now that their training was complete, he and the other Navajo were leaving San Diego for their first tour of duty among the islands of the South Pacific.

"Quiet down Marines," Staff Sergeant Philip Johnston exhorted. As a civilian, he had founded the code-talker program. The rank of staff sergeant was new, a recent field promotion.

Chester Nez took a seat across the aisle from Whitehorse in the bus. They had known each other since they were boys. "I guess this is it," he said. "We are going to the South Pacific. We are going to war."

Stanley Whitehorse allowed a quizzical smile. "Before three months ago, I had never once left the reservation, not even to go into town. Now I have been to California, San Diego no less. And now I am leaving America for a foreign country, an island in the middle of the ocean, if you can believe that. Until twelve weeks ago, I had never been on a beach before, never even seen the ocean. Now I am about to cross the largest one."

"It will be okay," Chester said. "It will be okay."

Stosh was comforted by his friend's words.

"Get settled, Marines," Staff Sergeant Johnston called out. "It is about thirty minutes' ride to the pier from here, maybe a bit more."

Whitehorse didn't need any encouragement to settle down. He was exhausted, as tired as he could ever remember being. Sleep would come easily.

The bus was barely out of the gravel parking lot when his eyelids grew heavy and closed. His unconscious mind slipped back to those early first days at Camp Elliott, three months ago, May 1942.

•

•

"Semper Fi, Marines. Welcome to Camp Elliott," Marine Lieutenant Colonel James E. Jones barked at the nearly three dozen men standing before him. To his left stood two other men, one in uniform, one not. Neither man had yet been introduced.

For several months now, Colonel Jones had been shepherding the code-talker program through a complicated genesis. "It is about time you boys woke up and smelled the gunpowder. You men are to be here at Camp Elliott for eight weeks of basic communications training. Your assignment while you are here is to work alongside my people and to develop a workable code based on the Navajo language. This is vital work we will be doing. — And top-secret. So keep your mouths closed at all times."

Twenty-nine Native American recruits stood at attention in the small, high-ceilinged barracks. The air was thick with dust and dry summer heat. This was southern California at the hottest part of the summer 1942.

Camp Elliott was a Marine training facility for the 2nd Marine Division. It was known within the Corps as having one of the better ranges for rifle training. The training camp was located twelve miles northeast of downtown San Diego, where it was framed by a pair of steep desert hills.

Their journey to this location began on the morning of May 4, 1942. On that day, these nearly three dozen Navajo recruits boarded a bus in Ft. Defiance, Arizona, and left the reservation, some never to return. From Ft. Defiance, they were first transported to the induction center at Ft. Wingate, New Mexico. Then, after lunch, overnight to Marine Corps Recruit Depot, San Diego, for administrative in-processing. Then came seven weeks of standard Marine Corps basic training.

Lieutenant Colonel James E. Jones continued his introductory remarks. "Your guides over the next eight weeks will be these two men — cryptographic officer Christopher Burlingame and program founder Philip Johnston." The lieutenant colonel nodded to his left, in their direction. "For the time being, Mr. Johnston is a civilian. He is not to be saluted. But he is to be treated with the same deference you would accord a Staff Sergeant, which is what his rank will be once the Corps acts on my request and makes it official. Is that understood?"

Twenty-nine closely-shaved heads bobbed up and down as if to say "yes." These men had just completed a seven-week-long course of basic training, the first all-Navajo platoon to graduate. June 27, 1942. Platoon Number 382.

"Mr. Johnston, please escort these men down to the code hut. They been eating our chow and crapping in our latrines all summer long. It is high time these Indian warriors began to earn their keep."

"Yes sir, right away."

Philip Johnston, the principal driving force behind the Navajo code-talker program, led the squad of lean and muscular men down the dusty path to the new code hut. Johnston had fought in the First World War, which made him at least twice their age. In the intervening years, Johnston had managed to keep himself remarkably lean and fit.

"I think all you men know that this code school began as an experimental pilot program."

Philip Johnston opened with these words once the group had made their way down to the code hut and taken their seats. There were four rows of closely-spaced folding chairs.

Johnston continued. "I learned to speak Navajo as a boy, became fluent. I lived on the reservation as a child, same as you. I played with Navajo children growing up, probably your parents, maybe your grandparents. That was more than forty years ago. All I ask from you now, today, is that you try and do your best. I have a lot at stake here. So does the Corps. But my reputation is on the line. I want to see this program succeed."

A tentative hand went up in the third row.

"Yes, Marine? What is on your mind?"

The man in the third row stood. According to custom, he remained at attention as he spoke.

"My name is Chester Nez. My people are a proud people. We are proud to serve. But why the need for all this secrecy?"

PFC Chester Nez remained at attention and politely waited for his superior to answer.

"I know who you are, Marine."

In Philip Johnston's estimation, Chester Nez was a man perfectly suited to the United States Marine Corps. As a boy, he had often slept in the open air, more than occasionally on hard ground. Hours of hard physical labor did not deter him. Nor did danger. He was a Navajo warrior at heart. It was in his blood. Personal danger was something the man took in stride.

In the Marine Corps, chow was plentiful, a happy change from Chester's childhood when he was often stung by hunger. Plus, the service uniform accorded him a measure of respect wherever he went. He was normally easygoing. Some things bothered him, though.

His given name was not Chester. Nor was his surname Nez. Whatever his name had been at birth, that name had been stripped from his memory at boarding school. The white world of his youth had tried to civilize him, tried to make him one of their own, tried to wash away his Navajo past.

Like Whitehorse and many of the other recruits in that room, they forced Nez to speak English, a language he had never heard spoken before. To break him of speaking the filthy gibberish language he had grown up with, the same filthy gibberish language he still insisted on using, the matron of the boarding school would brush his teeth with bitter laundry soap.

But the cruel measure did not succeed. Even at that young age, the culture of the Navajo was already deeply ingrained within him. His mother was of the Black Sheep Clan; his father, the Sleeping Rock People. Chester was already fluent in one of the most complex languages on the planet, verb-rich and adjective-poor.

Verbs did most of the heavy lifting in the Navajo language. By adding prefixes and suffixes, each verb-root could be made more complex. Plus, each verb was capable of taking on seven modes as well as twelve aspects. The Navajo language lacked punctuation, for it had no written counterpart. Thus, intonation constantly came into play. Four combinations of tone, plus glottal, and aspirated stops. A shift in any one of them could significantly alter the meaning of a word.

So now, when Chester Nez rose from his seat and questioned Philip Johnston about the need for secrecy, Johnston had to answer him simply and directly.

"At ease, Marine."

Chester Nez did as instructed and took his seat. Philip Johnston continued.

"This is the 382nd Marine Platoon. We all know it to be a fictional unit. But a fictional unit built for an absolutely serious enterprise. From this moment forward, you may not speak with other Jarheads about what you do. You may not speak with members of your family, not your parents, not your children, not your girlfriends, not your wives, not your brothers or your sisters."

A second Marine raised his hand.

"Stand and be recognized."

"Private Whitehorse, Sir."

"Go ahead, Whitehorse."

"I do not mean to speak out of turn here, Sir. But you do understand that we have no prior experience in such matters, no special knowledge of signaling or code?"

"Oh, but you do," Johnston said. "You just don't realize it yet. And when the Camp Elliott School is done with you, you will have more. The United States of America cannot win the war in the Pacific without help from the Navajo Nation."

"Sir?" Marine Private Stanley Whitehorse was still standing.

"Our military codes are weak and cumbersome. They have already proven to be a fatal weakness. But you men can help us solve this problem. Now be seated, Marine."

Philip Johnston turned to introduce a new man, Camp Elliott's top cryptographic officer. "Captain Burlingame, would you like to weigh in here?"

"Thank you, Mr. Johnston."

Captain Christopher Burlingame was a no-nonsense Marine. He possessed a keen and agile mind. He cleared his throat now to speak.

"This code-talker program began as an experiment, like the man said. Marine commanders were initially skeptical. But now that the case has been made, the experiment is complete. A message that takes any other military unit of ours one hour to encrypt, transmit and decrypt using our existing mechanical system can be transmitted orally by our Navajo code-talkers in just over forty seconds. Not a single member of our signal corps or our code cracking unit has been able to break the Navajo code."

The twenty-nine men sat a little taller in their chairs, their chests now pumped up with pride. As Native Americans confined to a reservation in the western United States, they were often considered by other Americans to be second-class citizens.

But now, dressed in a snappy Marine uniform, they could visit bars and restaurants that would normally bar entry to a Native American. Now they possessed a scarce and valuable resource, their Navajo language.

Unbridled pride was a feeling that did not come easily to men like Stanley Whitehorse or Chester Nez. To look someone directly in the eye was considered a sign of disrespect in their culture. To raise one's voice or shout at a man was perhaps the most disrespectful act of all. When Chester Nez spoke, which was not often, he spoke in low even tones.

Captain Christopher Burlingame continued. "We began this experiment with just three men. When Pearl was attacked, Mr. Johnston was working for the Los Angeles water department as a civil engineer. He recruited four Navajo who were working in the Los Angeles shipyards and arranged a demonstration of their skills for Marine General Vogel. They proved to the General the value of using the Navajo language to transmit military communications."

Marine Private Stanley "Stosh" Whitehorse raised his hand for a second time. "Mr. Johnston. You said you lived on the reservation as a boy. Would we perhaps have met?"

"How old are you, Whitehorse?"

"Twenty."

"Then perhaps not. I am old enough to be your father."

Several men chuckled. Johnston continued.

"I was born in Topeka, Kansas. This was before the turn of the century. My father William was a missionary. He brought our family to Flagstaff in 1896. His mission was to serve Navajo residing on the western part of the reservation. I was only four years old at the time. When we arrived on the reservation, there was a great deal of tension between the Navajo and the neighboring ranchers. The two were on the verge of open warfare. My father worked hard to keep the peace. There was a confrontation between the two sides, what is known today as the Padre Canyon Incident. It had to do with livestock rustling. My father stepped in to help defuse what could have been an extremely violent clash."

"That was your father? The Reverend?" Whitehorse asked, properly impressed. "My grandfather told me a story once about the Reverend. After your father helped resolve the Padre Canyon Incident without bloodshed, Navajo leaders allowed Reverend Johnston to build a mission nearby."

Philip Johnston nodded. "Yes, that was my father. After the dispute was settled and the mission built, my father worked with the tribe and with the federal government to expand the boundaries of the western part of the Navajo reservation. He viewed the expansion as part of a longer-term solution to the ongoing livestock rustling disputes. Not long afterward, my father traveled to Washington, D.C. along with the Navajo leadership. The purpose of their trip was to speak with the new president — President Theodore Roosevelt — about enlarging the reservation. This happened not long after President McKinley was assassinated. Since I knew both languages, English and Navajo, I was asked to accompany my father as the translator between the two parties, the Navajo leadership and President Roosevelt."

"But you were just a boy."

"My youth may have actually helped. It may have helped persuade a reluctant President Roosevelt to issue an Executive Order adding more land to the Navajo Reservation. I would like to think I had a hand in it anyway. Years later, during the Great War, when I enlisted and got shipped off to France, I heard how Comanche Indians were being used by the U.S. Army as code-talkers. That is how I came to think of this project."

Philip Johnston continued. "Initially, I thought the Navajo language could be used as-is to transmit military communications, using conventional Navajo. But before the actual demonstration got underway, my Navajo recruits received samples of the various military expressions they were going to be asked to convey to one another in code. That is when a strange thing happened. My recruits informed me that in order to send the military messages, they would have to use word and letter substitutions throughout. That seemed cumbersome. So we quickly huddled and began to build a list of Navajo words that would stand-in for their English equivalents. Later, the Navajo were split into two groups and put in separate rooms at opposite ends of the building. Each room was equipped with a field phone.

"The two opposing Navajo teams transmitted the long list of common military expressions by verbally encrypting, transmitting, and decoding the messages nearly verbatim from English to Navajo and then back again into English. After seeing the limitations to using conversational Navajo for military communications, I was inspired to use letter and word substitution methods to encrypt Navajo. What we need to do now, you and me together here at Camp Elliott, is to develop a codebook, commit it to memory and then destroy it. No printed matter in the field where it might be captured by the enemy. All in your head. Is everyone clear on the objectives?"

•

•

Suddenly, the bus hit a pothole in the road and everyone jerked awake.

"We there yet?" Whitehorse muttered.

"Yes, just about," Chester answered.

"Okay, Leathernecks. Eyes open, heads up!" Staff Sergeant Johnston boomed. "It is about time you Jarheads woke up and smelled the gunpowder. We all be going to war."

SATURDAY
AUGUST 1, 1942
5 p.m.

Riverfront Levee, New Orleans

"Hector, he come to me last night in a dream," Kentucky Rose said as the two Negroes walked along the riverfront levee in the direction of the passenger ferry terminal at the foot of Jackson Avenue. She was upset and shaking like a leaf.

"Who come to you last night in a dream?" Hector asked. From their present location atop the levee near the foot of Canal Street, the river was nearly half a mile wide and running strong. A series of busy wharves lined both shores of the river. Men could be seen unloading ships and cargo of every sort, mainly produce.

"Dat dead man, dat who. Dat Heinie Kraut who crapped off in mah bed. He come to me last night inna dream, dead an' all covered wid maggots."

Hector shook his head. "Did I not tell you de death of dat man gonna be bad *juju*? But maybe you be okay in de end, girl. After alls, you still have your *gris-gris* to protect you. Anyways, today we cross de river to see de voodoo queen Thelma over dere in Gretna. She mights b'able to do us both some good."

"How so?" Kentucky Rose gave him a quizzical look.

Hector brushed off her question with a bothered expression. Helping Rose adjust her *gris-gris* was not Hector's only agenda in this evening's visit to the voodoo queen. In Hector's world there were good luck charms and bad luck charms. The gold signet ring in his pocket, the one he had filched off the dead man's finger two nights ago, was a case in point. Maybe the gold ring was itself bad *juju*. Hector intended to have the voodoo queen pray over it, have her whisk away any bad spirits, cleanse it for him that he might safely wear the thing without fear of trouble.

But Hector dare not tell Rose the truth. She would be furious to know that was Hector's only reason for accompanying her to see Thelma.

The two stopped a minute on the levee above the river's edge to catch their breath. The late afternoon sun was blazing hot.

Below them, at the base of the levee, the expanse of muddy water seemed in no particular hurry to get down to the ocean as it flowed by with great deliberation. Here, near the end of the powerful river's thousand-mile journey from headwater to sea, the river writhed like a crouched snake between the hardened, yellow-clay banks of the encircling levees.

The dark current carried driftwood, small boats, even oceangoing vessels downstream toward the open sea. Sea gulls swept in from the Gulf. They soared above the churning water, searching for a bite to eat, perhaps a small fish. Every now and again, the shadow of a passing summer cloud would darken the water's turbulent surface. But the shadow would be fleeting and then the sun would pop through the clouds again. The accompanying wind wrote mysterious script in swiftly changing ripples that swirled above the river's eddies and whirlpools.

The greater portion of the city would suffer from floods nearly every year were it not for the artificial levee system that surrounded it. The built-up section of the city was drained by a series of canals and pumping stations, and was completely enclosed by levees constructed along the river, as well as along the lakefront and the neighboring waterways.

"It was terrible, mah dream," Rose said sadly. "Like when I was a little girl. Dere was dis chimney sweep . . . "

"Nothing to fear from no chimney sweep," Hector said, gazing into the brown water. During the winter, a thick fog would often blanket the river's surface. On those days, the sound of fog horns could be heard echoing their warning message between the hidden shores. In late spring, when the river's waters were swollen by the icy melt of its tributaries, the river would rush past the city with great fury. The fast-moving water would gnaw at the imprisoning banks which, before the arrival of mankind, once had the privilege of overflowing.

"Chimney sweep dun molested me when I was just a girl." Her eyes were filled, now, with tears.

"Say it ain't true," Hector said. He had heard this sad story before and did not care to hear it again. The river was more interesting. A dredge boat could be seen churning up the mud. During summertime's low water, it would work dredging silt away from the dockside to maintain the boat channel's required depth. The current of the river shot toward the west bank. Silt would accumulate on the east bank in front of the wharves, unless it was removed.

"But 'tis true," Rose exclaimed. "Sweep was dis tall, very black nigger, black as midnight. He had crooked toes. Dey peeped out of shufflin' shoes. His trousers was all torn an' tattered. He wore an old frockcoat. It be all threadbare and smellin' like burnt cinders. The dirt of a hundred chimneys. Cocked over one eye be this ginormous top hat. Most'a de crown was bashed in. He carried dis big ole bundle of rope and broom straw and bunches of palmetto."

Hector grinned knowingly through a mouth of crooked teeth. "Palmetto. What Creole folk call *latanier*. Fans, hats, baskets, brooms, chair seats — dey all made from dat palmetto plant. Strips of *latanier* still carried by Negro chimney sweeps. But not many sweeps left dese days. Not many coal peddlers neither. Nowadays peoples gots gas heat. Adieu, *ramoneur*!" he said wistfully.

"In mah dream, sweep yelled dat very t'ing in the streets below our flat — R-R-R-R-R-RAMONAY! R-r-r-ramonez la chiminee du haut en bas! — Then Marie Laveau came to me in mah sleep."

"De Voodoo Queen Marie Laveau, who be buried in Materie Cemetery?"

"One and de same. It may have been real; it may have been a dream. When I was but a little girl, mah mother took me to stand before dat woman Marie Laveau. Dat woman said I be afflicted with demons ... But in mah dream, it was the chimney sweep who took me to see de Voodoo Queen, to get for me some *goofer* dust."

"Again with the *goofer* dust?" Hector said, entranced by the frenetic activity along the riverbanks. He stood watching men unload bananas from a South American freighter. In spite of the river's obvious hostility toward Man, it held a certain fascination, a calming influence on those who gazed upon it. The eloquent silence told of strange and distant places from whence its waters came, and of the history that once unfolded along these banks.

"Hector, surely you must know 'bout *goofer* dust. In mah dream de *ramoneur* took me to de old St. Louis Cemetery. It be late afternoon. De sun be low in de sky. De sexton at de gate won't be letting in no strangers. De sweep whispers somethin' to dat man in French or Creole. Den de sexton dun bows, and we enters de gate. We wander about 'mong the old, crumbling whitewashed tombs. Dey look like little houses. Small, wrought-iron fences be in front of each tomb. Dat cemetery be like a miniature city, city of de dead. Dere be street names and everythin'. Some'a de tombs be blindin' white under de hot sun. All dem big tomb hab a place for flower vases. Most'a de oven vaults haves a small shelf for de same. He an' me walk a spell. Den de chimney sweep stops afore a tall tomb. He puts his finga to his lips. Dat tells me to be quiet, den he climbs to the top of de tomb like a cat burglar. Moments later, he come back down with a handful of damp earth. *This be Marie Laveau's grave*, he says to me.

"I asks him: *Who dis Marie Laveau?*"

Kentucky Rose continued. "He say to me: Only de most famous, most powerful of all de Voodoo Queens. On Saint John's Eve, de needy come here and put coins in de chinks of de grave to have her spirit answer dere prayers. *Goofer* dust be earth from a grave, any grave. But I thought I wanna get you earth from Marie Laveau's own grave. Dat would make de *gris-gris* charms twice as potent, he say, smiling. People comes here often. They leave hoodoo money at de base of de tomb, small sums, two-cents or 'leven-cents. They believe de hoodoo money gonna bring dem good luck or else bad luck to dere enemy. Marie is said to conversate with her followers through de walls of her oven, giving up such information as dey desires."

"Oven?"

Even as Hector asked the question, his attention was directed elsewhere, on the activity down by the riverside wharves. Upstream, to his right, coffee beans were being unloaded at the Poydras Street Wharf, many hundreds of bags each month. Concrete ramps led to the second story of the wharf, on the city side, for the convenience of drivers and their trucks.

But to Hector, the most interesting aspect of the coffee unloading process was the flag system the shipping companies employed to organize the freight. Most of the dockhands were illiterate. They could neither read nor write. For them, a written sign would hold no meaning. And yet, a method had to be devised to properly sort materials as they came off a ship. Thus was born the flag system still in use today.

The flags were a foot or more in size and of various colors and designs — stars, moons, birds, even alligators. The flags were placed wherever different shipments or lots of merchandise were to be piled. The longshoremen, as they passed up the ramp with their loads, would be tapped on the shoulder by a foreman. He would indicate the pile the carrier was to go to by shouting out the color or design of the appropriate flag. The system was quite efficient. It provided employment to many workers of low intelligence or limited skills.

"A tomb be like an oven," Kentucky Rose said. "It be like an oven to cook de dead flesh away. Most tombs gots a crypt where de bones are kept. They be sealed up real tight to stop de gases from escapin' de decayin' bodies. Sometimes de vaults be built in layers. They be like great, thick walls. They be called ovens. After a period 'a time set by law, de tombs be opened an' de coffins be broke an' burned. Remains den be deposited in dem crypts. Dis a'way one single tomb may be used by de same family for gen'rations."

Hector said. "In some'a de graveyards vaults can be rented for a certain period 'a time. When time be up, de body be removed 'n' den be buried in some out-of-de-way corner of de graveyard."

"Ain't dem gravediggers got no heart?"

"It ain't 'bout heart, Rose. It be 'bout space an' money, mainly money."

"It always be 'bout money," Rose sighed. "But den me an' de sweep we dun took our leave of dat cemetery. We still be talkin' 'bout Marie Laveau. She would charm po'licemen sent to take her into custody. She waves her hands an' dey be unable to move. We talked of how her *tignon* — her turban headdress — be tied in a way no other woman be permitted to tie hers. Also, how she be said to conversate with those who inherited her church after her death; and of many other sin'ster things."

As Rose told him her story, Hector watched with growing interest the activity on the riverfront across the river. Green bananas were being unloaded at the Thalia Street Wharf used by the United Fruit Company. Three or four times each week, the same scene played out at the same location.

The Thalia Street Wharf had two sheds, one for bananas and another for passengers. The greatest activity on the waterfront could always be found where the larger steamship companies made their landings. When a passenger boat docked, there was always a lively scene. Half a dozen railroad spurs ran into the banana shed at right angles and extended out to the riverside platform. Here were located the banana conveyers, constructed so that they could be lowered by hand into the open hatchways.

Workmen in the hold of a ship placed the bunches of bananas in the conveyer pockets which lifted the bananas up to the level of the wharf. From there, the bunches were taken by carriers who toted them on their shoulders to railroad cars after being sorted, at sight, by men skilled in the profession. There was an element of danger in the work as tarantula spiders and large, green tree snakes, as well as small boa constrictors, often hid in the bunches. The overripe and broken bunches were sold to peddlers, who resold them in the city streets from wagons and trucks.

Kentucky Rose continued with her story. "Den dat bad man molested me down by St. John's Bayou. I was only ten, but already tufts of hair had taken root down dere. He did things to me, terr'ble things. Afterward, I cried an' cried. I could not stop. So mah moms took me to Mother Catherine, High Priestess of N'Orleans. She dead now. But in mah dream, she be alive. Brother Isaiah be dere too."

"The White Prophet? At de Church of Innocent Blood?"

Rose nodded. "I seen it. Brother Isaiah cured sick an' lame white folk with prayer an' a magic touch. But he refused to cure Mother Catherine from what ailed her, 'cause of her dark skin color. This set her mind to thinking. She was stirred to pray more deeply for religion an' for better health. *De Lawd healed me*, she contended. *He healed me. Ah heals all colors.*

"Mother Catherine wore no partic'lar uniform. The Lord told her what to wear each day. Usually it be a ginormous white dress an' white cap. A large key dangled from a blue cord tied 'round her waist. The members be permitted to kneel at her feet an' make wishes as dey kissed her key.

"Mother Catherine did not wear no shoes on her ugly fat feet during church services. She reminded her people that *de Lawd went widout shoes.* Mother Catherine always entered de church through a hole in the roof of a side room. It made people think she be sent down from Heaven or somethin' to preach de gospel. The men of de congregation helped her to the top of de church on'a ladder. She made a right solemn entrance an' de entire aud'yence remained quiet until she had blessed every last one'a dem.

"But when she begin to speak her sermon, hysteria sweep like a flame throughout de room. Groans, n' shouts, n' tapping of feet, swaying of bodies. Us black folk say de church gets 'hot'. Den a rhythmic outburst of chantin' voices an' stampin' feet begin as she start to preach. De High Priestess stands in de center of de altar. She raise her hand in blessin'. *Chillen, Ah's come here to do good, not evil.* De response from de aud'yence be approvin' in every way. — *She sho did*, someone shouts. — *Look a here, she done cured me*, shouts another. — *Ah believes in ya, Mother* — came from whites as well as blacks.

"Mother Catherine did never bother with no Bible.   She could 'member everythin' in it. *Ah's read de Bible all de time. Ah's gonna gib ya dah facts.*   Dats what she dun said.   When de congregation starts to singin', much improvisin' be done by Mother Catherine an' her co-workers.   Dey all be clad in long white robes an' sits in de front-most pews."

Rose continued to drone on, but Hector ignored her and continued his slow walk along the levee toward their destination. He clutched tightly to the stolen ring in his pocket.

Rose followed behind at a distance, blabbering on and on. Now Hector could see the Robin Street Wharf which began at the foot of Terpsichore Street.   From here, he could see a surprising variety of merchandise being unloaded — hogsheads of tobacco, farm machinery, automobiles, cartons of carbon black, stacks of raw food products, and canned goods of every description.   Lumber and millwork and bales of cotton would likely be found in every transit shed.

At the foot of Market Street, opposite the Market Street Wharf, stood the massive power plant of the New Orleans Public Service Corporation.   Submarine cables from this plant carried power across the river bottom to the west bank.   Nearby was the site of the old city waterworks which, for many years, supplied unfiltered water to the business section of the city.

The Jackson Avenue Ferry, which connected the city with Gretna on the other bank, made for another break in the wharf line.   This is where the two of them were headed.   There at the ferry landing, in warm weather, as well as at other points along the docks, boys could be seen diving and swimming in the unforgiving river.   It was a dangerous sport, one strongly discouraged by the port authorities.   But, until recently, the river was the only swimming hole available to the poor.   Indeed, many of the city elders learned their first strokes beneath those same wharves.

Kentucky Rose chattered on.   "When a brother or a sister wanted to be healed, he be escorted to de altar by a co-worker. Mother Catherine looked over de candidate real close-like an' asked: *Has de Lawd got His rod on ya?   Ah cain't cure anyone what's got de rod on dem.*   De candidate first took his castor oil or black draught, den Mother Catherine would pray over him, making all kinda motions an' calling — *Hear me, Sperrits* — while dat man just stands dere real quiet like afore her.

"If he be not healed, someone woulds say — *Sumpins wrong wid him.   Boy, clean yo soul for' de debbil gits ya too much.*   Cripple and wheelchair folk be rubbed an' prayed over with de help of unseen spirits. De lame be whipped with a wet towel an' told to run outta de church. De most spectac'lar cures be those of dah blind. Easy cases be treated wid blessed rainwater. In stubborn cases, Mother Catherine called *lightnin' right down from hebben* to clear de clouded visions of dem folk. Dat High Priestess don't charge no fee for all dem services or remedies. But, with a finger pointed towards de money box she woulds say — *Ah's gotta pay mah expenses an' eat, ya know.*

"She cured by *layin' on ob hands an' anointin' dere innards* wid a full tumbler of warm castor oil, followed by a quarter of a lemon to kill de taste. *Ya gotta do as Ah says if'n ya wants to be healed an' blessed*, she told those who objected.

"Other folk step forward to be cured. Dat voodoo queen talks to the white folks, 'splaining — *Ya be hoodooed, too. Dat one was hoodooed, wasn't ya, child? I cures ev'rybody, white an' black alike. Makes no diff'rence to me.*"

Hector was now practically beside himself. "E-nuff already, Rose! I kin listen to no more'a this. We gonna get ourselves onto yon' ferry and over to d'other side'a de river. There be a healer there I kin take you to. Thelma gonna cure you of yor bad dreams and fix yor *gris-gris* once and for all."

Hector knew of what he spoke. The practice of making and wearing charms or amulets for protection or for healing or for the harming of others was a key aspect of Louisiana Voodoo. The *ouanga* was a charm used to poison an enemy. It contained the toxic roots of the accursed fig tree — the *figuier maudit*. It was brought to the Americas from Africa and preserved in Louisiana. The ground-up root of the tree was combined with other elements — bones, finger nails, roots, holy water, holy candles, holy incense, holy bread, or crucifixes. The administrator of the ritual frequently evoked protection from Jehovah or from Jesus Christ. The tentative nature of African belief allowed for the adoption of many Catholic practices into Louisiana Voodoo.

"We be here now, girl," Hector said as they walked the few remaining yards to the passenger ferry terminal above Gouldsboro Bend. "We gonna cross dat river to de voodoo queen in Gretna and she gonna cure you of all yor troubles."

Near the ferry terminal on both sides of the river were street vendors of every sort, but none in greater number at this season than the berry men and the berry women. Men sold only strawberries, women only blackberries. No one knew why. That was just how it had always been.

Street cries from sidewalk vendors had been a hallmark of New Orleans life from its earliest colonial days. They were little more than crude rhymes composed by scruffy looking peddlers. The peddlers would saunter along the streets hawking their wares, crying out their rhyming pitch to housewives and servant girls, in fact to anyone who would listen. The blackberry women, having just walked miles from the woods and bayou banks, wore skirts tucked gypsy-fashion around their waist and bare legs. Faint traces of dusty travel showed on their weathered skin, as they called out in a melancholy tone:

> *Come get yor blackberries fresh an' fine;*
> *I got blackberries, fresh from da vine;*
> *I got blackberries, three glass fo' a dime.*

A dime was not a great deal of money, just two American nickels, ten lousy cents. Small coins of all sorts circulated in the local economy. These were a product of the long history of conquest and commerce in the Louisiana Territory. The oldest piece still in circulation was the *picayune* — one "bit" — a Spanish half-real made of silver and worth six and one-quarter cents. The locals used the word *picayune* in many different ways, either to describe a small sum of money, like a penny or nickel, or to describe a small or worthless individual. The word was borrowed from the French like so many Creole terms. In French, *pécaillon* or *picayon* was slang for money or cash. Both words descended from *piquar*, meaning to ring bells, not unlike the sound of coins jingling in one's pocket.

Hector and Kentucky Rose dug deep in their pockets for small change. Between them they came up with a collection of pennies and nickels. They paid the ferry fare, bought a portion of berries, and boarded the flat-bottomed boat for the trip to the other side.

The trip across the broad river would take no more than fifteen minutes. They stood on the deck, stared out on the water. From here, in the middle of the river, the entire dock and wharf system took on a new perspective. Now it could be observed in all its rich frenetic activity, stretching up and down the river on both sides, for miles. Vessels flew the flags of every seafaring nation.

The flags fluttered at the mastheads. Sea gulls followed the ships, searching for food.

Presently, the banana wharf was abuzz with activity. A banana ship had docked within the hour. Now, hundreds of laborers carried the green fruit to the waiting cars. Old Negro women, fat and wearing snowy turbans on their heads, moved about the crowd selling the workers sandwiches and sweet cakes. Those who tasted their wares found the dainties toothsome and appetizing.

All day long the groaning conveyors would lift bunches of bananas from the hold of the ship, and all day long the men would move like robots in a line carrying them. Darkness would fall and the great lights would flash on and yet, the work of unloading would continue into the night. Before long, there would be long swaying shadows, and the fruit would appear doubly green in the artificial light.

The hours would pass and the men would continue at their labor. Then, suddenly, the foreman would give a great shout and the outsized conveyors would stop moving. The ship was empty. The line would break and the men would briefly scatter. Then, as if on cue, they would form up in line again, this time in front of the paymaster. Every dock up and down the river was the same — coffee, cotton, molasses — all busy scenes of activity.

To Hector's mind, there was no finer place to live than New Orleans, nor finer time to be alive. He was a happy man. He would be happier still once the ring in his pocket was cured of the dead man's evil spirits.

SUNDAY
AUGUST 2, 1942
8 a.m.

South Pacific

The wind swept across the thin, uninhabited stretch of open beach. A flock of seagulls hung lazily in the warm tropical air. The island of Fiji might have been a paradise, if not for the presence of the 1st Marine Division.

"All due respect, Colonel. Why do you have my men scratching around in the sand digging foxholes on this quiet speck of land in the middle of the South Pacific? The only action my men have seen so far are sand crabs fighting each other to the death on the beach."

"You questioning my orders, Captain?" Colonel Daniel Morrison asked, refusing to step out from beneath the protective shade of the large canvas dining fly.

"Not even."

"Good, because this place will not remain quiet much longer. Any day now I expect our 1st Marine Division to receive orders to break camp and set sail."

"That is good to know," Captain Whittaker said. "These boots are fresh from training. They are all keyed up, ready to shoot at anything that moves. You know as well as anyone how quickly Jarheads can get bored. After Pearl, about the only thing these Leathernecks want to do is go out and kill themselves some yellow-skinned butterheads. The men want in on the fight."

"And fight they will," Colonel Daniel Morrison said. "Soon enough. For the next day or two, stay with the boat drills. Keep practicing with those Coast Guard boat drivers. They have the experience, the know-how, and the guts."

The canvas over their heads snapped in the breeze. Out here, in the middle of the Pacific, at this time of year, the wind never stopped blowing. And when it did stop blowing, watch out. A storm was brewing somewhere over the horizon.

"I have been to the briefings, Colonel, same as you. The attack on Pearl crippled our fleet. What the Nips want now is to totally neutralize our navy."

"Yes, and seize possessions rich in natural resources. The Nip homeland lacks the basic resources necessary to wage war against a country as big and powerful as ours. They need stuff that is hard to come by — and lots of it. Good stuff like oil, rubber, lumber, and steel — stuff like that. Their strategy is to take what they need from others."

"What they really need to do is establish a string of strategic military bases. They need those bases in order to defend the Empire. They have already captured the Philippines."

"And let's not forget Thailand," Colonel Morrison said.

"Yes, and Singapore. Burma. Wake Island. The Dutch East Indies. The list goes on. Every last one of them once belonged to the British or the Dutch or the Aussies."

"So you know your history, Captain. Bravo. But let's get something straight from the get-go. This island-hopping-shit our Semper Fi are about to engage in is going to be a bitch. Not like a land war at all. Certainly not like an ordinary naval battle. Each beach assault is going to be worse than the one before. The closer we get to the home island, the more vicious they will become. Plus, the Jap Navy has been pushing hard to extend its defensive perimeter."

"And we have begun to push back, Colonel. Battle of the Coral Sea three months ago early May. Battle of Midway two months ago. We kicked the living crap out of their carriers at Midway. It was sweet revenge for Pearl."

"Yes, Midway was a clear naval victory. And a big one. Coral Sea, not so much. Tactical stalemate. At least that's what the higher-ups say; though I am not entirely sure myself. Personally, I place the Battle of the Coral Sea in the win column, a strategic Allied victory. But you are right — Midway was a big win. That one significantly degraded the offensive capability of the Imperial Navy's carrier fleet."

"No one is arguing with you, Colonel. But even Midway did not alter the Jap mindset. The Nips see it as only a temporary setback. They are still on the offensive, still as brash and brazen as ever."

"You are talking about their effort to assault Port Moresby over the Kokoda Trail."

Captain Whittaker nodded grimly.

"Not to put too fine a point on it, Captain. But that is precisely why we are down here in Fiji practicing maneuvers with our Higgins boats. I suppose you must know it by now, but the Southern Solomon Islands are to be our target. Guadalcanal is the first prize, near the top of the list. Tulagi and Gavutu are likely stepping-stones to the bigger prize. Here, take a look at these maps."

Colonel Morrison directed Captain Whittaker to a large table in the center beneath the canvas-roofed dining fly. Maps of different scales were laid out everywhere on the table, as well as detailed aerial photographs. Bricks and rocks and chunks of driftwood weighted down their various corners.

"The Glorious Sons of the Rising Sun are building a large airfield here, at Lunga Point on Guadalcanal." Morrison pointed. "They have imported thousands of forced laborers from Korea to help them build the damn thing."

Captain Whittaker slowly shook his head. "That is not good news, not good at all. Japanese long-range bombers could threaten the east coast of Australia from such a base. Most of their citizens live along the east coast. If the Japs capture islands far enough to the east, those bombers might one day be able to even reach our own Pacific Coast."

"Now you have the picture square in the frame. If the Nips are allowed to complete work on that airfield, then Guadalcanal becomes a staging area for every manner of attack against Samoa and New Caledonia. Our Navy would never again be safe anywhere in SOPAC. The British might have to surrender Australia."

"So what is the plan?"

"Admiral King's plan," Colonel Daniel Morrison said. "King has proposed an offensive to deny the Japanese use of any of the Solomon Islands as bases to threaten our supply routes. Roosevelt has agreed to the plan, though it is not yet a priority for Army General Marshall. For Marshall and most of the other brass, it is Europe first, then Japan. Pacific operations have to constantly compete with the likes of Patton and Montgomery for the resources and personnel we require."

"But things are moving faster now that Admiral Chester Nimitz has been named commander-in-chief over all Pacific forces," Captain Whittaker said. He was still poring over the maps and aerial photographs of Guadalcanal and the three nearby islands of Tulagi, Gavutu, and Tanambogo. The last two seemed to be connected by a manmade causeway. "I understand that Admiral

Nimitz has dug in his heels. I hear tell he has gone so far as to say that the United States Navy and U.S. Marine Corps are prepared to carry out the operation, even without support of the Army."

Colonel Morrison chuckled. "It certainly hasn't hurt that we have been able to break the Jap naval codes. The JN-25 Code has proven far easier for us to crack than what the Brits have faced trying to break the Kraut Enigma machine codes. The Krauts keep changing the number of rotors on those infernal machines, as well as the rotor settings. I understand that Bletchley Park has been pulling their hair out. But so far they are keeping up. Here in the Pacific, things have been different. The Nip naval codes have been easier to crack. Plus, our Indian code-talkers have performed brilliantly, beyond expectations. We have been able to use them to disseminate disinformation to the enemy, information the enemy seems to be acting on. There is every indication the Sons of Nippon believe we are reinforcing Australia, not preparing for an attack on the Solomon Islands. Admiral Nimitz is pretty damn sure they took the bait."

"Indian code-talkers? What the hell are you talking about?"

"Yeah, that bit of intelligence is probably above your paygrade. The Camp Elliott program is pretty much hush-hush. I probably shouldn't have said anything. Technically, telling you is a court-martial offense. Very interesting story, though."

Captain Whittaker looked around. "I won't be pressing charges if you wish to spill."

Colonel Morrison debated. "I can't see any great harm in telling you. I will be leaving the Pacific Theatre before long anyway. Take a seat, Captain."

The two men sat and Colonel Morrison began. "The exact details are not known, even to me. What I do know is this. Adolf Hitler is a student of history. He knows that code-making and codebreaking are one part of waging a successful war. The Romans used it back in their day, same as the Greeks in their day. This megalomaniac thinks he is building the Third Reich, the third Roman Empire. That is what the Wehrmacht's Enigma machine is all about, coding and decoding. That infernal machine is a product of their advanced mathematics. And it is a constant thorn in our sides. Hitler clearly knew, even before the war began, that our Signal Corps used bilingual Cherokee and Choctaw Indian code-talkers to great success in World War I."

Captain Whittaker frowned. "How can you be so sure that Hitler knew?"

"Because I came up through the Office of Naval Intelligence. Even before the 1938 Munich Agreement, when Britain caved to German strength, Hitler dispatched thirty anthropologists to the United States. Their assignment was simple enough: to learn Native American languages. At the time, we did not know their mission objectives to a certainty. But we were damn suspicious. We vetted the thirty men and women, made excuses to block the entry of two or three of them, granted the others travel visas, kept an eye on them, watched where they traveled, who they talked to."

"If you knew all this beforehand, why the hell weren't those enemy agents arrested?"

"Well, for one thing, there wasn't a war on at the time. Accredited scientists conducting legitimate research from public sources is not a crime. But more to the point, the anthropologists failed in their mission. Too many languages to learn. Not enough people on the Indian Reservations eager to teach them. Too many dialects. Hardly any of them written down."

"The inscrutable prairie nigger."

Colonel Daniel Morrison stopped what he was doing, his face now beet red with anger. "I do not want to hear those ugly words come out of your mouth ever again, Captain. Is that understood? Make no mistake. I can have you broken down to Second Louie in nothing flat."

"Yes, Sir. Sorry, Sir."

"There are damn few Redskins who are bilingual, fewer still who are willing to risk their lives to help the United States of America kick Nazi and Nippon ass."

"Yes, Sir. Sorry, Sir."

Colonel Morrison continued. "Like I said. The Office of Naval Intelligence knew of the anthropologists' mission, even if that mission failed to produce results. So, after Pearl Harbor, when the United States came into the war against the Nips and the Nazis, the Army decided against any large-scale use of Cherokee or Choctaw code-talkers in the European Theater. It was a precaution, just in case we were wrong and Hitler's people had actually learned something useful from their trip."

"So if we are no longer using these Cherokee Indians as code-talkers, what are we doing to encode our messages so the enemy cannot read them?"

"Ah, here is where it begins to get interesting, Captain. Here in the Pacific, the Corps has been taking a different tack from that taken by the Army in Europe. Station Hypo in Hawaii is staffed with some impressive fellows. Every last one of them is a genius, believe me. Joseph Rochefort. Edwin Layton. Joseph Finnegan. Their cryptographic skills practically won the Battle of Midway for us."

"How so?"

"Until our guys at Station Hypo got started with their codebreaking magic, we could do little more than guess where the Imperial Jap Navy might strike next. Would it be Midway? The Aleutian Islands? New Guinea? No one knew for certain, and we could not possibly protect them all. But then one of their number came up with a ruse; Rochefort, I think. The ruse was designed to make the Nip bastards show their hand. His idea was brilliant. He suggested we fake a water supply failure on Midway Island, then have the Navy broadcast an unencrypted emergency warning to the fleet. The hope was to provoke a Japanese response."

"And did it?"

"You know how the Navy works," Colonel Morrison said. "No one takes a dump without someone else first cutting orders. Rochefort took the idea to Layton, who put it to Nimitz. Nimitz approved. They broadcast the emergency bulletin and the Japanese took the bait. The Japs broadcast instructions to their fleet to load additional water desalination equipment. This broadcast confirmed two things simultaneously — Midway was to be their target and Rochefort had figured out an ingenious way to crack their code."

"Cagey fellows, those mathematicians."

"There is more. The Jap radio message produced an unexpected bonus. They revealed that the assault was to come before mid-June. Now we knew the time *and* the place. We had the upper hand."

"But that still doesn't explain how we are encoding our own messages so they cannot be broken by the enemy."

"I am coming to that, Captain. Like I said, here in the Pacific the Corps has taken a different tack. Instead of Cherokee and Choctaw, we have put other groups of code-talkers to work in the Signal Corps coding our traffic. Enter the Navajo. These fellows speak a language hardly anyone knows and even fewer can translate; that is, unless they are Navajo themselves. Not even other Indian tribes understand it."

"But how does this code-talking thing work? You never explained that."

Colonel Morrison nodded his head and began to lay it out. "Most codes are substitution codes. Take any number you wish, say the number 53. Raise it to the second power. Add 1. Substitute that sum for the letter 'A' wherever it appears in the message, that sort of thing. The problem is that substitution codes, no matter how sophisticated, can be broken if a man works at it long enough and throws enough brainpower at it. Indeed, codebreaking is a form of mathematics, way above my IQ level. Witness the success of Bletchley Park. All those people are mathematicians, top-drawer. The genius of using codes constructed from obscure languages or from languages which are not widely spoken is that the substitution method becomes much tougher to crack. In an obscure language, ordinary words can take on completely new and different meanings."

"Now you have really gone and lost me, Colonel."

"Before the white man arrived in the New World, the Native Indians had never seen a cannon. They had no word for cannon in their language. So they made up a new word for it, more of a descriptive term than an actual word, like flaming candle or something along those lines. In similar fashion, the Comanche code word for tank is *turtle*. Bomber is *pregnant airplane*. Machine gun is *sewing machine*, maybe because of the sound it makes. Adolf Hitler becomes *crazy white man*. The Navajo have equally unlikely words. Bomber is *buzzard*. Submarine is *iron fish*. Stuff like that."

Colonel Morrison continued. "The Navajo coding experiment began with a guy named Philip Johnston. He was a veteran of the Great War, one who had grown up on a Navajo reservation. His father was a missionary to the Navajo, an important guy. To this day, Johnston remains one of a relative handful of non-Navajo who can speak their language fluently. The Navajo language has an exceedingly complex grammar. There is no written version of their language, no books, no newspapers, no dictionaries, nothing. Its syntax and tonal qualities make it unintelligible to anyone without extensive exposure and training. But Johnston was smart. He had been a soldier. He understood perfectly well how their language answered the military's need for an undecipherable code.

"The long and the short of it is that Johnston arranged a demonstration for Major General Clayton Vogel. As you undoubtedly know, Vogel is the commanding general of our Amphibious Corps. The general was impressed and the first batch of Navajo Indian recruits has already completed Marine Corps boot camp, about thirty men. They have been spending a lot of time at Camp Elliott near San Diego, refining a Navajo codebook. The code will never be written down. It must be memorized by the code-talkers word for word. The code they are developing is modeled on the Joint Army/Navy Phonetic Alphabet, plus a stable of Navajo descriptive terms to help shorten coding time."

"I don't follow."

"Okay then, a few examples. The word *shark* to describe a destroyer, or *silver oak leaf* to describe a lieutenant colonel. Even simple stuff like *ink stick* to describe a pen."

"Got it."

"I was brought into the circle maybe fifteen weeks ago, as this current operation was being planned by Admiral King. One group of thirteen Navajo code-talkers has been assigned to the 1st Marine Division, our division. They will be going in with us when we assault Guadalcanal."

"That's the mission then? Guadalcanal?"

"Operation Watchtower. That is what the brass are calling it. Several thousand men. Seventy-five warships and transports. Tentatively set to commence 7 August 1942."

Captain Whittaker's jaw dropped. "That is five days from now. When the fuck do we sail?"

"Could be as early as tomorrow morning," Morrison replied flatly. "But orders have not yet been cut. Commander of the Allied expeditionary force will be Vice Admiral Frank Fletcher. You know the man?"

"Everybody knows the man. Medal of Honor. Navy Cross. Operational Commander at the Battle of the Coral Sea. Officer in Tactical Command at the Battle of Midway. But no, I have never actually met the Vice Admiral in the flesh."

"Fletcher's flag will be on the Saratoga."

"Big mother of a ship. Lexington-class. One of our first large aircraft carriers."

"That is the one. Nickname *Sara Maru*."

Captain Whittaker chuckled. "Some of our more religious boys call her *Sister Sara*."

"Call her what you will. Sara is one tough broad."

"Who is our direct commander?"

"That would be Rear Admiral Richmond Kelly Turner. Once my boss, now your boss. Kelly will command the amphibious forces."

"Terrible Turner. That's what they call him."

"If I were you Whittaker, I would call him Sir and not much else."

"Some say Turner missed key intell that might have blunted the attack on Pearl Harbor."

"I have heard that too. But until you see that assertion in print and attached to a general court-martial, I would keep that ugly thought to yourself."

"I would not have it any other way, Colonel."

Colonel Daniel Morrison drew his captain closer. "Between you, me and the canvas over our heads, I should tell you this. Supplies down here are going to be tight for our fighting boys. Coast Guard crews are going to land supplies fast as they can. But if our Marines get bogged down in the sand, men are going to die. Ops planners are in such a rush to get the 1st Marine Division into battle, they have reduced our supply cache from the usual ninety-day inventory to just sixty."

"So the rumors are true."

"Rumors?"

"Call it scuttlebutt then. The men of 1st Division have begun referring to the coming battle as Operation Shoestring. My gunnery sergeant tells me there is just ten days' worth of ammunition on hand, a meager supply, hardly anything, if you ask me. This will not do, Colonel. We cannot go into battle this way. The pucker factor is going to be high enough as it is. What if we lose just one supply ship along the way? We will be fucked in the ass without Vaseline."

"Don't go all FRED on me, Captain."

"I don't get your meaning, Sir."

"FRED. Fucking Retarded Enlisted Dude. We'll get you your supplies. I am leaving later today for Hilo, then onto Camp Pendleton. One of my assignments is to try and improve our supply-chain. But I am actually needed elsewhere. A new team has been formed under the spanking new Office of Strategic Services, the OSS. Bill Donovan has been put in charge. He has asked to speak with me face-to-face, probably on account of my work with the code-talker program. The battle here in the Solomons will be long done by the time I return. Do not let me down, son. It is going to be a bitch."

"We won't let you down, Colonel. Semper Fi!"

"Semper Fi."

**SUNDAY
AUGUST 2, 1942
1 p.m.**

New Orleans

"Ma'am, dere be a man downstairs. Says his name be Sebastian somethin' or other. Looks to be one pissed off peckerwood."

Hector spoke quietly to the madam of the house, Lady Belle. She stood proud and strong at the top of the stairs, gazed past Hector onto the lobby below. By now, the other girls of Mahogany Hall had gathered around them both at the top of the stairs.

Lady Belle gave Hector a quizzical look. "Name of Sebastian? I never seen him 'round here before. Any you girls know this cracker?" It was one o'clock in the afternoon, an unusual time for visitors. The day normally did not get busy until 4 p.m. or later.

Lady Belle looked around the group. But all her girls shook their heads. The madam spoke again to Hector. "What's this peckerwood want?"

"Say he be looking fer his father."

"Ain't we all?" one of the girls quipped. "My pappy left when I was but seven."

"No, I mean he be looking for his actual father. I think he be meaning his real-life father."

"What does dat fella down dere in de lobby think this place be? Some kinda Lost 'n' Found?"

"He can have me if'n he wants me," one of the girls said. Her name was Petunia. She was of mixed-race, just like the others. "Drives a mighty fine automobile, a flash sedan. I was outside on de balcony; saw de man roll up sweet as you please. Got outta one of dem new Packard luxury cars. Custom super something or other." A covered balcony wrapped around the second floor of the whorehouse on three sides. The girls could access it easily from any bedroom window.

"How you know so much 'bout cars, girl?"

"No, she be right," Hector said, peering out the window. "Dat be de Custom Super Eight sedan Packard Company just come out wid. The Super Eight One-Eighty they calls it. I heard Nico talkin' 'bout it d'other day. Said how he would give anythin' to have one just like it, but dat dey be in short supply on account'a de war."

"Forget dat man's wheels already," Kentucky Rose said as she pulled Hector aside out of earshot. "What d'ya think?" she quietly said, fingers on her new *gris-gris*. Just yesterday he had taken her across the river to see the new voodoo queen in Gretna. "Could de john who died in mah bed actually be dis moke's father? Has de son actually now come'a lookin' fer de papa?"

The madam glared at Kentucky Rose talking quietly in the corner with Hector. "This got anything to do with dat peckerwood who kicked off in your room early Thursday morning?"

"You knows 'bout dat?"

Lady Belle laughed her best laugh. "You thought you could hide somethin' like dat from me? Sweetie, I knows just about everything dat goes on in this house, night or day. Nico told me right off. Luca knows all 'bout it too."

"Well den you knows we gots nothin' to hide," Kentucky Rose said. "Invite dat peckerwood in. Nico Carolla long ago d'sposed of de body, and de little book right along with it."

"Book?" the madam questioned. "What book? And why this be the first I be hearing of it?"

"Dat probably be what dis Sebastian feller be here for, dat fuckin' book," Hector said, nodding his head. "Some kinda German guide book."

"You got rid of it, right?" Kentucky Rose said sharply.

Hector turned away without reply.

"Hector! What de hell hab you gone an' done?" Kentucky Rose exclaimed. "Nico tole you to bury dat book 'long with de body and you disobeyed him? Now you gone and made a liar of me too. What if Nico finds out? What if'n he learns de truth?"

"He won't. Not less'n you or Luca tell 'im."

"I would never rat on you, you knows dat," Rose said. "Where de hell is dat book now?"

"I hid de book behind the medicine cab'net in de upstairs bathroom, where nobody would think to look."

"Honestly, Hector! Dat is 'bout de fust place anyone would think to look."

"Okay, enough," Lady Belle snapped. "Petunia, I want you to go downstairs. Make dat man feel welcome. See whether you can charm off his pants. Help de man find his wallet. Let's find out what de fuck he really wants."

"Yes, ma'am."

"Rose, you and Hector hang 'round downstairs until we see's how things go wid Petunia. You other girls, go wash up and try yor best to look pretty."

Petunia put her backfield in motion and worked her way slowly down the staircase. She was one of the younger girls in the house and one of the prettier, with chocolate-colored skin. Any man would be lucky to have her. Kentucky Rose came down the staircase right behind her.

"Hello, big fellow," Petunia said in her most sultry voice. "Can I interest you in anythin' today?" She peeled back a corner of her nightie to expose some more skin.

"I make it a rule never to dirty myself by sharing a bed with a colored woman," Sebastian Grimm said. He wasn't in uniform today, but he was dressed crisply nonetheless.

Petunia purred. "They say once you go black, you never go back."

"I promise you — they do not say that where I come from."

"And where 'xactly do you come from, darlin'?" Petunia asked, touching his arm lightly. By now Kentucky Rose had joined the conversation. Hector held back, upstairs, hands shoved deep in his pockets.

"Where I come from is really none of your business," Sebastian Grimm answered brusquely. "You are nothing but a curbside swallow, a *bordsteinschwalben*."

"Curbside swallow? You mean like a blowjob on de street?" Petunia was offended. "I ain't no streetwalker. I don't live in no crib. And I don't give no blowjobs on de stroll like a common whore. I work indoors, like a proper lady. An' don't you ever forget dat!"

"Curbside swallow or *huren*; all women are the same — stupid and unclean."

"Are you a cop?" Petunia asked, suddenly becoming uncomfortable. "On account of you look like a policeman to me." Grimm's cold demeanor was getting in the way of her usual playfulness.

"Common mistake," Grimm said. "I am with the military police, not the local police. For the moment I am off-duty."

"We wants no trouble with no police," Kentucky Rose said, "military or otherwise."

"I am not here looking for trouble. And I am certainly not here to have pay-sex with a colored."

"Then why de fuck you here, big boy?"

"I am here looking for my father. I know for a fact that he frequents this place, this Mahogany Hall. The last time I spoke to my father, he was headed here, to this very house."

"Okay," Petunia said. "No pay-sex. But to find yor father, we gonna need more to go on than de little you hab said so far. We see lots of men in here over de course of a week. What is your father's name? What does de man look like?"

"Big man. German accent. Pushing sixty years old. First name of Henry. Henry Brock. This would have been about two days ago, maybe three. Please. This is important. Think hard."

"Have a seat, soldier," Petunia said. "Let me an' Rose go upstairs, ask de house manager, talk to some of de girls. Give us a few minutes."

"I give you five," Sebastian Grimm said, tapping the face of his wristwatch as if he meant to time her down to the second. "Make it snappy."

Petunia nodded and Sebastian sat down. The sofa was lumpy, the pillows not much better. The parlor was comfortable. The spinning fans overhead made the temperature tolerable. The summer heat had come full-force to New Orleans.

Sebastian was all keyed up. But he tried to relax. He had gone house to house in the past twenty-four hours, following the listings in the *Blue Book*, slowly narrowing down his list of targets. *This had to be the one*, he thought.

Mahogany Hall was past its prime, hardly the place it once was. He had seen E.J. Bellocq's photographs of the original establishment. They were haunting photographs. They harkened back to a time when the place was beautiful. Fifteen bedrooms. Each with its own adjoining bathroom. Elegant furnishings. Huge chandeliers. Expensive oil paintings. Tiffany stained glass windows. Sculptures. Works of art. A stable of octoroon girls.

Sebastian Grimm glanced at his watch, decided he had waited long enough for an answer. He jumped to his feet, moved quickly across the room. He gripped the banister and started up the staircase. One of Nico Carolla's beefier henchmen met him on the landing.

"You cannot be up here unescorted," Luca said, blocking Sebastian Grimm's way.

"I don't want any trouble," Grimm said, eyeing the revolver in the other man's shoulder holster. "But if you know what's good for you, I would advise you to get the hell out of my way. My father died in this place. I want to know why. And I want to know what happened to his body as well as his personal belongings."

Nico's man Luca grabbed Sebastian Grimm by the arm. Grimm reacted like the Waffen-SS infantryman that he actually was. With his other hand, Sebastian Grimm grabbed Luca's arm and in one fluid motion spun the man around, then pressed him hard up against the wall before Luca could reach for his gun.

"Touch me again and I will break your arm," Grimm said icily. He removed the .38 from Luca's holster, made sure the safety was on, and tossed it clattering down the stairs.

Hector stepped out onto the landing to see what was going on. "Heh, you cracker! Let go'a dat man!"

"I don't take orders from some spade coon dog."

Hector became incensed. "And you an' I don't knows one another well enough for you to speak to me like dat."

"Yes? And what are you going to do about it? It is my word against yours. Who are the authorities going to believe? Some nigger? Or some white man in a uniform? They don't even let coloreds serve in the United States Army."

Nico's man Luca tried to wriggle free of Sebastian's grip, as Hector drew closer, meaning to help him.

"Hold still, you Guinea swine." Then he glared at Hector. "You two pathetic fools don't think I can kick both your asses at the same time?"

"I would like to see you try," Hector taunted.

Sebastian poked Nico's man in the kidney with fingers hardened by practice. Luca winced in pain and dropped to the floor.

Then Sebastian turned to face Hector straight on. That is when he saw it, the ring on Hector's finger.

"Where did you get that?"

"What?"

"That signet ring."

Hector looked down at his hand. Any lie he told now would have to be damn convincing. "It be a family heirloom," he said.

"Yes, it certainly is. But not your family."

"What you be accusin' me of, cracker?"

"For now, I am accusing you of nothing. But that will change rather quickly if you do not hand over that ring this instant."

"And if'n I refuse?"

"Then I will have no choice but to remove it from your dead, black hand."

"Take your best shot."

Sebastian Grimm, Captain in Heinrich Himmler's Waffen-SS, drew his combat infantry knife from his belt. Hector saw the trench knife and took half a step backwards. He had expected fisticuffs, not a sharpened knife.

That half-step backwards was not nearly enough to place him beyond Captain Grimm's long reach.

Grimm gripped the knife in the manner he had been taught in infantry school and, without making a sound, slashed Hector lethally across the throat from left to right.

Arterial blood spewed across the floor and the wall behind him.

Hector gagged, spit blood from his mouth, and quickly dropped to the floor, his hands still reaching upward.

Petunia screamed. Kentucky Rose screamed louder and approached Grimm with balled fists. Lady Belle, her eyes filled with tears, grabbed Rose from behind before she could strike him the way she intended.

But Grimm ignored them all. He knelt down beside the blood covered body, cut off Hector's ring finger with his combat knife.

Then he removed the signet ring from the severed finger, wiped off the blood on Hector's shirt tail, and stuck the ring in his pocket.

"Call the police," Lady Belle said to no one in particular.

"Forget the *polizia*," Luca said, still smarting from the kidney jab. "We don't want them here, no which way. Mr. Carolla don't want them here. Damage is done. We handle this ourselves."

"Smart move," Sebastian Grimm said. "No police."

Sebastian rifled through Hector's pockets. "Where is the book?" He looked up at Kentucky Rose, still hovering nearby. To his eyes she looked guilty.

"You were close to this man," Grimm said to her. "I could tell that about you."

"Yes, we was close," Rose blubbered, gripping her *gris-gris* tighter than ever.

"You know where the book is."

"No, I do not," Rose lied.

"If you make me come back here to this cesspool for a second time, I will return with something more lethal than a knife."

"I don't know nothing 'bout no book."

"You can have it your way," Sebastian said. Then he got up from the floor, walked calmly back down the stairs into the lobby. "I will be back. I want that book you stole. And I want Henry Brock's body."

After the door closed behind Grimm on his way out of the whorehouse, Kentucky Rose went directly to the medicine cabinet. She explained it to the others.

"Hector told me he hid dat man's book behind this here medicine cab'net. It must be very important. How do we gets dis cabinet off dat wall?" she asked, scratching at the plaster.

"Forget about that for the nonce," Lady Belle said. "We have much bigger fish to fry. We now have a second dead body to dispose of. And Nico needs to be told what went down here dis afternoon. He not going to be happy, no which way. Plus, we need protection. If dat evil man comes back, he means to kill us all."

SUNDAY
AUGUST 2, 1942
2 p.m.

Bay St. Louis, Mississippi

Deputy Marshal Nolan Greeley let the cigarette butt hang from his lips as he gripped the steering wheel of the decade-old Chevrolet sedan and slowed the box-shaped automobile to a stop about two hundred yards from the water's edge. The smoke from his half-burned cigarette curled slowly out the open driver's-side window.

"Must you smoke incessantly?" Marshal Duncan Baxter asked, hunched down beside Greeley in the passenger seat. Baxter was the senior member of this two-man investigative team. They had driven up here from the main office in New Orleans. It was a dusty, muggy drive and the day's humidity had already begun to bite down hard.

"The local sheriff found another floater in the bay this morning," Marshal Greeley said as he opened the car door and exited the vehicle. "He radioed it in to headquarters about six a.m. this morning."

Greeley's head was still pounding from a binge that ended only three hours earlier. He knew he needed to stop drinking. But this made the third time this week that he had really tied one on. Smoking that cigarette while they drove up here from the city had not improved matters.

"That would make the second floater in the last week." Greeley burped out the words, then slammed the car door shut. He stared with derision at the automobile they had just arrived in. It was a so-called "Stovebolt" Chevrolet built with one of the industry's first inline six-cylinder engines. The contraption had four doors and was, in his opinion, far too old to still be on the road. The engine block was leaking oil.

"Local sheriff still has not identified the last one," Marshal Duncan Baxter replied as they walked from the car toward the edge of the swamp. Flies crowded around their heads. "What the hell are we looking at here?"

The smoke of Marshal Greeley's cigarette hung heavy in the wet humid air of Bay St. Louis. "This one's kind of a scrawny fellow compared to the last one."

"Not to mention, this one is a Negro. The last one was a big fat white fellow."

"So you think these two deaths are unrelated?"

"I didn't say that. But let's first review the facts as we know them to be," Baxter suggested.

"I'm game. First guy was a big white guy. Two hundred ten pounds, probably a bit more. Had been dead at least two days when we found him. Not a pretty sight at all."

"Corpses never are. A pretty sight, that is. Leave one floating long enough in putrid water like this and it can bloat up something fierce." Baxter had worked these bayou waters long enough to know.

"You don't seem to be bothered much by dead bodies, do you?"

Deputy Marshal Nolan Greeley was new to the Gulf Coast area. His previous assignment had been in the Colorado Rockies, not far from where he grew up, the oldest son of German immigrants. His parents and kin still spoke the language at home. So did he.

But that job in the mountains had gone south on him when he kept showing up in the field half-drunk. So the U.S. Marshal Service transferred him down here, to the Gulf Coast District. For the moment, Greeley rented a home from a woman he met in a local bar his first week on the job, a ramshackle house near New Orleans on the so-called "German Coast." If he screwed this up, the Gulf Coast would be Greeley's last stop before a forced retirement.

"Nolan, times have been tough. First, the Depression. Now the war. People get cashiered every day. The South has all kinds of problems. We got white trash. We got coloreds who are poorer still. We got mulattoes dumb as sand. We got crime families. We got bootlegging. We got whorehouses and loan sharks and gambling halls. Every damn thing you can think of. New Orleans is a cesspool, and it is but an hour's drive away from here by boat or by automobile. So ... if you ask whether I am nonplussed, the answer is yes."

"Okay, Duncan. Let's talk about that first body. I took a whole roll of Kodak film at the crime scene. Had the prints developed at my own expense. Here, take a look at these snapshots. That first fellow had been stripped of his clothes. He didn't get where we found him on foot. Or by swimming. Someone probably dumped his body in the bay. Seems like an unlikely suicide. Probably didn't die of natural causes either."

"What makes you say that?" Marshal Baxter asked. "That big, fat white guy could have been out fishing naked in a rowboat, for all we know. Maybe he was masturbating in the boat, had a heart attack and fell overboard."

"You do like to spin a yarn, don't you?"

Duncan Baxter smiled.

"Here, read the coroner's report. Take a look at this one photograph of mine."

Duncan Baxter stopped, took the clipboard from the other man and studied the coroner's notes.

"Do you see it now?" Nolan Greeley asked.

"The man's tongue is missing."

"Still think it was a heart attack?"

"What are you saying here, Greeley?"

"The man's tongue is missing, for fuck's sake. It wasn't eaten by some hungry catfish. It was cut out by another man. This is something straight out of a <u>True Crime</u> story. Plot goes like this: mobster gets angry, cuts out tongue of rat who blabbed to the police, end of story."

"Now who's got the active imagination?"

Deputy Marshal Greeley gave his counterpart a look of consternation.

Baxter returned the favor. "So you are trying to make a case that one of Nico Carolla's men did that first killing?"

"Maybe the second one as well."

By now the two men had reached the point in the marshy trail where the local sheriff had fished out the dead Negro's body. The corpse sat roasting like a dead fish in the hot, morning sun.

"Whew, what a smell," Duncan Baxter said.

"This nigger be cooked," the local sheriff said. "Where you boys been? I been waiting out here in the hot sun for nearly an hour."

"Sorry, sheriff. We got lost on some back road after we left Kiln pushing south on Highway 43."

"Not surprised. Half the roads out here don't go nowhere. Used to, though. Back in the Prohibition days, this be a lively place."

"Do tell," Duncan Baxter replied, half interested.

"No, it's true. Kiln was once the source of much sought-after moonshine. Al Capone himself sourced booze from down here. Ran a whiskey-making operation out by the old sawmill. Called his swill *Kiln Lightning*. Back in the day, that illegally made hooch was known on the streets of Chicago by that very name. Hell, the feds chased Capone's ass all over this fucking swamp. Come the late 1920s, Capone's men blew up a bridge on Highway 43 for no better reason than to prevent federal agents from getting down here into this bayou from Picayune."

"Okay, sheriff. Story time is over. Tell me about this corpse."

"Tain't like the other one. Colored, like I said. Kind of scrawny. Shot at close range with a shotgun."

Deputy Marshal Greeley knelt over the body and studied it carefully. He had a rudimentary background in forensics. During his years working as a marshal in the agency's western division, before he came down here, he had seen every manner of gunshot wound. Greeley could tell the difference between a wound made by a hunting rifle and one made by a shotgun.

"This man was shot by two different weapons," Greeley said. "I reckon the cause of death to be a bullet from a high-powered hunting rifle. That single bullet is probably what killed the man. The buckshot in the face was simply to make identification more difficult."

"Well lookie here what the north wind brought in — Sherlock Holmes himself," the local sheriff parroted.

"Poke all the fun you want, sheriff. But I stand by my analysis."

"So you still think this was a gang hit?" Duncan Baxter quietly asked his partner.

"Only one sure way to find out," Greeley answered.

"You want to go talk to the mob boss himself, don't you?"

"Only way to eliminate him for certain," Marshal Greeley replied.

"Or else piss off the entire Carolla clan."

"Your call, boss," Greeley said. "I am the new guy in town. If you don't want to rock the boat, I understand."

"No boat to rock, the way I see it," Duncan Baxter replied.

"Well if you boys are going to make a federal case of this, I am outta here," the local sheriff said, wiping the August sweat from his brow.

"Not so fast, sheriff. See to the body, will you? Get it to the morgue. Have your coroner do an autopsy."

"Not happening, boys. We got no budget for such things. And certainly not for some out of town nigger. You want the body put on ice, you do it your ownselves."

"Okay, what say we call Lent Rice? You know who he is, right? Mississippi Attorney General. What say me and Marshal Greeley tell Greek how helpful you have been?" Duncan said, without hint of threat.

"Greek?"

"Lent Rice likes to be called Greek by his friends," Duncan Baxter explained. "Greek Lent Rice. I know the man well."

The local sheriff reconsidered. "Okay, we put the corpse on ice. But any autopsy is on your dime."

"Agreed."

"So where you boys headed next?" the sheriff asked.

"One of Silver Dollar Sam's grandsons. Nico Carolla. Me and the Carolla's have had dealings before. If Nico will agree to a meet on neutral turf, that will be our next stop."

"Try not to get lost this time. Ain't no one out here in these swamps to rescue your sorry butts from the gators if'n you get yourselves lost again."

"Thanks, Sheriff," Greeley said. "I'm the one doing the driving and we will definitely keep that in mind."

SUNDAY
AUGUST 2, 1942
8 p.m.

Bletchley Park, England

Constance McCallister was a single woman. Twenty-eight years old. Unmarried. Of below-average looks. Destined to be a spinster.

She looked at herself in the mirror, now, and frowned. Boys were not attracted to her. Her mouth was too large and her breasts too small. The only man who ever thought she was pretty was her father, and he had been dead and buried five years already.

But what Constance McCallister lacked in the looks department she more than made up for in intelligence. The woman was very, very smart, the sort of intelligence that could not be easily measured with a test. When Constance McCallister saw a flower petal or a commodity index charted against time or the fine outlines of a jagged coastline, she saw not pictures or drawings or charts but numbers. Big, bright, beautiful numbers. The Fibonacci series. Mandelbrot numbers. Heisenberg's Uncertainty Principle. Fractal shapes. Pi to one thousand places.

She thought back. Her stunning brilliance made for a lonely childhood. What neighborhood girl wants to play with the girl next door, when the girl next door refuses to put on a pretty dress or wear jewelry or is entirely bored playing with dolls? What boy wants to date a girl with little tits and an oversized brain? Not many.

The 1920s was not an easy time to be an adolescent girl in Great Britain; the 1930s were no better. Britain still lived in the shadow of the Great War, a war that had cost the nation dearly. It had taken the lives of an entire generation of young British men, men cut down by German bullets and left to die in the forests and hedgerows of France. Even today, twenty-five years later, men of marrying age were still in short supply. They could have their pick of women. Constance McCallister rarely made the cut.

Constance reached adulthood lonely. Lonely. Starved for affection. Suffering from depression. If not for an enlightened, somewhat frisky male teacher in secondary school, her gift for mathematics might have gone unnoticed. Women her age were supposed to have babies. At age seventeen Constance McCallister was still a virgin.

Then came 1931. That was the year Constance lost her virginity. She lost her virginity to the man who handed Constance her first book of calculus; the same man who taught her how to solve that book's many differential equations. His name was Liam Fieldstone. He would enter university in the fall. But the ten weeks before he left for Cambridge were grand. For the first time in her life, Constance was happy.

For Constance McCallister, a world that could be described with numbers or equations, that could be proven either correct or incorrect was a knowable world, a certain world, a predictable world. Constance McCallister could live in such a world, perhaps even prosper.

Less than a decade later, when war came again to England, this time against a much more diabolical enemy, the Admiralty instructed its top universities to put out a call for the best mathematicians in the land. The Admiralty wanted accomplished chess players, crossword experts, and linguists.

But most of all, they wanted mathematicians. That is when Liam Fieldstone, now at Cambridge and working alongside Alan Turing, remembered Constance McCallister, that exceptionally smart girl he had once seduced with a book and a kind word. She was here today, this very instant actually, in his tiny office, at his invitation.

Hut 4 wasn't much to look at, a long wooden building adjacent to the Mansion, where Naval intelligence was headquartered. Hut 4's job was to analyze Naval Enigma, as well as Hagelin decrypts. Turing used the tower room in the stableyard cottages.

The property first became known as Bletchley Park after its purchase by Samuel Lipscomb Seckham in 1877. The estate of nearly six hundred acres was later bought by Sir Herbert Samuel Leon, who expanded the then-existing farmhouse into its present, atrocious admixture of architectural styles — Tudor, Victorian Gothic, and Dutch Baroque — or, as some of the more cheeky girls called it: Lavatory Gothic. More recently, in 1938, the mansion and sixty adjoining acres were bought by Admiral Sir Hugh

Sinclair, head of the Secret Intelligence Service, for use by SIS and the Government Code and Cypher School in the likely event of war.

Working conditions inside the huts were not great. Hours spent on a horrid wooden chair, bent over a wobbly trestle table, trying to make sense of a gaggle of coded enemy messages. Each worktable was illuminated only by lights that hung down from the ceiling on strings. In winter, the drafty wooden huts were kept warm by a frightful old stove placed in the middle of the room. In summer, the temperatures inside the huts could be stifling, the circling flies a constant annoyance.

Now, as Liam Fieldstone gazed again at the unremarkable face of Constance McCallister, this time from across the top of his small wooden desk in Hut 4, Bletchley Park, he remembered their few short weeks together that torrid summer. Constance McCallister had been an unimaginative lover. She performed sex as if trying to recall a set of instructions from a lovemaking manual.

First do this, then do that, then end with this.

Making love to the woman was utterly routine, humdrum at best. She reminded him of a gray-haired librarian re-shelving a returned book — Grasp book tightly. Enter stacks. Locate nonfiction section. Proceed to third shelf. Look for empty space on shelf. Shove book firmly into place.

But when it came to numbers and ciphers, no one worked them better than Constance McCallister. That is why she was standing in front of him today.

Bletchley Park was known as "B.P." to those who worked there. What the men and women of B.P. did in the buildings and huts of this place was above top secret, Ultra secret, as the Admiralty kept reminding them. To the outside world Bletchley Park had several cover names. London Signals Intelligence Centre. Station X. Government Communications Headquarters. For the women of the Women's Royal Naval Service — the so-called "Wrens" — who were assigned to work at Bletchley, their official posting was to HMS *Pembroke V.*

Everyone on staff was expected to sign the Official Secrets Act of 1939, from the lowliest cook in the mess to the men holding the top posts. They were also to abide by a more recent security warning. The warning emphasized the importance of discretion, even within Bletchley itself.

Do not talk at meals. Do not talk in the transport. Do not talk while travelling. Do not talk in the billet. Do not talk by your own fireside. Be careful even in your Hut . . .

"Am I to work for you then?" Constance McCallister stammered, staring blankly at the signature line on the Official Secrets Act form.

"For me, Constance. Not under me. For me." He thought that perhaps she was still carrying a torch. His team had just cracked the latest version of the Nazi Navy's Enigma Code.

"By under, do you mean beneath? As in you on top, missionary style?"

"Am I that transparent?"

Her face reddened. But she did not answer.

"I did not promise you love, Constance. You know that, right?" he said defensively. "I gave you what you wanted, no strings attached."

"I understand that now. I cannot say that I understood it back then."

"We are agreed then?"

"About the strings? Oh, yes. Quite clear."

"No, what I meant to say was that there would be no shenanigans here. Given that we have had a prior relationship, what I need to know from you this very instant is whether or not you can work for me. Once you sign this piece of paper, agreeing to keep our secrets, there will be no going back. Is that understood?"

"Yes, of course. Please hand me a pen."

MONDAY
AUGUST 3, 1942
5 a.m.

South Pacific

The troop ship bobbed peacefully up and down in the blue-green waters of the South Pacific. The LST was one of five similar troop ships anchored in the lagoon offshore Navua, a tribal village on the southern coast of Fiji. When the practice landings came, the Marines of 1st Division would assault the nearby snip of land called Beqa Island.

"Alright men, quiet down."

Gunnery Sergeant Forrester waited while the rambunctious chatter drew to a whisper. Then he continued.

"Don't be misled by the sandy beaches and pleasant waves, boys. The waters around Guadalcanal will not be near as calm on the day of the assault. The Japs will likely be expecting us. They will be hurling every god damn thing they own at us, including rocks and mortar rounds. The Nips are plenty pissed off because we handed them their asses at Midway. Sons of Nippon are going to want payback. The closer our landing craft get to shore, the easier it will be for their machine-gun nests to reach us in the water. Things are bound to get choppy real fast."

Sergeant Forrester looked across the deck of the LST and continued. "A troop ship like ours is designed to take the fight to the enemy. It can carry two hundred of you Jarheads, all your gear, plus howitzers, artillery guns and six of these smaller landing craft. We call these bad boys Higgins boats. This is on account of the name of the guy who builds them, Andrew Jackson Higgins. Each of these boats can make about eight knots fully loaded and carry an infantry platoon of thirty-six men to shore.

"This needs to come off like clockwork, boys. No SNAFU, no FUBAR, no fuck-ups. We unlimber the Higgins boats. We drop them in the water alongside the troop ship. Then we hop over the gunwales and climb down into them boats on those fancy rope ladders that hang down over the side of the ship. We do this maneuver well out from shore, hopefully out of range of the enemy's guns."

One of the men spoke up. "Gunny, aren't our asses pretty much exposed to the world when we're climbing down those scramble nets?"

"Seriously, private? This is a question you have to ask outloud? Our asses are pretty much exposed damn near everywhere we go in this man's war. Get with the program, Semper Fi, or I will expose your ass to the wind myself and blast away until I hit something important."

Another Marine chuckled then said, "These landing craft ain't nothing but plywood swamp boats, Sarge. You 'spect us to pilot these flimsy nothings to shore on our own? No escort? No cover? No armor?"

"Nah, you ain't bright enough for such work. The actual piloting will be done by Coasties — Coast Guard boatcrews. There isn't a Leatherneck among you smart enough to drive a rubber ducky through a bathtub filled with hot water and soap bubbles, much less a small boat through a coral reef in shallow waters and rolling surf."

"Leatherneck?"

"You never heard the word, Marine?"

The man shook his head.

Gunnery Sergeant Forrester explained. "Back in the days when marines were actually boarding ships with sword in hand, climbing up ropes and over gunwales, men wore thick neck collars made of tough leather to protect their throats and necks from being slashed by a cutlass."

"Did not know that," the man said. "Thought all us Marines were Jarheads."

"Oh, that you are, that and more. But here's the thing. Coast Guard boatcrews will man virtually every transport and landing craft we use here in SOPAC. Ferrying Marines. Landing troops. Landing supplies. Extracting wounded. Getting exhausted troops to safety. Ferrying them back to Coast Guard transports for rest and treatment."

"Why no Leathernecks at the helm of these small Higgins boats, Sergeant? Why only boat drivers from the Hooligan Navy and not from the blue water Navy?"

"Don't let them ever hear you talk that way, Marine," Forrester said. "They don't like that name, Hooligan Navy. Dates back to Prohibition. In those days, Coasties were short of men.

They recruited any halfway decent man who had been discharged from one of the other armed services — even the misfits."

"Isn't that what I just said? Hooligans?"

"Let me tell you something, son. Handling these smaller boats takes a steady hand. It is a specialized skill. Navy men ain't trained for it. Coasties are. The CG coxswains learned this skill handling small boats in rough surf at coastal lifesaving stations. But then the war came. Some of the best ones volunteered to drive these boats. Every last one of them is a graduate of the Higgins Boat Driver School in New Orleans. They have undergone extensive classroom and hands-on training on every aspect of these boats."

Forrester continued. "You need to trust these men. They know the absolute best ways to load and unload soldiers, jeeps and the wounded. They know how to land the boat on a hostile beach, and how to repair their boat under combat conditions. Like I said, these Coasties we got working for us are by far the most seasoned small boat handlers in government service. Show 'em a little respect, will you? One of these hooligans may save your ass before this island-hopping shit is done."

Forrester continued. "An amphibious assault begins far out at sea. Each Higgins boat will be outfitted with a pilot, a Coastie for a coxswain, a scout, and a gunnery sergeant. The two forward-most men operate the machine guns, which we use for defense. But yes, each boat makes its own way to shore. Try not to shoot your buddies hunkered down in the boat ahead of you."

Nervous chuckles broke the tension.

"I know it sounds obvious. But it really isn't. Friendly fire in choppy waters is a big risk. So is drowning."

"Every last one of us knows how to swim, Sarge," one of the men said.

"Do you? Can you? In full combat gear? In choppy seas? In water over your head? With bullets flying every fucking where? With a rifle in your hands over your head so it don't get wet?"

"Well, what I meant . . . "

"I know what you meant, Marine. But consider this. A man falls overboard. He is wearing a heavy backpack. He may be wounded, though not mortally. Or he is moving onshore. He slips and falls backward under heavy fire. Or the surf knocks him from his feet. I have seen it happen. Don't get cocky. Men drown all the time. Even in shallow water. Even good swimmers."

Now, suddenly, there was absolute silence among the two hundred plus men standing on the deck of the LST troop ship. Reality was beginning to sink in.

"Now about these boats. You complain that they are made of plywood. You say they look flimsy. They are anything but. Since the 1930s the Marine Corps has been looking for a practical boat it could use to land troops on a foreign beach. About five years ago the Corps conducted experiments with a variety of boats, plus lighters and launches, that kind of thing."

"Hey, Sarge. What if we get seasick in one of these wooden tubs?"

"Tough shit. Puke in your helmet."

The men laughed and Sergeant Forrester continued. "I was fresh out of boot camp around the time the Corps was conducting some of the original tests. It was my first post, 1936. Many types of craft were considered. Some came from the Navy Bureau. They were pieces of shit. Others were commercial fishing boats. Still others were experimental prototypes. Several sported ramps that deployed over rollers on the bow. The brass experimented with every single one of them. Some boats were overwhelmed by the surf. Others proved impractical for one reason or another. But the twenty-eight-foot lighter designed by the Eureka Tug-Boat Company of New Orleans proved to be the best. A good sea boat. Superior at beaching. In those days they were called *Eureka* boats."

"So, Sarge, you telling us the Navy is now in bed with the Sicilian mob?" Private Brock asked.

"What makes you say that, Brock?"

"There was a time when the Carolla crime family used those *Eureka* swamp boats to move bootleg gin and outrun the Coast Guard during the Prohibition."

"You know this how?" Forrester asked.

"My uncle on my mother's side was one of them."

"I heard the same stories," Forrester admitted. "But they are just that — stories. The boat model we tested was based on an early version of the company's spoonbill-bowed craft, their so-called *Wonder* boat. It was used by trappers in the bayous of the Mississippi River Delta. The boat's draft was amazingly shallow, only eighteen inches. It could cut through vegetation and slide over partially submerged logs like they were nothing. And it could do so without damaging its propeller in the process. The amazing thing was that the boat could be run up on shore and then extract itself from the beach with no damage whatsoever."

Sergeant Forrester continued. "I was present for several of the company's sales demonstrations. I can vouch for the seaworthiness of these boats, plywood or not. I saw a man — I think it was Higgins himself — run one of these boats up on the concrete seawall of Lake Pontchartrain, no problem at all. I saw him run it up on that seawall, off-load a shitload of equipment — motors, tool chests and the like — then slam it in reverse and back the damn thing right back into the lake in nothing flat. So if you tell me that rumrunners once used these sorts of boats to outrun the law, count me in as a believer."

The Gunnery Sergeant took a breath, gathered himself, then pressed on with his instruction. "The Corps didn't take the boats from the Eureka Tug-Boat Company as-is. There was a problem with cavitation at low-speed. But Higgins solved that problem with a redesign of the hull. They say he modeled it to mimic the shape of a blue whale's jaw and forward belly. I don't know if that's true. What I do know is that our original specs for the boat called for a crew of six with the ability to carry one squad, twelve men. The boats had to be capable of making fifteen knots and of being hoisted on a standard U.S. Navy davit. The general lines of the boat were accepted by the Corps nearly two years ago, before Pearl was hit. The brass struck a contract with the Eureka Tug-Boat Company located in New Orleans.

"But that contract was for a larger craft than first envisioned, one that could carry up to twenty-four fully equipped troops. The original smaller *Eureka* boat was stretched in length to thirty-two feet, then later to thirty-six. Plus other changes were made. Reinforced plywood. Armor plating on the front and sides. Watertight front gate ramp. Powerful marine engine. The newest versions of the boat — the version we will be using — can carry ashore three squads, thirty-plus men. General Holland Smith, commander of the 1st Marine Brigade, had a hand in its development each step of the way."

Now Forrester's demeanor changed as oral instruction ended and hands-on training resumed. He pointed to a man with a double chevron sewn on his sleeve.

"Okay Corporal, let's see what you can do. The boat first has to be properly secured to the davit. Then it has to be lowered over the side and into the water without it spilling over and chucking out the contents. Take those three men, Corporal.

Attach the cables and lower the Higgins over the side of the LST."
Forrester pointed out Brock, Woods, and one other man to assist
the Corporal.

All the troops had practiced these steps on shore and again
in shallow water. Now they were going to do the real thing in
deeper, choppier water.

The young corporal gripped a lever, released the ratchet,
and the chain tightened. Brock, Woods, and the third man
steadied the Higgins boat as it was raised off the deck of the LST
and the davit pivoted to lower it over the side. It swayed in the
wind.

"Don't get caught up in those cables," Forrester shouted at
Private Woods. Woods took half a step backwards. "That's better,"
Forrester said.

The chain uncoiled and the Higgins boat descended slowly
into the ocean. The entire process from start to finish took under
half a minute.

"Okay. Coasties first. Down the scramble net and into the
boat."

The Corporal did as instructed. He followed the Coasties
over the side of the LST and down he went. The scramble net was
actually a series of rope ladders laid side-by-side. Easy to climb up
or down, wide enough for three or four men to descend at one time
together. The ladders had thick ropelike strands that ran both
vertically and horizontally. The men were told to grab the verticals
and step on the horizontals. To do otherwise risked a smashed
hand or a broken finger when the guy above stepped on the
horizontal you were holding onto coming down.

The Corporal descended quickly. His feet touched down on
the gunwale and he jumped aboard. He lowered himself into the
seat of the Higgins, pushed in the choke and turned over the
electric starter. The craft shuddered and black smoke belched
from the rear of the craft. He would act as coxswain. An
experienced Coast Guardsman sat beside him.

The sound of the diesel motor coming to life accompanied
by the smell from clouds of choking diesel smoke jolted Russell
Brock back in time. Suddenly he was a boy again, back in New
Jersey, the transit buses of his youth, that sound, those smells.

"Okay, boys, that is how it is done. You have your boat
assignments. Lower all the boats into the water, one after the
other. As soon as your boat is in the water, down the nets and into
your boat. Back each boat quickly away from the LST so the next

boat can be dropped in the water. Then form up your boats about a hundred yards away. We will move in formation, along with the boats from the other troop ships, and take the beach."

Forrester pointed to the slip of land four or five hundred yards downwind across the lagoon, Beqa Island. Behind them, on shore, was an abandoned sugar mill. For the next day and a half, during the boat drills, it would serve as their temporary regimental headquarters.

Cargo nets hung down from the sides of each of the five troop ships. The men clambered down the cargo nets. Then they had to leap from the scramble net into the boats, which were bobbing up and down in the water. Each man had to time his jump. The boats rode up and down and sometimes from left to right on the ocean swells. It would be far worse out in open sea.

Thirty-five men in full combat gear shoehorned into each boat. If a man timed his jump wrong or messed it up in any way, he could slip between the sides of the troop ship and the Higgins boat and go straight to the bottom of the sea. No rescue attempt would be made.

Private Brock cinched his backpack tight. He slung his carbine over his shoulder, gripped the ropes of the cargo net and climbed down towards the waiting boat below. The man above him descended faster than he did and kicked Russell in the helmet, nearly knocking the helmet from his head and nearly knocking Brock from the ropes.

"Heh, you fuck! Watch where the hell you're going!"

"Shut up down there and move faster," Sergeant Forrester yelled. Waves slapped against the side of the boat, splashing the men as they cleared the gunwales.

Loaded now, the boat Brock had been assigned to jerked forward. Water splashed over the bow. The men were crowded in the Higgins boat like sardines in a can. Then Gunnery Sergeant Forrester began passing out condoms.

"What the fuck are these for?" Woods asked.

"I have no idea," Brock answered. "Party favor?"

"Slip them over the muzzle of your rifle," Forrester shouted over the din. "Keep the business end of your weapon dry."

Brock understood. The condom would keep the corrosive seawater out of the bore.

"Get an extra one for me," Woods said. "I saw a sweet young thing last night that may soon need saving."

Forrester barked at them both as the boat picked up speed. "If you come back from this with your balls still attached to the underside of your dick, consider yourself lucky. Otherwise, you won't be needing that condom, I assure you."

The faster the boat went, the more it rocked. Its shallow draft saw to that. Brock was sure he would be ill.

"What did the Sergeant mean by that?" Woods asked.

"I think he means we won't all be coming back from the fight when we do this shit for real. Semper Fi."

By now all boats were moving forward, each on course for its assigned stretch of beach. High-speed American PT boats would play the part of the enemy, harassing the incoming LCVPs and firing the occasional live round over their heads. The landing craft were to outflank the American patrol boats, maneuver over the shallow reef, and go straight into shore. Once onshore, the men were to jump from the boats and chase up the beachhead. Today was a practice run. There would be no actual enemy fire. But next week . . .

On the water, there was no boat faster or more dangerous than the Higgins PT boat. Pound for pound, it was easily the most lethal American boat deployed in the war. Their niche in the coming battles would be to attack enemy troop and supply barges. The Patrol Torpedo boat relied on stealth to attack, and on speed and maneuverability to make a clean escape.

In today's game, the rapid approach of the menacing PT boats startled the inexperienced coxswain at the helm of Brock's boat. The man was so unnerved by the live-fire experience that he took them to the wrong beach the first time in. Then, after the men had off-loaded, he rammed the craft into reverse so fast, the last guy had to jump from the ramp as it was going up.

God, save us. Forrester thought grimly. *On the big day, Lord, give me an experienced Coast Guardsman at the wheel, not one of these newbs.*

"Okay," he shouted. "Now let's go back and try this again. Back in the boats, my pretties. Next time, let's see if we can't get this fucking thing right!"

MONDAY
AUGUST 3, 1942
10 a.m.

New Orleans

"*Madre di Dio!*" Nico Carolla exclaimed. "Let me see if I have this straight."

Nico had just come from the Carolla family *trattoria* and was still incensed by what had happened the previous afternoon in the lobby of one of his more profitable establishments. The upstairs carpet was still bloody and the girls were still all worked up. Not good for business, not good at all.

Nico was red-faced. "A man comes into the house, claims to be that dead man's son, kills Hector, cuts off his finger, then nearly breaks Luca's arm? Is that what you are saying to me? Then, when the man fails to get back the book he originally came here for, he just walks back out into the street sweet-as-you-please and disappears? *Che cazzo?* What the fuck? That is the story you are going with?"

"It be the story we are going wid 'cause it be the absolute truth," Lady Belle said, not backing down. "Ask your man if you think I am lying."

Nico looked at Luca, his soldier and confidante, who nodded his head in agreement. Luca was embarrassed. Sebastian Grimm had disarmed him in a fraction of a second and tossed away his gun like it was nothing.

"Okay," Nico said. "This mysterious man, this man who came here yesterday afternoon and caused all this trouble. Where the hell did he go after he left the premises?"

"Don't know where he went," Belle said. "Was my impression dat before he landed on our doorstep he been going house to house looking for his father, if dat be who the dead man actually was."

"Was this troublemaker on foot?" Nico asked. There seemed to be no end to the troubles at this whorehouse. He was growing weary of all the turmoil and was beginning to wonder whether the family ought to be in this line of business at all.

"No, de cracker arrived by car," Petunia said.

"That's it? That's all you can tell me? That the cracker arrived at the house by car?"

"No. There is more," Petunia said. "I saw de car he be driving."

"Now we are getting somewhere," Nico said. "Can you describe the car? Maybe we can track it down."

"It be a Packard, a new one, a custom super sedan, all black an' shiny. White sidewalls. Fancy front grille."

"*Cazzo!* How would you know what kind of automobile he drove?" Nico asked. "You hardly seem the kind of girl who would have a mind for such things."

"No need to be mean 'bout it. I'm only repeatin' what Hector say to us before he . . . before he . . . was killt. Hector say you wanted a car just like it, a Custom Super Eight."

"Goodness. The man came here driving a flash car like that? How hard can a car like that be to track down? There have been so few of them made, none that I know of since the War Production Board got involved. Anything else?"

"It be sporting Miss'ippi plates."

"How would you know such a thing, girl? You can't even read."

"Don't need to read. Know de diff'rence. My papa 'splained it to me. Papa be a conga drummer and a horn player in Jelly Roll's jazz band. They get gigs here and there, travel by car from state to state. But a Negro on de road face many dangers. Papa gots a copy of de *Green Book*. It cost him only two bits, twenty-five cents."

"What the hell is this *Green Book*?" Nico asked. "I never heard of it before."

"Green not be de color; Green be de name of de man who wrote it. *Negro Motorist Green Book*. Helps a Colored stay safe when he be out on de road traveling by car."

"How so?"

"Many white-folk businesses refuse to serve Colored. Garages refuse to repair their vehicles. Hotels refuse to sell dem a bed for de night. Diners refuse to sell dem a meal. In white 'sundown towns' a Negro cannot be out after dark. A man like dat could get strung up if'n he's out after dark. The *Green Book* gots names and 'dresses of hotels and taverns and night clubs and such that cater to black folk, even de odd barber shop or beauty parlor."

"Life isn't fair," Nico said. "Everyone knows that. But now I understand why you know about cars. Your father travels; he knows about car license plates; and he explained it to you."

Petunia nodded. "Yes. My papa 'splained it to me. I know Miss'ippi starts with de letter M. Seen it on de bridge over de river. I know Lou'siana starts with de letter L. I kin tell de diff'rence. Plus, my papa 'splained it. Lou'siana has automobile plates of all diff'rent colors and sizes. Miss'ippi just one size. Plus, it says MISS on the plate, 'cept the MISS reads from top to bottom vertical-like down the center of de plate, with numbers on either side. Dat fancy ole Packard had Miss'ippi plates, of dat I be sure."

"I am impressed, Petunia," Nico said. "You are indeed quite observant."

"Have to be in my business. And there be one other thing I seen."

"Yes?"

"Dat man's car be stickered 'X'. Dat mean he kin get all de gas'lene he want. Plus, there be a big H in de upper left-hand corner of de license plate, some important word I cain't read dat starts with de letter H."

Nico's man, Luca, who had been listening to the exchange, spoke up. "She may be right, Nico. Mississippi puts the name of the — how you say? — *contea . . .* "

"County," Nico translated. "In America, they say county."

"Yes, county. Mississippi puts the name of the county that an automobile is registered in on the face of the license plate. That H could stand for Hancock County. Hancock is the county in Mississippi closest to the Louisiana border."

"How many Custom Super Eights can possibly be registered in Hancock County? How many have an 'X' gas ration sticker on the windshield? Those stickers are hard to come by." Nico reflected. "It can't be many. Perhaps only that one."

"Automobile registrations are — how you say? — public information," Luca said. "Maybe we can just send a man over to the county courthouse in Bay St. Louis and have him take a look at the logbooks."

"It may not even require an automobile trip across state lines. Perhaps a Western Union cable will do the trick, especially if that cable were to come from a lawman."

"You have someone in mind?" Luca asked. "What about your brother, Earl Ray?"

"*Madre di Dio.* No, my brother would never help me. I have an altogether different man in mind, a United States Marshal. Grandfather knows him. A man by the name of Duncan Baxter, Marshal Duncan Baxter. Our family — our *famigghia* — has had dealings with Baxter in the past."

"But how do we protect the girls? How do we protect the house against another . . . how say you *incidente* . . . ?" Luca asked in broken English.

"You think dat horr'ble man actually be coming back here again?" Lady Belle asked aghast.

"I do," Luca replied. "And when he does come back, he will be coming back more heavily armed than before. No knife this time, guns. My men only carry revolvers. We need to be more heavily armed ourselves."

"And you will be," Nico assured. "I will put spotters on the rooftops and the street corner, and I will place two armed *Mafiosi* inside. Now what about that goddamned book this *merda* came looking for? Who's got it and where the *cazzo* is the book now?"

"Here," Kentucky Rose said. "Here 'tis." She handed Heinrich Brock's map book to Nico.

Nico looked at the book and immediately recognized it. "*Dio cane!*" He swore in Italian. "Again with this *cazzo* German book? I thought I told Hector to put this book back on the body before we hauled the corpse away and dumped it in the swamp?"

"Why not just hand the fuckin' book back to de man if'n he shows up here again?" Kentucky Rose asked as if it were the logical thing to do. "There don't need to be no shooting."

"Of course, there has to be shooting," Nico said. "*Madre di Dio!* A lesson must be taught. This man has cost me money. He has cost me time. And he has cost me a good man in that Negro Hector. He also may have given Mahogany Hall a bad name. Our businesses are a matter of Carolla family pride. I cannot have some Heinie Nazi pig coming in here, killing my people and causing a ruckus. A lesson must be taught. We track down that Packard. We take the fight to him."

"And what becomes of the book?" Luca asked.

"I give the book to Duncan Baxter."

"That United States Marshal? I thought you said you didn't trust the police."

"I don't trust the police, not one little bit, not since the old country, not since the Carabinieri. But Duncan Baxter is not ordinary police. He is a United States marshal. Marshals work for the federal government. Anyway, where else can I go with this? The U.S. Navy? The Navy has agreed to look the other way with kickbacks down by the docks; that much is true. Just as we have agreed to help them with the invasion plans of Sicily. They probably have people on the payroll who can translate the foreign mumbo-jumbo in this book. But Duncan Baxter, he is definitely *il mio uomo* — my man."

MONDAY
AUGUST 3, 1942
10:30 a.m.

New Orleans

Still angry about what had happened, Nico walked out the front door of the brothel, turned north out of the French Quarter and up Orleans Avenue to the closest streetcar stop. He paid the conductor the 7-cent fare and rode the car to the end of the line. From there, he went across the bridge, over the slip of water, and left onto one of the diagonal cross streets, alleys really, to City Park Avenue. As was his habit, Nico's pistol was in his pocket, just in case.

The Higgins Industries boat plant was located at the foot of City Park Avenue, a large multi-building facility. Nico was to meet Andrew Higgins here at the plant later this morning. Now Nico walked north past the giant plant entrance, up the path toward Big Lake in City Park. The ground was wet and spongy from a recent rain.

Nico liked to walk. It calmed him when he was angry. Some days he would stop at the nearby cemetery where his father was buried. Greenwood Cemetery, at the corner of City Park Avenue and Canal Street. Row after row of above-ground crypts. He and his father would talk graveside, mostly about the old country, what it was like to live in Sicily, the family history. Nico would pause a moment at the Fireman's Monument before leaving the sacred grounds and pay his respects. The monument was the centerpiece of the entire cemetery. It had been built before his time to honor the memory of volunteer firemen who had lost their lives in the line of duty — a life-sized, marble likeness of a man, a volunteer fireman, standing beneath a cluster of Gothic arches.

Then Nico would move on, continue walking. He enjoyed these times in the morning, these quiet times before the city became fully alert. The simple fact was that Nico preferred to be alone, to just walk in peace and quiet. He would walk this same route, sometimes south toward the river, but more often north toward the park. Louisiana air was wet in the morning, the dew often heavy.

The city of New Orleans would soon wake and come alive in every way. By this time there might already be street vendors on the sidewalks with their carts hawking their wares, food or clothing or housewares. Downtown, nearer the French Quarter, the street carts peddled *muffuletta* bread. It was an old-world recipe, Nico's favorite, a large, round, somewhat flattened loaf. Common laborers might buy a loaf from a cart on their way to work. Then, at lunchtime, they would secure from their favorite grocer a portion of cured meat, a wedge of cheese, and a serving of *giardiniera*. The workers would find a place to eat, a bench or soapbox or quiet spot beside the river, split the loaf open sideways and assemble the ingredients between the loaves of the bread. It was a filling meal, enough to get them through the rest of the day.

At night, after the workday was over, the city never went to sleep. Music, dance, drink. Fiery lyrics, grotesque dance moves, vibrant energy. All dark. All carnal. All sexy. All taboo. Sweat mixing with bourbon blended with tobacco. Black people, mulatto, strange tongues, boisterous gestures.

But during the day, like now, especially in the morning, the Quarter was quiet, almost subdued, exhausted by the events of the night before. That is when the other senses came most vividly alive. Sound. Smell. Taste.

The smell of fish down by the docks and along the lake. The sounds of seagulls barking overhead. The buzz of flies or cicadas. The stench of urine in the streets. The distant shriek of a hawk hunting its prey, fish or rats or small mammals. In the Quarter, narrow streets with overhanging balconies, splendid wrought-iron and cast-iron railings, great barred doors and tropical gardens.

There was much confusion in Nico's life. He wasn't sentimental. His wife Fiona had given him a son and a daughter. He loved Fiona, but not in the way he once had, not in the way he once hoped he still would. She had gained weight, cut her hair too short, slapped on make-up, no longer reached out to him in the middle of the night.

He and Fiona had drifted apart. Now he thought he might be in love with Martina. *Nonno* said it was infatuation. *Nonno* said it was inappropriate for a man of Nico's station.

But the horrible truth was that Martina was off-limits to him emotionally. They had sex together, great sex. They did business together, good business. They sometimes made each other laugh. But it could never be more than that. This made Nico sad.

Loneliness began and ended at the water's edge. Every day he walked alone here, in every season, in all kinds of weather, no Luca, no Vittorio, no Fiona, no Martina.

Every day he walked here among the waterfowl, the bald cypress trees, the bubbling water. He listened to the world around him, enjoyed these few quiet minutes before the business day began. Loons, gulls, alligators, the odd snapping turtle, the occasional weasel, egrets, hawks, and snakes, many of which were poisonous.

City Park was a modern wonder. The sixth-largest municipal park in the United States. Magnificent groves of live oaks heavy with Spanish moss, floats of yellow pond lilies, palmetto thickets, crêpe myrtle trees, magnolia, a formal rose garden. Then there were the manmade improvements. A swimming pool, a fountain, thirty-three tennis courts, three baseball diamonds, a large football stadium, two 18-hole golf courses, a bridle path, a bandstand, and a natatorium. At one corner, the Delgado Museum of Art with six Ionic columns across the portico. Beside it, Dueling Oaks, a favorite spot among the trees where affairs of honor were settled by sword or pistol back in the days when satisfaction for an insult was obtained by spilling blood.

Nico exited the park, walked swiftly across the small bayou bridge, down to City Park Avenue, up to the front gate of Higgins Industries.

"*Signor* Carolla. *Buongiorno!* Good morning. It is so good to see you again." The burly man at the front gate was one of Nico's own, a young Sicilian man of limited intelligence. "You here to see Mr. Higgins?"

"*Ciao*, Paolo," Nico nodded quietly, greeting the man in Italian.

"He is in the workshop arguing with *Signor* Tucker again. Just follow the sound of the yelling. You will find them soon enough."

Nico again nodded quietly. Preston Tucker was getting to be a problem. Nico knew it to be true. Higgins had told him as much. The two men were constantly at each other's throats. It would erupt in a brawl any day now.

But Nico knew something else equally true. If the government's boat contracts were to be fulfilled on schedule and within budget, the problems between Higgins and Tucker would soon have to be set aside or solved for good.

In the meantime, Nico needed to talk with Higgins privately — and without Tucker present. It could not wait. It had to be now, today. Tomorrow would be too late. The men from the Navy were coming to the plant, and he and Higgins needed to iron out some financial details ahead of time.

Nico crossed the gravel parking lot and entered the large production facility through a side door. At five million square feet and with a six-hundred-foot-long assembly bay, it was the largest boat-building facility in the world. This is where the thirty-six-foot LCVPs were assembled. The deadly PT boats were fabricated next door. Two production lines, side by side, with a raised walkway between them. The walkway allowed workers to have access from above, from below, and on all sides at the same time.

After Nico entered the plant through the side door, he saw Higgins almost immediately. Higgins was standing in his usual spot, midway along the elevated catwalk at the opposite end of the immense building. The catwalk stretched from outside wall to outside wall and overlooked the expansive factory floor. Higgins was yelling out instructions to someone working below him on the factory floor. Tucker was nowhere in sight, a small bit of good fortune in Nico's eyes.

Nico quickly walked the length of the building and scrambled up the open mesh metal stairs to the level of the catwalk. The walkway was elevated about twenty feet above the second-floor production area.

Higgins greeted him with a warm handshake. The two men leaned against the safety rail to observe the proceedings below. The factory floor was a huge cavernous affair, far larger than an aircraft hangar, three stories tall, open on the interior with no inside walls dividing the workspace. A series of large rectangular windows ran along each sidewall of the building near the pitched roofline.

Below the two men on the factory floor were dozens of plywood boats, all being worked on at the same time, all at various stages of assembly. Even from this distance, above the din, the boat assembly area was uncomfortably noisy and filled with fumes and odors of every sort — sawdust, fuel oil, metal shavings, human body sweat, lacquer, cat urine, rat droppings.

In the immediate foreground, beneath their feet, were partially assembled boats resting upside down on their gunwales.

At this stage, the landing craft were little more than wooden skeletons held together by a series of regularly spaced ribs. While their assembly looked haphazard, it was anything but.

Large detailed blueprints lay open and unrolled on tables either side of the main assembly line. The workmen consulted the blues frequently. Each rib and strut, each piece, had to be cut to match the blueprints' strict specifications. Nothing could be left to chance. The workers, while not highly educated, were skilled and exacting. A world war was being fought. A great deal was at stake here and each laborer wanted to do his part.

Forty or more boats were being assembled simultaneously, four production lines set side by side. Each boat began life in the identical way, as a hardwood keel. Fastened to the keel were twenty-five wooden ribs of various length, each rib expertly cut to fit according to the blueprint. The boat frames were formed with the use of jigs and templates. Once the ribbing was bolted to the skeleton, then came carefully crafted planking for the bottom and sides of the hull.

The planking and other woods used to build a boat were cut next door in the adjoining mill. Raw logs of Philippine mahogany were cut, glued, and pressed together inside an autoclave to produce a sturdy marine plywood, layers of wood and glue heated to form bonded wood. This multi-ply laminate was the raw material used in all of Higgins' wood boat designs.

Other important woods used in the construction were oak, spruce, and loblolly pine. Most of the structural supports and fasteners were galvanized iron or bronze, and most mating wooden surfaces were sealed with dolphinite bedding compound. This was a heavy bodied compound applied with a broad-bladed putty knife. It was used in the marine industry to waterproof planking, bedding, or batten, wherever two pieces were fitted closely together.

The boats sat four abreast across the factory floor and ten rows deep. The boat assembly teams moved laterally across the rows from boat frame to boat frame. Each plywood section had to be screwed into the canvas and dolphinite bedding, then laid flat to the keel and flush to the chine before being covered in canvas. Last to come were garboard planks fashioned from three-quarter-inch mahogany.

At the height of the production day, the floor was an ocean of people, machinery, tools, and noise. The factory was fully integrated. Negroes worked alongside whites. In the months ahead, women would begin to work alongside the men as well.

Every known dialect spoken in the South or the Caribbean could be heard at one time or another on the factory floor.

Once a given row of boats had completed a given step of the assembly process, all rows were moved haltingly forward. The moving was done using a lifting sling. It hung above the workplace from a hoist and a gantry crane. The sling had two large leather harnesses, one at either end of the lifting beam. When the harnesses were not in use, they were draped loosely over the ends of the perpendicular crosspieces attached to the ends of the lifting beam. When the two fabric harnesses were needed to lift and move a boat chassis, they could be easily unfurled at either end and looped by hand under the bow and stern of the boat under construction.

Finished boats rolled out the second-floor factory exit at the far end of the building, even as fresh planks of unplaned wood and inventories of parts and screws arrived at the ground-floor factory entrance in suitable quantities to assemble the next row of four boats. The parts list for a single boat — materials and fasteners — ran into the many dozens of items.

Item 43 —TRANSOM PLANKING
        Quantity 2 — Mahogany plywood — 5/8" X 4'6" X 4'8"
Item 83 —WASHER (SPECIAL)
        Quantity 17 — Galvanized Steel — 1/8" X 1 1/2" X 2 3/4"

And so on, for pages.

Once the hull planking was fastened to the ribs, the boat was flipped over onto its bottom with the help of the overhead hoist, and the assembly line continued. Soon came legions of metal screws, the marine motor, the propeller and shaft, two machine-gun turrets, the 150-gallon fuel tank, and the all-important steel ramp. The fuel tank was itself a piece of engineering. Thirty-six separate and distinct pieces, each fabricated from 18-gauge galvanized iron plates and welded together to form an internal honeycomb of vertical and horizontal baffles.

At the end of the building process, when a completed boat reached the far end of the factory, it was lowered by elevator onto a flatbed railroad car and sent to Bayou St. John for testing and acceptance.

The racket inside was constant and incessant and painful to the ear, a chaotic symphony of angry noises played out at high volume. Hammers banging. The zing of metal planers. The grinding and banging of machine tools at work. The sudden roar of a lathe. The whine of a sharpening stone. The clanking rumble of a conveyor belt. Workers cussing and shouting at one another.

Tools were everywhere, on the floor, on the gunwales of the boats, in the workers' pockets, hanging from their belts, clanging inside toolboxes of every size. Hammers, levels, awls, metal punches, screwdrivers, handsaws, hand drills, wrenches, pliers, crowbars.

A latticework of beams and girders flanked each side of the long assembly line. The girder wall ran the full length of the factory floor along both sides of the assembly area, at least one football field in length and nearly as wide. The latticework frame supported electrical lines, multiple overhead cranes, hoses, paint sprayers, hooks and hoists, plus fan belts, catwalks, roller conveyors, skids and ramps.

The boat frames were assembled one by one on large moveable wooden pallets. The overhead crane raised, lowered, and moved each boat frame forward from pallet to pallet as needed. On the far wall of the factory, painted high overhead the work area in giant letters four-feet tall were eight words:

THE GUY WHO RELAXES
IS HELPING THE AXIS

Guilt and patriotism and painful memories of the Great Depression just ended were the fuel that got much of the work done each and every day.

The most distinctive sound on the factory floor was the sound of a circular saw. It was different from the sound of an up-and-down reciprocating saw, a distinctive buzzing sound which earned it its nickname — buzz saw. Two men could not possibly have a conversation within earshot of a whirring buzz saw.

Every now and again a worker would steal a furtive glance in the direction of the two men as they stood shoulder to shoulder on the catwalk overlooking the factory floor talking quietly. Each man was feared by others in his own way.

"You understand I need this Navy contract, yes?" Andrew Higgins said.

"No less than I," Nico replied. "You and I have an understanding. You share a percentage of the take with me. I give you manpower and labor peace."

"Yes, yes, you will get your cut. But without a steady stream of new procurement orders from the armed forces, this place goes bust. You got that, right? My overhead in this shop is enormous."

"What are you asking of me, Higgins?"

"Behave. That is what I am asking of you. When these Navy people come tomorrow, treat these people with respect. Do not give us away. Do not ask them for too much."

"You know very well what I want from them."

"I do know. And they may very well be willing to grant you your request. But if they are not willing, I am asking you to please back down. Do not press them. We both need this contract, me as much as you."

The buzz saw started up again and the two men instantly fell silent. There wasn't anything further to be said today anyway.

TUESDAY
AUGUST 4, 1942
8:30 a.m.

City Park Avenue, New Orleans

"They come off the line on the factory floor, either City Park Avenue or Industrial Canal, then get outfitted with a single 225-horsepower diesel engine from Gray Marine Motor Company and two Tucker machine-gun turrets that we manufacture ourselves. From there we throw them in the water, wet-test them, and run them through their paces. We seal any leaks with dolphinite. Then, when everything is shipshape, we haul them out of the water and load them onto a cargo ship or railcar for delivery to the U.S. Navy. We are building between three and four landing boats a day, plus an equal number of PT boats each day."

Andrew Jackson Higgins, president of the Eureka Tug-Boat Company, sat behind his worktable desk in his City Park Avenue office, drink in hand, and stared hard across the floor of his immense workspace at the two men in uniform, Marine Colonel Peter Morgan and Navy Vice Admiral James Carmichael. Louisiana days did not come much hotter than this one, and Vice Admiral James Carmichael was once again sweating profusely.

"Not nearly fast enough, Higgins," the Vice Admiral said. "We need nearly five times that number. We may need a third factory — or even a fourth. Perhaps one on the west coast. In any case, here in New Orleans we need you to devote more square feet of factory floor space to the assembly of these landing craft and PT boats."

Andrew Higgins shook his head in irritation. "Listen, Admiral, the new boat I showed you last Friday will take longer to build. It is more complicated. A steel ramp. Two machine-gun turrets. More materials. I cannot get my hands on enough good quality plywood. Gray Marine is having problems keeping up with my demand for engines. I only have one rail line coming in here. Plus, with more and more boys enlisting in the army every day to fight the Hun and the Yellow Horde, it is getting harder and harder for me to find qualified people to work in my shop. I already use

Cajuns, Indians, old people, and Negroes. We will be adding women to the workforce before Thanksgiving. Hell, my lumber mill next door runs night and day already. We are about to start up an autoclave to manufacture our own plywood."

"Maybe if you didn't drink so much bourbon, you might be able to build more boats faster."

"You're a fuck, Admiral. Did anyone ever tell you that? I only drink when I'm working. But since I work all the time, I keep several bottles of Old Taylor right here in a cabinet beside my desk. Care for a snort?"

"You're incorrigible."

"I may not be able to spell the word, but I know what it means. Anyway, the men love me."

It was true; the men did love him, even the union bosses. They would go to the ends of the earth to keep Higgins happy. Whenever a dispute arose on the floor, Higgins would take the union rep up to his office and they would thrash it out the old-fashioned way, nose to nose, eyeball to eyeball. But, in his turn, Higgins was also a vocal champion of workers' rights. Just four months ago he attended the Southern Conference for Human Welfare in Nashville, an event for which he was roundly criticized by other businessmen. Higgins made a short speech on the rights of Negroes in which he said that he would hire Negroes at equal pay up to their percentage of the population. Mrs. Roosevelt, the president's wife, also attended. She termed him one of the most enlightened businessmen she had ever met.

"Yes indeed," Higgins said. "The men love me."

"Can we please dispense with the dramatics?" Vice Admiral James Carmichael implored. "The Navy needs more boats, and they need them sooner than later. That's all there is to it."

"You have to understand, Admiral. There are certain physical constraints I have to deal with here. This is an absolutely perfect location from which to operate and produce, ideally situated. But this plant, the City Park Avenue plant, is too small. We need to expand. But we are boxed in physically. On one side of the property are the Southern Railway System tracks. That piece of railroad track is essential for bringing in supplies and for taking out finished boats. On the other side of the property is the Delgado Trades School. I depend on them for workers. In front of the plant is City Park Avenue itself, an important thoroughfare. I cannot expand in that direction either. My only other choice is a piece of ground adjacent to the back of the shipyard and owned by the Holt Cemetery."

"The cemetery company has sold you some of its ground to build on?"

"Not exactly."

"What exactly then?"

"I preempted an unused portion of the cemetery grounds."

"Define preempted." The Admiral seemed to be sweating even more than before.

"We are building on it. In fact, we have already completed building on it."

"Without the cemetery's permission?"

"Forty percent of the expanded facility is now built on cemetery land."

"On land you do not hold title to? Land you do not legally own or control?" Vice Admiral James Carmichael shook his head with disgust.

"You want more boats or not? Doing it this way was the only way to increase output at minimal cost and without further need for delay. Let's forget about the cemetery, shall we, and talk business. The original boat, the *Eureka* boat we were selling to the Brits before we entered the war, had several drawbacks, you know that. When men or equipment had to be off-loaded from that original boat, it had to be over the sides of the boat, very dangerous. It exposed the men to enemy fire in a combat situation."

Marine Colonel Peter Morgan, who had been quiet all this time, interjected. "But your brilliant redesign changed all that, didn't it? You fit the boat with a full-width steel ramp at the front. Now troops can leave the landing craft *en masse.* The new boat is wider, wide enough to carry a small vehicle like a Jeep. The Navy has even given your new boat a new designation. LCVP. Landing Craft, Vehicle, Personnel. The boys in the field ignore the official designation. They simply call it a Higgins boat. The boys definitely prefer it now that you have repositioned the machine-gun turrets. Plus, they love those bilge pumps you installed. No more bailing with helmets."

"I am flattered, to be sure. But I cannot take all the credit. Repositioning those guns was actually Preston Tucker's idea."

"Where is Tucker anyway? I haven't seen the man all morning."

"Me and Tucker have been arguing quite a lot these past days. Tucker hasn't much more in the way of ideas to offer this company. The real geniuses in this place are my draftsmen and engineers — Graham Haddock, George Huet, Art Fleitas, Captain Richard McDerby."

"Well kiss Tucker and make up. There is a lot more tinkering to do in the days ahead, and we need the man's smarts."

"What kind of tinkering?"

"We need you to build us a bigger boat yet, one able to carry and quickly unload a thirty-ton Army tank. And we definitely need your thoughts on how to build a smaller version, one we can drop from the air as a lifeboat for downed air crews. Supplies of marine plywood may soon become less of a problem, because the newer boats will need to have a metal hull."

"Slow down, Admiral. One outrageous demand at a time. Talk to me first about this larger boat you have in mind, the one able to carry a tank. I could probably have a working model in your hands this very afternoon."

"How is that even possible? Has the liquor finally gone to your head?"

"Not at all. This is what the big fight with the Bureau of Ships this summer has been all about, a tank lighter," Higgins said. "Or haven't you been paying attention?"

"I've read some of your testimony before the Truman Committee, if that's what you mean," Carmichael said.

"I hope you didn't skip the part about the near-disaster in Norfolk ten weeks ago. In the competition that day between the Bureau's boat and my boat, the Navy's Bureau of Ships got its comeuppance in front of an entire swarm of generals and admirals and political types."

"We'll know the official outcome soon enough. The Truman Committee is scheduled to make its report public any day."

Higgins could barely contain himself. He remembered the day of the competition like it was yesterday. Norfolk, Virginia. May 25, 1942. The day was cool and overcast. A stiff, twenty mile-per-hour wind was blowing. Whitecaps carpeted a moderately rough sea. Two boats in the water, each carrying a 30-ton Army tank. When the two boats rounded Cape Henry north of Virginia Beach, and turned south into the open ocean, trouble began. The Bureau's lighter dipped bow down into the waves and began to take on water. Out came the hand pumps and the life jackets and the Navy crew began to bail water. Suddenly, the lighter began to roll and sway dangerously. The coxswain reduced power, afraid the boat would capsize and the tank would be lost, not to mention the boat and crew. He slowly turned his lighter back toward safe harbor. Higgins' boat completed the course without mishap and successfully landed its 30-ton Army tank dry on the beach in the designated location.

Higgins was thoroughly enjoying himself now. "You are aware, aren't you, that I am already in possession of a pre-publication copy of the Committee's report?"

"No, I was not aware," the Admiral said red-faced. "And have you already read it?"

"Indeed I have."

"And what does it say?"

"It says that I am right and that you are wrong."

"I see."

"Admiral. Due respect. Do you even know the history of our tank lighter design? The boat we built and tested and won the competition with at Virginia Beach was based on a shallow-draft boat I previously used to great success on the Amazon River. If you give me a moment, I can show you the plans for that very boat."

Higgins slid past his drafting table to a multi-drawered wooden cabinet at the opposite end of his office, where he stored all his blueprints. He opened the third drawer from the bottom. "Yes, here it is, right where I left it."

Vice Admiral Carmichael nodded. "You really are full of surprises, aren't you?"

Higgins smiled but said nothing. He unrolled the Amazon River boat blueprints and set them out on his drafting table for the Admiral to see. Colonel Morgan pushed in front of him and took an immediate interest in the drawings.

Carmichael continued. "One of the LCVP's strengths, the shallow draft, is also one of its weaknesses. It sways like a son of a bitch in choppy seas. Seasickness onboard is legend. Plus, it offers limited protection against enemy fire. The sides and rear are made of plywood."

"Yes," Higgins said. "But an armor plated boat will take longer to build. It will require more materials. It will be heavier. It will require an even larger motor. When it is in operation, it may take longer to beach and longer to unload. An experienced Coast Guard crew can run the current LCVP right up onto the shoreline, off-load a platoon of thirty-six men and their equipment, reverse itself off the beach and head back out to the supply ship for another load in under five minutes."

Marine Colonel Peter Morgan looked up from the drawings. "Let's first see how the current version of the LCVP fares in battle. The first Pacific landings are already underway and much has already been learned from the practice landings. Reports from the field are good. Coasties — most of whom you trained right here at your school — suggest the hull sides be made flatter, which should make them easier to build and easier to plate with armor. The helm should be moved forward from the center of the rear deck to a lower position next to the engine compartment. But you have already done that in your new design. They recommended that light machine-gun turrets be added to the aft deck, but you have already done that as well."

Morgan continued. "The Pacific island assaults will involve many landings and evacuations on shallow beaches. The bottom of the boat is going to receive hell. The skeg section of the keel, near the stern, will need to be made longer and more substantial to better protect the propeller and rudderpost."

"All doable," Higgins said.

"Which brings me to our current thinking on upcoming invasion plans," Vice Admiral Carmichael said.

Higgins drew a sharp breath. "I thought such information was top secret, something I was not privy to. Does this mean you now finally trust me?"

"Andrew, I have never questioned your patriotism. And there has never been a time when I did not trust you. But I have people I must answer to. They do not know you as well as I do. In any case, you are not the one the brass is worried about. He is."

Vice Admiral Carmichael motioned to the factory floor. Nico Carolla and three of his men were working their way along the length of the factory floor and to the stairs that would take them up to the second floor and Higgin's office. They were here at the Navy's request. Higgins recognized two of the men at a distance, Luca and Vittorio. They all looked to be packing heat and very much out of their element.

Vice Admiral James Carmichael spoke hurriedly, now, before they came to the door. "I want you to know that senior commanders have considered our options. They are agreed that we have no choice but to share select pieces of top secret military intell with this mobster, the *Don* of a Sicilian crime family. But that doesn't mean the sharing doesn't worry them. They are worried sick about leaks, information leaks. It worries them a lot, day and night."

"Honestly, Admiral, that man out there is sharing more with us than we are with him. His family — an uncle of his, I believe — has already given the Allies valuable intelligence — road maps, terrain markers, safe houses, even the names of other Sicilians willing to risk their all and help. These are people the Allies can turn to at any time, to get more information. Let's invite him in now. I really don't want to keep a man like this cooling his heels outside my door for long."

Andrew Higgins went to the door when they knocked. "Thank you for coming, Nico. The Admiral would like to speak with you alone."

Nico growled his disapproval.

"Just you, Nico."

"*Madre di Dio.* These fuckers still don't trust me?"

"Just you, Nico," Higgins quietly repeated. "Like we discussed."

Nico nodded and calmly motioned to his men to remain outside in the anteroom. He and Higgins had discussed this scenario yesterday morning when they met privately here at the plant. *Put up a little stink*, Higgins said. *Make it look real but do not protest too much. Be polite to the Navy boys even though we both know they are assholes.*

As Nico entered the room, Vice Admiral James Carmichael extended his right hand. "Please come in." He bid Nico enter and have a seat.

"And this person is?" Nico asked.

"Colonel Peter Morgan, United States Marine Corps."

"A lot of brass for one poor Sicilian. A colonel, an admiral. What, no brigadier generals on hand to greet me?"

"Nice to make your acquaintance, as well," Colonel Morgan said, acid in his voice.

"Yes, yes, yes. Enough with the pleasantries," Admiral Carmichael said, turning to Nico. "Mr. Carolla, the United States of America would like to thank you and your family for all the help you have given the Allied war effort so far."

Nico nodded. "And I would like to thank you and your Uncle Sam for all the many good-paying jobs you have steered our way, given our dockworkers. Also, for the handsome sums you have passed our way."

"This is a subject me and my Uncle Sam would rather you not dwell on. No one must ever know about that money."

"Of course. How crude of me. But surely you must know that there are some things in life more precious than gold."

"I find that hard to believe coming from a Carolla. But do go on."

"Freedom, Admiral. Freedom."

"I do not get your point."

"My grandfather does not want to be deported back to Italy," Nico said.

"And he will not be. The war has seen to that."

"Nor does he wish to go back to prison."

"That is out of our hands, isn't it? Your grandfather needs to keep his nose clean. The courts will not look kindly on him should he happen to commit another murder. You understand that, right?"

Nico nodded but continued to press. "A man who is a U.S. citizen cannot be legally deported. That applies in equal measure to law-abiding citizens as well as to those held in a house of detention."

"What are you saying? That your grandfather, the *Don* of a major crime family, has been recently reborn as a god-fearing flag-waving patriotic American?"

"Even dirt-poor Sicilians can understand sarcasm."

Vice Admiral James Carmichael stared back hard at the other man, but did not reply in kind.

"What I am saying is this, Admiral. Find a way to grant my grandfather U.S. citizenship. Place a stop on his deportation order. Not a stay. A complete and permanent stop."

"What you ask . . . is not easily done. I do not have that kind of juice."

"I do not understand *juice*."

"Juice. Pull. Influence."

"Well then, Admiral, you must find yourself a ripe piece of fruit and squeeze it until the juice runs clear, for that is the price to be paid for our continued cooperation — citizenship for my grandfather. I need a personal guarantee from you that *Nonno* will not be deported."

"Now that is a new one on me. *Nonno?*"

"A Sicilian word. It means grandfather."

"Okay then. I will run it up the ladder, as you ask. But let's not lose sight of one very important fact. What you ask is a political decision, not a military one. People higher up the food chain than me will have the final word on your request."

"If you give me your word that you will try, I can perhaps live with that."

Carmichael acquiesced, though he was surprised that Carolla gave in so easily. It suddenly dawned on him that Higgins and the Sicilian might be working from the same playbook.

"So tell me, Admiral. What can the Carolla family do for the United States government today?"

"What I am about to tell you is highly classified information. We are little more than three months away from an Allied invasion of North Africa."

"That is good to know. *Che cazzo?* Only about time."

"I would rather you not swear at me in Italian."

"Sicilian."

"Okay, Sicilian. I would rather you not swear at me in Sicilian. Mr. Carolla, you must understand that neither I nor Colonel Morgan can give you any operational details. But there are certain things we still need to know, things you may be able to help us with."

"Such as?"

"For the moment, what worries the brass most are troop movements on the island, both German and Italian infantry positions. Where exactly on the island of Sicily are they bivouacked? How dug in are their forces? What size guns do they possess and how many? How many men and where? How many trucks? How many aircraft? Ship movements. Convoys. Storehouses. Ammo dumps."

"You want a lot, Admiral."

"A lot is at stake."

Nico Carolla nodded. He understood. Sicily was the soft underbelly of Italy, the doorway into central Europe. "For the proper sum of money, I believe I can get you much of that information."

"Tell me how. I need specifics."

"I have two cousins who live in Sicily, both with children. Then there is my great-uncle's family. The children have free run of the island. The Italians and the Germans ignore them totally. The boys can tally numbers of German soldiers in the field just as easily as they can tally sheep. Also, many of the local fishermen are loyal to us. We can count on them for much information. Already, they have been keeping score of the comings and goings of

German ships. Supplies. U-boats. Plus, there are burro trails. Every two days, we send men on donkeys from Palermo over to the other side of the island. They carry goods, deliver mail, return with textiles and other goods."

"We need these men to do much more."

"Tell me. What do you have in mind?"

"We need intell on airstrips, on fuel supplies delivered and stored, on armored vehicles, ship movements, yards of concrete poured, things like that."

"This may be possible. These Nazi pigs need *puttana* to service them all day and all night long."

"*Puttana?*"

"Yes, *puttana*. *Troia*. *Zoccola*. Hookers, prostitutes, local women. These Nazi pigs will fuck anything with two legs. But *puttana* can also be a great source of intelligence. Such women can give us counts on troop strength. Truck movements. The comings and goings of senior personnel."

"Okay, then perhaps we can strike a deal. If you can provide us with such intell, I will see to it that your family is well paid, same as before, with deposits to that same bank account in Havana."

"That is agreeable. Shall we shake hands on it?"

"Yes, of course. But there is one more thing. I would like for the two of us to meet again in two days' time."

"*Madre di Dio*. What about this time?"

"We know there is a large Sicilian population living in Tunis. The Allies are going to need their help ahead of the landings."

Nico looked doubtful. "That will be more difficult."

"Yes, we know that. But we do have a man, codename Rygor, who is already positioned in North Africa. What we need from you is the name of a man loyal to the Carolla family that Rygor can make contact with. Do you know such a person?"

"I may be able to provide you with a name," Nico said. "But first I have to make some inquiries."

"Good. Excellent. Thank you. Can we meet again in two days' time? Can you come up with a name that quickly?"

"Yes, I think that I can."

"Two days then. Thank you."

The two men, uneasy allies, shook hands. Then Nico Carolla left the plant with his men via the way they had come in, down the long corridor and out past the loading dock, where a hammerhead lifting crane could be seen loading and unloading nearby railcars.

Andrew Higgins watched through the glass as the mob chief left the premises. He and the Carolla family were thick as thieves. Then he threw off the thought and turned back to Morgan and Carmichael. "You were saying something earlier about needing a lifeboat model?"

"What we need is a powered lifeboat that can be dropped into the water by a fixed-wing aircraft."

"That is a tall order. Who are we trying to save with these lifeboats? And under what circumstances?"

"Let me answer that, Admiral."

"Go ahead, Colonel."

"We are losing airmen in the water nearly every single day — pilots, navigators, gunners — good men who survive an emergency water landing, but then die in the water from other causes. Even when we are certain where an aircraft went down, we often cannot get a surface vessel to the crew fast enough to save their lives. They drown or are eaten by sharks or else freeze to death in cold water. If only we could fly a lifeboat out across the ocean to the scene of the aircraft downing, the survivors might be able to crawl into the lifeboat and get out of the water long enough for us to arrive with a surface vessel and rescue them before they perish."

At first, Higgins did not say anything. Then the wheels began to turn in his head. Higgins was a natural-born problem-solver. "And how would this airborne lifeboat arrive on the scene?"

Vice Admiral Carmichael nodded his head. "It would have to be sturdy, obviously. We see it being carried aloft by a heavy bomber, maybe a B-17 Flying Fortress. The bomber would have to be specially modified to handle the external load of the lifeboat. We picture it being dropped into the water by parachute."

"Like I said, a very tall order. Has anyone ever attempted a stunt like this before?"

"Yes, actually they have. A man named Uffa Fox. From the United Kingdom. Uffa is a sailboat designer by trade. He is said to have designed what the Brits are calling the first airborne lifeboat. It looks a bit like a canoe. A twenty-seven-foot-long boat designed to be dropped by parachute from beneath a Vickers Warwick. We want you to evaluate the Fox boat and see what you think."

"Arrange a meeting. Better still, get me some drawings and photographs of the damn thing. I will put together a team of my best men to study it."

Vice Admiral James Carmichael nodded his approval. If anyone could build the thing, it would be Higgins. The man had a reputation for skipping the drafting board and just charging ahead and building test models. When Higgins wanted a development in a hurry, he would call a group into his office, fire questions at them, taunt them with their stupidity, push them into arguments, swear at them if he thought it might help, and insist they keep at it until a solution presented itself. Over the course of the war, his people developed some remarkable devices. A ship-to-shore telephone system. A smoke generator that operated independently of a boat's engine, yet was capable of laying down a screen several miles long. A one-horsepower pump the size of a grapefruit yet powerful enough to pass nearly 200 gallons a minute. A semiautomatic clutch and reverse-gear mechanism that enabled a boat operator to handle the clutch, reverse gear, spark and throttle with a single lever.

"Okay," Carmichael said. "You will get your drawings and your photographs. An actual meeting with Fox may not be possible. But I will talk to the Brits and see what shakes loose."

"Let's call it a day then, shall we?"

TUESDAY
AUGUST 4, 1942
10 a.m.

French Quarter, New Orleans

"I bring news from Aldo," the dark-haired beauty said.

In this setting, she was careful to maintain a respectable distance between herself and the swarthy man she often shared a bed with. Today's rendezvous between her and Nico was a business meeting, not at the apartment, but at the Carolla supper club, the *Trattoria Sicilia*. The club was the focal point of the crime family's operations. Somewhere in the back of the *trattoria* lurked Nico's grandfather. The old man, who Nico affectionately called him *Nonno*, was watchful but hard of hearing in one ear.

"And how is my uncle Aldo?" Nico asked, breaking the crust from his bread. Sometimes, to keep up appearances, the two lovers met to conduct family business where Luca and the others might observe. Such meetings greatly cut down on rumors.

"Great-uncle, I thought you said."

"Yes, great-uncle. *Nonno*'s youngest brother. Uncle Aldo was the youngest in a family of twelve. Now he is senior *Don* of the Palermo Mafia families. What is your news?"

"It is not good," Martina said. She dipped a corner of her bread into the small glass bowl. The bowl held a measure of virgin olive oil, plus pepper, spices, and tiny bits of diced onion. She brought the morsel of bread hungrily to her lips.

"*Che cazzo?* The news out of Sicily has not been good for some time," Nico said. "Ever since the Fascists came to power in Italy, the *Mafiosi* have suffered."

"I am not political; you know that."

"Not political. Historical."

Martina Amerada dipped her fork into the bowl of cooked spaghetti and twirled the fork several times gathering the pasta into a ball. Then she dipped the loaded fork into the steaming hot bowl of meat sauce. She slowly chewed the mouthful, savored the taste. Then she spoke, choosing her words.

"Nico, it's your cousin, not your great-uncle. There has been an assault."

The color drained from Nico's face. "Josepha? *Madre di Dio!*" He looked toward the back of the *trattoria*, where his grandfather stood straining to hear what was being said.

Martina nodded in the affirmative. "Yes, Josepha."

"How do you know this?" Nico asked, suddenly angry. Josepha was his favorite, a girl of perhaps fifteen.

"Aldo told our courier after we made the last money exchange in Palermo. She has been raped by soldiers."

Tears came to Nico's eyes. "What are you saying?"

Martina was struck by the sudden onset of emotion.

Then his tears turned to anger. "Has there been no retribution? My uncle . . . he is not the sort of man to let such a terrible thing go unpunished. *Merda.* The Carolla family . . . our name . . . we have been disgraced by these . . . by these *bastardi . . . .* these bastards."

"I am told two men have been caught, both soldiers. One man was beaten to death, the other castrated. The crime has not gone unanswered."

"Mother of God! The country is in shambles. That is how the Mafia first came to be. You know that, right?"

"The history you were talking about?"

Nico nodded. "A hundred years ago, Sicily was lawless, just like it is today. Bandits roamed the countryside then, just as they do now. The bandits harassed people. They interfered with commerce, stole from merchants, terrorized innocents. The central government was weak. The judicial system was ineffective. The first *Mafioso* were employed as private enforcers. Their job was to protect the property of merchants and landowners from the thuggery of thieving brigands."

Nico continued. "The strength of the *Mafiosi* grew right along with the need for protection. Before long, they were a bigger menace to the citizenry than the bandits had ever been. In the 1920s, the Fascist regime began to push back against them. That is when Benito Mussolini appointed Cesare Mori to be prefect of the island. Mori was a rabid dog. *Un cane rabbioso.* Mussolini gave Cesare Mori carte blanche to eradicate the *Mafiosi.* Mori had at his disposal all the resources of the regime, both the Carabinieri and the regular army, such that it was."

"Carabinieri? This is a word I do not understand."

"National military police. The Carabinieri were used by the government to bind the kingdoms of Italy into a single nation. In Sicily the Mafia made a mockery of Mussolini's power. He was enraged by the putdown. So, to legitimize his rule, Mussolini the *bastardo* Fascist unleashed all hell upon the Mafia. He laid siege to towns, tortured suspects, took women and children hostage. The hostages were to be bargaining chips used to encourage suspects to give themselves up. Now, today, you come here in the middle of the week to tell me that some of Mussolini's thugs have ravaged and raped my beautiful innocent Josepha? *Cazzo.*"

"We don't know the particulars yet, Nico. It could have been one of Mori's Fascist thugs. Or it might have been a Nazi soldier. Hitler's people are crisscrossing the island scouting for highly defensible locations to set up their artillery. The Nazis want to command the high ground in the event of an Allied invasion. Aldo exacted retribution against those two soldiers, mostly as a show of force. He is not yet actually sure who is responsible for the attack — and Josepha is not saying."

"Nor am I entirely sure what went on at my whorehouse the other day."

"So you said."

"A man came to the door of Lulu White's old place. He claimed to be looking for his father. He murdered Hector, cut off his finger to retrieve a special ring, hurt my man Luca, then walked calmly back into the street, threatening to return again later more heavily armed."

"You have any leads as to who that man might be?"

"Only one. The man drove a brand new Packard sedan, the type they call the Super Eight One-Eighty. One of my girls said it had an 'X' gas ration sticker on the windshield. I thought only ministers and police and firemen were permitted 'X' stickers?"

"Such a car should not be difficult to find. I know people inside the government — bureaucrats mainly — who might be able to help us locate an automobile of that sort."

"What aren't you telling me, Martina? Are you some sort of *poliziotto*? Do I have reason to be worried?"

"Yes, yes. You caught me, Nico. I am a super sleuth, a spy. I launder money for crime bosses then report everything I do to Internal Revenue."

For a brief instant, Nico took her seriously. Then he laughed. "If you worked for Internal Revenue, I would already be behind bars, just like Alphonse Capone. Find me that Packard, if you can. It is likely registered in Hancock County, Mississippi."

"I will try," Martina said. "But promise me that the next time you and I meet, it will be in a spot quieter than this."

"Yes, next time. I promise. But the first thing I need you to do is find me a way to get a message through to Aldo. He and I have much to discuss. Then you need to try and track down that Packard."

Martina stood up under the watchful eye of *Nonno*, extended her hand in a professional and courteous manner and left the small restaurant. Her network of connections was about to become quite valuable indeed.

TUESDAY
AUGUST 4, 1942
4 p.m.

Bletchley Park, England

"Shaun Yardley is simply one of our brighter lads here at Station X. A bit of a dandy, true. But smart as a whip."

The speaker was a bespectacled man, Liam Fieldstone, a mathematician from the University of Cambridge. Like so many of the wunderkind on staff here at Bletchley Park, Liam was bright and inquisitive, if peculiar.

Indeed, the entire staff at Bletchley Park ranked high on the peculiar scale, both men and women. All brilliant. All inquisitive. All sworn to secrecy at the highest levels. Chess champions. Linguists. Mathematicians. Crossword puzzle experts.

The women of Bletchley Park were under the jurisdiction of the Admiralty, all part of the Women's Royal Naval Service, the Wrens. Their official posting was to the HMS *Pembroke V.*

"What exactly are you getting at, Fieldstone? Your shop is doing a bang up job for us. Everyone says the same. Bletchley is practically winning the war for the Allies singlehandedly. Even the Prime Minister agrees."

The speaker was Commander Ian Fleming, later the author of James Bond fame. He had been recruited into the service before the war by Rear Admiral John Godfrey, Director of Naval Intelligence of the Royal Navy.

Fleming was Godfrey's personal assistant. He served as Godfrey's liaison to the intelligence services. This included MI6, which was the British Secret Intelligence Service, as well as Bletchley Park and the Special Operations Executive, better known as the SOE. Fleming's codename was 17F. He worked out of Room 39 at the Admiralty where he made regular reports to the Prime Minister.

"I am glad that Mr. Churchill is so happy with our work," Liam Fieldstone replied. "But as I was saying, Shaun Yardley is one of our better cryptographers, chief analyst actually. Earlier this year, June in fact, he and his B.P. team in Hut 4 cracked the latest version of the Nazi Navy's Enigma Code."

"With a little help from the Polish, don't you mean?" Commander Ian Fleming interrupted. "Might have happened sooner had they listened to me."

"I do not get your meaning," Fieldstone replied.

"Operation Ruthless."

When Liam Fieldstone replied with an unknowing stare, Commander Fleming continued.

"September 1940. I wrote the Admiralty a memo. In that memo, I described a plan to obtain details of the Enigma codes. My idea was to obtain a German bomber, man it with an English crew that spoke German and wore Luftwaffe uniforms, and crash the aircraft into the English Channel. When a German boat arrived on the scene to rescue their downed bomber crew, the English crew would attack their rescuers and bring the German boat back to England, along with its Enigma machine."

"That is a pretty sly plan for a desk-jockey. But I dare say, Commander — wouldn't the downed bomber have sunk to the bottom of the Channel in nothing flat?"

"Desk-jockey, is it?" Steam rose briefly from Fleming's eyes. Then he chuckled. "As it turns out, that is precisely why the RAF turned down my plan. But you can ask Alan Turing about it, if you wish. He was quite miffed at the time. Turing very much wanted to see Operation Ruthless carried out."

"So it is a good thing, then, that the Poles brought us their intelligence. Very smart people, those Poles. They were indeed the first to crack Enigma, not us. Poland's Cipher Bureau. The embarrassing truth is that we could not figure out the infernal thing until they showed us how."

"But now I understand the Nazis keep fiddling with the thing."

"Each iteration is tougher to crack than the last. That is where Shaun Yardley and his crew come in. Yardley is an ace, the brains of the bunch. Youngest son of an American cryptographer of some note. Herbert Yardley."

"Yes, I know the man. U.S. State Department. Founder of MI-8. Author of *The American Black Chamber*. Codebreaking hero of the Great War. Not held in such high esteem anymore."

"Yes, Herbert is the father. Son Shaun works for us. Seems like the boy has something to prove."

Fleming nodded. "Strange turn of events, would you not agree?"

"How so?"

"Herbert Osborn Yardley. American cryptologist. Born before the turn of the century. Founded and led the Black Chamber. Broke Japanese diplomatic codes in the 1920s. Furnished American negotiators with key intell during the disarmament talks, the Washington Naval Conference of 1921. Helped the Nationalists in China crack Japanese military codes about the time the current world war broke out in Europe. More recently, went to work for the Canadians. Last year, he helped the Canucks set up a cryptologic section."

"I don't follow. What was the strange turn of events?"

"Old Man Yardley was discredited by the Americans after he wrote his book about the Chamber. The book itself was quite popular. This was in the early 1930s. The man was a hero. But they no longer trusted him. Maybe that's why his son acts as if he has something to prove."

Fieldstone nodded knowingly. "The boy is an ace, like I said. Apple didn't fall far from the tree. I have assigned him to Block A. He has nothing to prove by me."

"Block A?" Fleming asked. "What is that?"

"You mean to tell me that Britain has secrets even Commander Ian Fleming is not privy to? Is that even possible?" Fieldstone asked.

"No one person should know everything. That is the very essence of successful spycraft."

"At Bletchley, the original huts were built of wood. Now we have newer blockhouses built of brick and concrete. Each blockhouse is designated by a letter of the alphabet. Block A is where we deal with Naval Intelligence. Shaun is now working in Block A, as well as in Block E, which handles incoming and outgoing radio traffic."

Fleming was growing impatient. The Commander thought in terms of broad strokes, not minutia. *Who in the world cared which concrete block building housed which operation?*

Two years ago already, Commander Fleming had authored the so-called "Trout Memo." His boss, Rear Admiral Godfrey, Director of British Naval Intelligence, circulated the memo widely throughout the intelligence community. In that memorandum, Fleming likened the deception of an enemy in wartime to fly fishing, hence the name of the memo. Fleming outlined a number of schemes that might be used against the Axis powers to lure U-boats and German surface ships towards British minefields. Number 28 on the list was an idea to plant misleading papers on a corpse that would be found by the enemy.

As Fleming wrote in the memo:

The following suggestion was used in a book by Basil Thomson. A corpse dressed as an airman, with dispatches in his pockets, could be dropped on the coast, supposedly from a parachute that had failed. I understand there is no difficulty in obtaining corpses at the Naval Hospital. But, of course, it would have to be a fresh one.

Fleming's memo eventually evolved into Operation Mincemeat, the successful 1943 plan to conceal from the Germans the intended invasion of Italy from North Africa.

The impatient Fleming now said, "You will presently come to the point about this Yardley business, won't you?"

"Yes, presently. As I said, Block E is tasked with monitoring radio traffic."

"So you said."

"Well, Station X is the information hub, the very fulcrum point for Operation Torch."

"Station X?"

"Still above your paygrade?" Fieldstone teased.

"Do get on with it, will you? I am a busy man and you are becoming quite tedious."

"Not much of a secret really. Station X. The Roman numeral ten. Station X is our Intelligence Service's tenth wireless station."

"Yes, quite enlightening. What surprises me is that you should know anything at all about Operation Torch."

"Perhaps not as much as you," Fieldstone replied tartly. "But Bletchley selected the very name of the operation. A torch to light the fire. The imminent landings in North Africa, with targets still up for debate. Hut 4 is tagging any German chatter which might suggest they know when or where or how. The Wrens have been working around the clock as the decision date draws nearer, one team in particular."

"That team include the new girl?"

"Constance McCallister?"

"Quite the bird, that Wren," Fleming said. He already had a reputation as a lady's man.

"You know her?"

"Signed off on her clearance before she came to you. Very talented girl. I understand you two have some history."

"Is that a problem?"

"That remains to be seen. But I told her that I would be watching."

Fieldstone harrumphed politely. "Only a matter of days ago, Shaun Yardley's cryptography team uncovered something it had not expected to find. An anomaly."

"I do not quite understand the problem. Don't your people stumble across unexpected things every single day of the week?"

"Commander, the problem is that what they have found has nothing at all to do with Operation Torch or with North Africa, not Casablanca, not Algiers, not Tunis, not any of it."

"So why the fuck are you bothering me with such rubbish? You know who I am, right?"

"All I know is what you have told me. You are from the Admiralty and you are Godfrey's assistant."

"All true," Fleming replied. "But you would be well advised not to treat me as some low-level paper-pusher. I am much more hands on than that. I would not be violating my oath if I told you that my most recent project has been to form a unit of commandos. The unit is composed entirely of men from other commando units that have been specially trained by SOE in intelligence gathering. Also, unarmed combat, safecracking, lock-picking and similar pursuits. The Admiralty has designated the unit as No. 30 Commando. Churchill has a pet name for the outfit. He calls it the 30 Assault Unit, or 30AU for short. 30AU's job is to remain near the front line of an Allied advance — sometimes in front of it — to seize enemy documents from previously targeted headquarters."

"Forgive me, Commander. It was never my intention to get on your wrong side today. So let me try to display more deference. The reason I am bothering you with such rubbish, as you say, is because my people think they may have stumbled onto a German plot to attack a facility or a location somewhere in the continental United States."

Commander Ian Fleming sat bolt upright. "That is big news, very big indeed. I must notify Rear Admiral Godfrey forthwith. Have you distilled any operational details?"

"No, not yet. What we do have thus far is this. Our listening post in Barcelona intercepted a message. We broke the cipher. Once again, we have to thank Constance McCallister and her cipher queens for that. The message originated at Waffen-SS Headquarters in Bremen. The recipient of the message was one Captain Wilhelm Kronenhauer. SOE has a file on this man. Maybe you have seen it. This is only my opinion, but I believe the pertinent part of the message, as it applies to us here today, is that our Captain Kronenhauer is an expert with munitions, RDX and the like."

Fleming nodded. "Actually, that file request of yours came through my office. I scanned the contents quickly before we released the file to your office. But until our meeting today, I had not made the connection. So tell me, Fieldstone. What were this man's orders?"

"It breaks down this way. Kronenhauer was ordered to Lisbon."

"No surprise there. Lisbon is a hotbed of spies and counterintelligence types. We ourselves have a large operation in Portugal and another in Spain. A story for another day perhaps."

"Yes, perhaps. Lisbon is many things. It is the main air transit point between Britain and the United States. Near as we can determine, our Captain Kronenhauer's orders were to board a Portuguese freighter, the *Vasquez*. We were instructed by MI6 to contact the HMS *Fidelity* and to ask her captain to dispatch a team to try and intercept Kronenhauer before he boarded the *Vasquez*. They were able to do so and we now have a detailed physical description of the man, as well as photographs. Those have been added to the SOE file on him."

"I know the *Fidelity* well," Fleming remarked. "The Admiralty has just overhauled her to operate as a commando carrier for operations in Southeast Asia. She has been armed with four 4-inch guns, four 21-inch torpedo tubes, and now carries two Kingfisher floatplanes, a motor torpedo boat, as well as two landing craft. You were lucky to get her. *Fidelity* has probably now served one of her last missions in the Med before joining a convoy bound for Southeast Asia."

"In any case, we obtained the photographs. But *Fidelity* was unable to get one of their crew onboard the *Vasquez* before she sailed."

"The men and the women of *Fidelity* have a broad portfolio."

"So I gather," Fieldstone said. "This was the first I had heard of her."

"I am not surprised. Most of her operations are quite hush. Until her recent reassignment, HMS *Fidelity* has operated off the coast of Southern France under SOE control. *Fidelity* lands agents onshore. She picks up escaped POWs, conducts small-scale sabotage operations, that sort of thing."

"I had no idea. What is her cover?"

"I am afraid that is above your paygrade," Commander Fleming said.

"I guess I deserved that."

"Indeed you did. Now back to Kronenhauer. *Fidelity* was unable to get a man onboard the *Vasquez*. So now we have lost track of him?"

"Not entirely. The ship did sail, as I said. But not before *Fidelity* made contact with the ship's captain. The Portuguese are our allies in this war, even if they are sometimes discreet about it. The captain confirmed Kronenhauer as a passenger onboard his ship from the photographs we showed him."

"You are right about the Portuguese," Commander Fleming said. "It would be doubly difficult for us to win this bloody war without their cooperation. The friendship between our two great nations is based on a five-hundred-year-old treaty. The Treaty of Windsor. Dates to 1386. The world's oldest diplomatic alliance. The treaty was renewed in 1899 and the current Portuguese government is still committed to it. They flat-out do not trust Hitler or the German people."

"I suppose that is one thing in our favor."

"So tell me, Fieldstone. Where the hell did that ship go when it left with our boy?"

"I have this secondhand from your people. But this is what I know. Twelve days after departing Lisbon, the *Vasquez* docked in Havana, Cuba, where Kronenhauer disembarked. The ship had intermediate stops in Tortola, the largest of the British Virgin Islands, and in San Juan, Puerto Rico. From what we can determine, she took on fuel in both ports and off-loaded cargo."

"Not much to go on," Fleming remarked. "Do we know where Kronenhauer went after he disembarked the ship?"

"One step ahead of you, Commander. Since we knew beforehand from the captain what the final destination of the ship would be, and since we already had in hand a complete physical description of the man, we radioed those details to your department's local contact in Havana, a woman."

"You brought a woman in on this?"

"Good enough to bed, but not good enough to employ as a spy?"

"No, women make excellent spies. But they make lousy soldiers. A woman is physically small. I do not know this Captain Kronenhauer personally, but based on his dossier I would expect him to be quite strong and physically fit. He would likely present as a formidable foe in a close-in fight, and, in such an encounter, the woman would be overmatched. He would kill her, and that would be a shame. Good spies take a long time to prep and train. A dead one doesn't do any of us much good."

"Not my call. The female belongs to MI6, not Bletchley Park. So if you have any complaints, feel free to lodge them elsewhere."

"This woman have a name?"

"I am confident that she does. But I do not know what that name is."

"No, I suppose you wouldn't. Martina Amerada. That is her name. Very bright woman. Very well-placed."

"Well-placed how?"

"Banco Nacional de Cuba. Vice President. Private Client Group."

"That sounds like code for money laundering," Liam Fieldstone said.

"You are not far wrong. Britain has many interests to protect. Not all of them can be conducted in the open."

"But money laundering?"

"You have heard of Alphonse Capone, yes?" Fleming asked.

"The American gangster?"

Commander Fleming nodded. "After Capone was taken down by the United States government for income tax evasion, the Sicilian mob families were forced to become more creative when laundering their illegal money. MI6 provided them with a way. We gained control of a Cuban bank charter. We put one of our own people in play down there. Martina Amerada."

"So now the Crown is in bed with the Sicilian mob?"

"The world is filled with uncomfortable bedfellows. But ask yourself, Fieldstone. Who is in bed with whom? They with us? Or we with them? We help them launder money, yes. But we see from where that money comes and to where it goes."

"Everything comes at a price, eh Commander?"

"Yes, it does. Now please tell me the rest of the Kronenhauer story."

"Since we knew precisely where the boat would eventually dock and since we had ample time, we sent a courier by air out of

Lisbon. The flight went via the Canary Islands to Havana. The courier was carrying with him pictures of our man. That way we would be sure to obtain an absolutely positive identification of Kronenhauer for our Havana contact — your woman — to follow when he got off the ship."

"I commend you. That was smart thinking."

"Not my idea actually. Shaun Yardley thought of it."

"Then what happened?"

"After two days in Havana, Captain Kronenhauer boarded a much smaller ship, one bound for the Port of New Orleans. Your girl Martina could not easily follow Kronenhauer onboard. The ship was too small, a crew of roughnecks. It would not have been safe for her, not even as a stowaway."

"So that's it then? We lost him?"

"No, not entirely. After paying off the captain of the *Vasquez*, your Cuban girl radioed in for instructions. MI6 gave her the name of a U.S. serviceman we could trust, a Marine Colonel posted at the Naval Air Station in New Orleans. The Marine — name of Peter Morgan, I believe — was contacted by wireless, given Kronenhauer's description, and told to meet the inbound ship and follow the man to his final destination."

"First-rate work," Fleming exclaimed. "In whose hands are the photographs now?"

"This question I cannot answer. Probably your girl Martina. I do know that this Peter Morgan, the Marine, picked up Kronenhauer's trail once he got off the boat from Havana in New Orleans. He reported that Captain Kronenhauer met with a second man, name unknown. Since our Colonel Morgan was working alone, he could not possibly follow both men after the meeting concluded. He had to make a decision. So our Marine stayed on Kronenhauer. The next day Kronenhauer went north out of the city and then east by automobile into the neighboring State of Mississippi. I can show you his approximate route here on the map. Our man lost him in the wilderness swamps. The Americans call them bayous or some such."

Commander Fleming looked at the map, became very quiet, lost in thought. "You have done some first-rate work here, Fieldstone. You should be commended. Perhaps you would like to come work for us?"

"Perhaps after the war. For now, I am quite happy where I am at. The work at Station X suits me well."

"Okay," Fleming said, still lost in thought. "I will take this to Godfrey. But I know what the man is going to say. He is going to say that this Kronenhauer business is not yet actionable."

"But look what we already have," Fieldstone objected.

"You have a great deal, I will admit. But nothing solid, only suspicions. You suspect that the Nazis have identified a military target in or around the New Orleans area. You suspect that whatever the target is, the Germans intend to blow it up, but with what sort of explosive you do not know. You base this second supposition on the arrival in the New Orleans area of a purported German bomb expert."

Fleming continued. "The plot is riddled with holes. You do not know when this hypothetical bombing is to take place. You do not know what the actual target is. You do not know what sort of explosive will be used. You do not know where the bomber is currently holed up or what he is using as a cover. I doubt whether he is traveling under his given name. Until we gather more intell, we will never know any of these things."

Liam Fieldstone frowned. "We need to tell the Yanks what we know. If there is an attack on their homeland and they learn that we might have warned them ahead of time, there will be hell to pay."

"I do not disagree. We ought to warn the Americans. And I know just the man to tell your story to. A Yank by the name of Colonel Donovan. Wild Bill is what the Americans call him. Donovan works with Colonel Daniel Morrison and the Yank codebreaking group. If anyone can crack this thing wide open and figure out the target, it is Wild Bill and his crew."

"What kind of name is Wild Bill?"

"Colonel 'Wild Bill' Donovan. President Roosevelt's special representative on intelligence cooperation between London and Washington. More than one year ago, May last, I accompanied Rear Admiral Godfrey to the United States. He and I helped Donovan write a blueprint for their new Coordinator of Information. This is the department which the Americans have since renamed the OSS, the Office of Strategic Services, though at the time I suggested a different name for the group, the Central Intelligence Agency or CIA. Britain's MI6 offices in America are located one floor below OSS offices in the International Building at Rockefeller Center, New York City."

Commander Fleming continued. "I have worked with Donovan on several hush projects since. Operation Goldeneye.

This is a plan I developed to maintain an intelligence framework in Spain in the event of a German takeover of the country. Godfrey made me responsible for its implementation. Goldeneye has involved maintaining communication with Gibraltar and launching sabotage operations against the Nazis. Donovan is a complete asshole. But I have found common ground over American involvement to ensure the Germans do not dominate the seaways."

"Commander Fleming, if your goal has been to impress me with your accomplishments, then by all means you have succeeded. As soon as MI6 gives me the go-ahead, we will gladly give the Americans whatever we have on this. But, as you said, we do not yet have all the pieces of the puzzle. A small portion of the original message that was recently intercepted by our listening post in Barcelona remains unintelligible to us. Three words, to be precise. They are almost certainly an anagram."

"I do not understand."

"We believe those three words to be an anagram for some other thing, perhaps the actual target in the United States. What those three words actually stand for remains a mystery. The only thing we have to go on thus far is an earlier message from the United States to that same Waffen-SS Headquarters in Bremen. The cipher queens broke it down a while back. Again, all but three words. And again, they would seem to suggest an anagram. The same thirteen letters, only arranged in a different order. In that earlier message, the sender had lost contact with his operative in the United States. I may have it here somewhere." Fielding began to shuffle through the papers on his desk.

"Codebreaking is not my forte. Tell me about this anagram."

"At least that is what we think it is. In the older of the two messages, three words. BEAUT KRAUT EGO. In the current message, the one that specifically mentioned Kronenhauer, four words. BOA AUK TREE GUT. Our team in Hut 4 thinks that both these word-groupings are anagrams for the same word or words, perhaps the Nazi target in the U.S."

Fleming understood. "Put Constance and the rest of the Wren nest to work on it."

"Already have. What they have produced so far is a nightmare. They have set up chalkboards all around the room with all thirteen letters from the two anagrams written in chalk on the boards. Then they have gone to work producing every possible recombination of those thirteen letters they can think of to produce other phrases of one, two, three, or four words. At last count they had produced 1,812 new anagrams from those same thirteen letters, none of which mean a goddamn thing."

"So we are nowhere."

"Precisely."

"And this is what you want me to tell Godfrey?"

"Please tell him anything but."

TUESDAY
AUGUST 4, 1942
8 p.m.

New Orleans

The sun was setting in the western sky and the streets of New Orleans were beginning to come alive.

Nico Carolla found solace in these quiet moments at dusk. The sky yellowed, then reddened, then grew steadily darker. The stars made their first appearance overhead. Then began the low drone of cicadas, a veritable symphony of noise accompanied by a percussion of sea gulls barking in the distance.

But darkness also brought risks, and Nico had to be careful. It was unsafe for him to be out at night alone. For protection, he always carried with him in his pocket a .25 caliber semi-automatic pistol, a *Bernardelli*.

Luca and Vittorio trailed after him, as they did nearly every night. They too were armed. *Nonno* insisted upon it. He feared for his grandson's life. Any number of rival crime families might want nothing better than to ambush Nico one night on the street and make a move onto Carolla turf.

From out of the darkness, a girl approached Nico on the street. "Heh, big fellow. Want a blowjob?"

He looked at her with unrepentant contempt.

"Only ten dollars," she said. Then she recognized Nico for who he was and switched to Italian. "*Bocchino?* Only ten dollars."

Nico shook his head, then shooed her away with a flick of the wrist. He kept on walking.

There were streetwalkers everywhere, not one of them high-class. They reeked of sweat and tobacco. This one, a dark-haired woman of average looks, next tried to sell her wares to Luca, then to Vittorio. Both men waved her off with equal contempt.

"Whore!" Luca said. "*Troia! Va fanculo.* Go fuck yourself."

She gave him the finger and turned away.

"Where we headed tonight, boss?" Luca asked. Both he and Vittorio were armed with revolvers and primed for trouble should it suddenly step out of the shadows.

"Same as every Tuesday night," Nico said. "Angelo's *taverna* off Bourbon Street. Angel runs a good game of poker in the backroom four nights a week; that is, if you can stand the constant racket from the coins spilling out of the slot machines. Plus, his mother makes a good *muffuletta*. We three can share a bite to eat before I join the game."

"Hard to protect you in that place," Luca said. "Rough crowd. Lots of dark corners. Too fucking many places to hide."

Nico knew the risks. If a man walks the streets of New Orleans alone at night, he is either looking for trouble or looking to get laid or perhaps looking to get drunk and party. Lonely men would often come to town looking for all three at once and at the same time.

The three men crossed the street shy of the corner, entered an alley, and came upon a drunk urinating against the wall of the adjoining building. He hadn't been the first to urinate in this spot. It was appalling. The smell assaulted the nostrils. Urine. Feces. Dog waste. Spilled alcohol. Tobacco smoke. Vomit. Soiled cigarette butts.

They exited the alley, crossed a second street, and then they were there, on the doorstep of Angelo's *Taverna Monreal*. The Sicilian tavern and gambling hall had a covered patio out front, with a canvas awning overhead, a few smudge pots outside for lighting beside the front door.

A guard stood beneath the awning at the entryway. The bulge beneath his coat said he was armed with a large weapon, probably a .45. The man was picky about who he admitted to the club. Most of what went on inside was illegal. Carolla-supplied slot machines were the backbone of Angel's business, along with roulette tables, craps, and high-stakes poker in the backroom. Up one flight of stairs was a brothel.

The slot machines were the product of years of sly political maneuvering between rival crime families. During the Great Depression, the mayor of New York City, Fiorello La Guardia, began a crackdown on organized crime. The one-armed bandits he chased out of New York City soon made their way to Louisiana. Sylvestro Carolla personally negotiated a deal for those machines with the New York mob, a deal brokered by Louisiana Senator Huey Long.

Gaming and vices were synonymous with New Orleans. Dice games, bull and bear baiting, gambling, dog and alligator fights — all products of the raucous, anything goes atmosphere.

Tonight, the gambling hall was loud inside, loud and gay. Off to one corner of the smoke-filled room was a four-piece band. It was busy hammering out a collection of spirited jazz blues. Brass trumpet, jazz piano, wood clarinet, and drum. Sometimes the musicians would switch instruments and the sounds of a trombone or saxophone would enter the mix, perhaps a banjo or guitar, sometimes a cello or bass violin. People were talking and laughing, hard liquor was flowing.

These days, jazz music was standard fare in a place like this. The music, robust and rhythmic, was played with gusto and brass instruments, usually second-hand military band instruments. The big names in jazz were all products of the New Orleans jazz scene. Louis Armstrong, the trumpet player, grew up only blocks away, in Storyville, practically next door to Lulu White's place.

"Something to eat?" Angelo asked Nico from behind the counter as the crime boss approached.

"One of your mother's *muffuletta.* Salami, provolone, prosciutto. Extra peppers on the *giardiniera*, if she doesn't mind."

"Enjoy the music five minutes, Nico. I will bring the sandwich to your table when *mia Madre* is finished making it. *Mettiti comodo, come a casa.* Sit, make yourself at home."

Nico relished the thought of food. He hadn't eaten since this morning with Martina. The *muffuletta* was a two-fisted working man's lunch, portable and hearty, a stable for the tradition-bound Sicilians that inhabited the French Quarter and the Trémé just north of it. Since the turn of the century, this neighborhood had been known to one and all as "Little Palermo." It included the Storyville red-light district.

Nico found a table where his back was to the wall and settled into a chair to enjoy the performance. Luca and Vittorio sat either side of him.

Nico knew his music. It was his one diversion. Martina had been the one to introduce him to Cuban *habanera*, said it was the earliest form of rhythmic jazz music played in the French Quarter. The most distinctive versions were accompanied by a Cuban conga drum, one of those tall single-headed drums played with the flat of a man's hand. This type music, with its lively beat and distinctive backbeat had deep roots in the African tradition.

The *habanera* rhythm was known to the locals by many names — conga, or tango-conga, or just simply tango. A simple man like Nico Carolla didn't know whether to dance to it with wild abandon or to cry with joy at its sound. He was known to do both.

Nico drew his chair up close to the table at the edge of the big open room and drummed his fingers on the tabletop. He tapped his foot with the beat, allowed his legs to sway idly to the music. A wave of emotion washed over him and, suddenly, he felt at ease, as if all his troubles could simply melt away with the sound. The melody was soothing and at the same time jarring, perfect for a man in his present state of mind.

Angelo approached the table, now, with a plate, napkin, and platter in hand. "Extra peppers, like you asked. *Mia Madre* was generous with the meat, cheese, and *giardiniera*. She warmed the bread a bit to melt the cheese. I hope you don't mind. Enjoy."

Nico had always eaten this type sandwich cold before, so warming it was a new taste. The bread had a dry, crumbly crust. But the *giardiniera* kept the sandwich moist, even a bit soft. The melted cheese added to the flavor. Every cook prepared their *giardiniera* differently — pickled vegetables marinated in wine or vinegar or olive oil. The medley of vegetables normally included carrots, cauliflower, gherkins, and a variety of peppers.

Nico cut the sandwich into three parts and pushed one slice across the table to Luca, the other to Vittorio. The three ate hungrily. When the door to the backroom opened, mealtime was over. It was time for the game to start.

Nico got up from the table, made his way across the smoky tavern to the backroom, where tonight's game was being played, 5-card stud, minimum ante fifty dollars. For the briefest moment, he thought he saw the visage of his estranged brother Earl Ray standing in the shadows near the far end of the bar.

Nico stopped, looked again, and the face was gone. *Must be imagining things*, he thought as he entered the room.

Luca and Vittorio followed close behind Nico into the backroom. They were nervous. Rumors were swirling. Capone's Chicago Outfit was still looking for payback. Twelve years ago, when Al Capone himself traveled by train to New Orleans, he demanded that Carolla supply his Chicago Outfit with imported alcohol and that they cut-off supplies to a rival Chicago gang. But Sylvestro turned the tables on the other man. With the help and assistance of three police officers, Sylvestro "Sam" Carolla disarmed and broke the fingers of Capone's bodyguards as they exited the train, humiliating Capone and forcing him to return to Chicago empty-handed.

Now, no sooner had Nico sat down at the poker table and anted up his fifty dollars, than his eyes locked on the man sitting directly across the table from him. This was Vinny, second man in the rival Provenzano gang, a gang that had recently allied itself with remnants of Capone's Chicago Outfit.

At about the same instant, Luca saw the man as well. His eyes moved rapidly around the smoke-filled room. There were two other suspicious-looking characters lurking in the shadows along one wall.

Luca's mind instantly jumped to the worst possible scenario.

It was a set-up! The Provenzanos had staked out Nico's usual Tuesday-night game and the rival gang was about to strike.

Luca nudged Vittorio on the shoulder, drew his attention to the presence of the other men.

The two *Mafiosi* loyal to Nico did not even have to work out a plan of attack. Instinct and long-standing practice defined their actions. Vittorio moved rapidly across the room, so as to block the line-of-sight of one of the two other men. If necessary, he would use his own body as armor to shield Nico from harm.

But the Provenzano men were having no part of it. One of the men instantly drew his gun and leveled it at Nico's head from about thirty feet away.

Vittorio drew his weapon at almost the same moment. He did not hesitate to pull the trigger, but immediately fired at the rival gangster who held Nico in his sights.

Crack!

There was an explosion of gunpowder and noise when the firing pin of Vittorio's .38 Special revolver connected with the business end of the shell in the chamber.

Now things moved rapidly. Nico had drawn his own semi-automatic pistol as soon as his eyes locked on those of the man sitting across the table from him. He hauled back, now, twice on the trigger at pointblank range. Everyone at the table dove for the floor. Chips and money flew in every direction.

Then the door into the room burst open. Two of *Nonno's* closest associates stepped in, Carlos Marcello, his lieutenant, and Fernando Marcos, his bodyguard. Each man held in his hand a sawed-off shotgun. Angelo lay dead on the floor behind them, his head bathed in a pool of blood.

Carlos took crude aim on the rival gang member still aiming a pistol in Nico's direction. He let loose a volley from both barrels of his shotgun, spraying blood and guts across the wall behind him. Fernando did the same against another man. It was all over in a matter of seconds.

Next, in stepped Sylvestro, Nico's grandfather. He was flanked by two additional men. These men held Tommy submachine guns in their hands, ready to spray the room with bullets if necessary. A Tommy gun was a devastatingly effective killing tool at this range.

"You okay, Nico?" Sylvestro asked.

"*Che minchia?* What the fuck?"

"You know better than to keep to regular *programma!*" *Nonno* barked angrily, stumbling on his English. "Make you easy target. Easy to stake out and kill. *Cazzo!* How could you be that *stupido*? Have I taught you nothing all these good many years?"

Nico wiped the spent gunpowder from his shirt, stood up from the table. "Angel sold us out?"

"Yes, but his son now shy two fingers and *sua madre* has two broken ribs. Eventually boy broke and gave up father."

"Only two fingers?" Luca asked. "Why didn't you take the whole hand?"

"Must leave something for sharks, no?"

"You have a plan for this *traditore?*"

"Oh, Nico, he much more than traitor. More like *doppiogiochista*. Two-faced double-crosser. Carlos and Fernando have boat standing by. Angel and son and brother are about to be chum for one of those great white sharks that circle out in Gulf. Those great whites going to sleep fat and happy tonight."

Nonno paused for dramatic effect. "Now may we all please go home, where we can be with families and sleep night safe and sound? Tomorrow, Nico, you and I will talk. Angelo not only one involved in attempt on your life."

"Who else?"

"Tomorrow."

Nico did not like being put off. "Can it be lunch? I already have plans for the morning. Luca and the boys are off at first light tomorrow morning to do a job for me."

"Sì. *Pranzo*. Lunch."

WEDNESDAY
AUGUST 5, 1942
9 a.m.

Kiln, Mississippi

"I think I was followed."

Captain Wilhelm Kronenhauer wore the look of despair, complete with worry lines on his face. Sleep had not come easily these past days. He was jumpy and on edge.

The two men, Grimm and Kronenhauer, were standing on the narrow porch of the old Jordan River Lumber Company Hotel, now vacant, in the tiny village of Kiln. The Mississippi air was thick with flies, humidity and suspicion. This was bayou country; standing water could be found everywhere.

"Just a case of nerves," Captain Sebastian Grimm said. Both men were sweating like mad. "The American South is dirt poor. Most people here are stupid and uneducated, not like we Germans at all. The locals are quite suspicious of outsiders. They know precisely who belongs and who does not. I mean just look at this place. *Baufällig. Schäbig.* Dilapidated. Shabby."

Captain Kronenhauer shook his head vigorously, then wiped his brow with the back of his wrist. He had done this same thing perhaps six times in the last hour.

"*Nein,*" Kronenhauer said. "This is not just a simple case of nerves. This is not my first field assignment. I have had this feeling for some time, this feeling of being followed. The first time was back in Lisbon, when I was briefed. My papers were in order. But I felt as if the ship's captain paid me undue attention when I boarded. Plus, in Havana there was this woman."

"Isn't there always?"

"*Mein Gott.* I didn't fuck her, if that is what you mean."

"Maybe she liked the way you looked," Grimm said. "It certainly cannot be on account of the way you smell. Your entire body reeks of something foul."

"It is this god damn heat! Plus, I have not showered in days. This place — this entire place — is one giant swamp, a cesspool that stretches for miles. It is worse here than being stuck onboard a U-boat. Sweltering heat. Crippling humidity. Bugs. Snakes. Disgusting filth. *Ekelhaften dreck. Schmutz.*"

Grimm shook his head. "Honestly. This isn't an overcrowded *Unterseeboot*, where there are no showers. America has bathhouses on every corner. Yet you reek of crotch rot. *Schrittfuchs.* Crotch odor. I can smell you from here."

"Fuck you! How I smell is none of your concern. If I have been followed, if the Americans learn that I am here to blow up the boat plant, this entire plan will end in a blaze of bullets. I will not be taken alive by these mongrel dogs."

"Trust me, Kronenhauer. No one followed you from Havana into the port of New Orleans. You said yourself that you were onboard a small ship, not the regular ferry. Anyone out of place would have been instantly noticed by the crew."

Kronenhauer nodded his head as if in agreement. He looked with derision out into the murky waters of the bay from the porch of the dilapidated hotel. The large, two-story hotel was made entirely of wood, once painted white, now peeling. A covered porch ringed three sides of the ground floor of the building in front of a graveled parking lot.

Kronenhauer continued. "And yet, I again had the same feeling of being followed when I got off the ship. I tried to avoid detection in the ordinary way, made evasive moves, up one block, over two, then double-backed to retrace my steps to the start. But some U.S. Navy sailors stopped me on the street to ask for directions. Why would a group of sailors do such a thing unless they were after me?"

"Maybe they were as lost as you were. Maybe they were drunk. How the hell should I know? New Orleans is a baffling city," Sebastian Grimm said. "But I do understand what you are driving at. This United States of America is indeed a strange country. I too have had some uncomfortable experiences in the weeks since I arrived."

"Yes, some of what has been revealed, I already know," Captain Kronenhauer said. His hand instinctively brushed against the Luger he carried with him at all times. Kronenhauer loved that gun, better than he loved most women. This type Luger was called the Parabellum, the Pistole Parabellum 1908, a toggle-locked recoil-operated semi-automatic pistol. It had been the standard sidearm for German Army personnel in both world wars. The Pistole 08 (or P.08) was dressed with a 100 mm barrel and chambered in 9 x 19 mm Parabellum rounds.

Kronenhauer continued. "I was privy to a — how you say *bearbeiten* in English?"

Grimm did not immediately answer, as if he could not find the right word.

Kronenhauer became impatient. "*Bearbeiten. Geschwärzt.*"

"Ah, yes, *geschwärzt*. In English, they say *redacted*."

"Yes, that is the word — redacted. I was privy to a redacted copy of Günter Kesselring's first cable to Waffen-SS Headquarters. Oberst Richter shared it with me. That is how I first learned that you might have lost contact with Henry Brock. What do you think actually happened to Brock? Have the Americans captured him? Have they perhaps already learned of our plans?"

"I lost contact with Brock days ago; that much is true. But I rather doubt whether the Americans have him in custody," Grimm said. "I think the man just got cold feet and ran away frightened. His disappearance is a setback. There can be little doubt of that. But the plan will go ahead with or without our Mr. Brock. I have been able to reconstruct much of the information he gathered from other sources. You may not know this, but there is a German settlement nearby. It is referred to locally as the German Coast. Günter Kesselring gave me the names of several people in that area, people who are sympathetic to our cause, one man in particular, a burgher of sorts, Rudyard Pfingsten."

"You should not have done that," Captain Kronenhauer said sternly. "Kesselring is an imbecile. You know that, right? His father is a brilliant *Luftwaffe* General Field Marshal, one of the few men ever awarded the Knight's Iron Cross with Oak Leaves, Swords and Diamonds. But his son Günter is an imbecile, an idiot, a fool. You should not have brought an outsider into this operation without my express permission. The more people who suspect what we are up to, the more likely we are to be found out."

"I am not grotesquely stupid," Captain Sebastian Grimm replied angrily, advancing toward the other man across the creaky wooden floor of the exterior porch. "In case you have forgotten, you and I are both of equal rank, both captains in the same Waffen-SS, both products of the same infantry school, both carry the same high-level security clearance. Do not presume to instruct me . . . "

"You are of course right," Kronenhauer said, trying to quickly mend fences. "You are right and I am wrong. Please accept my apologies."

Wilhelm Kronenhauer held out his right palm to shake the other man's hand in a gesture of good faith. But Sebastian Grimm batted it away.

Then Grimm continued. "As I said: the loss of Brock has been a setback. Surveillance of the target has become much more difficult without him in place. He was an old man. No one paid him any attention. He fit in, knew his way around. I do not."

"Talk about not fitting in. Explain this to me, Captain Grimm. Whatever possessed you to cruise around the countryside in such a fancy car? Such things draw attention, attention we do not want." Captain Kronenhauer pointed out the window to the gravel parking lot of the old hotel where a practically brand-new Custom Super Eight Packard was parked.

"Ah yes, the Packard. The car was definitely not my idea. Kesselring arrived here behind the wheel of the flaming thing when he drove down from Baton Rouge. He left the car here with me until he returns. But the car has been nothing but trouble. American cars! I had to register the finicky thing with the local county office just to get a fuel ration card. To do otherwise would have made people suspicious. The local sheriff will pull you over and issue you a citation for the smallest infraction."

"So you have had troubles of your own."

Grimm nodded. "My best guess is that Henry Brock died or was killed in a New Orleans whorehouse. The brothels are run by the Sicilian mob, the Carolla family. Those Guinea swine run everything down here. One of the whores nicked Brock's signet ring and his notebook. I recovered the ring, but had to kill a man to manage it. The book with all Brock's notes about the target and our mission, I was unable to recover. I was actually on my way back to the brothel to try and retrieve the surveillance notebook when you arrived by boat from Havana."

"Splendid work," Kronenhauer said with stunning sarcasm. "Just splendid. Now you have both the Sicilian mob and the local *polizei* scouring the countryside for you."

"Again with your mouth? No one will find us here, I promise you. This place is literally the armpit of America. Swamps. Alligators. Negroes. Banyan trees. Abandoned buildings. Flying insects. Snakes. Rats. A sewer, really."

"Well, good. Then we can do our work in peace. For now, you can forget about going back to New Orleans to recover that notebook. Your return will only attract more attention. I need to see with my own eyes what sort of explosive materials they have given me to work with. I asked for W-Salt, what the American military calls Composition B, what we call *plastiksprengstoff*. I also asked for rolls of detonation cord and a box of No. 10 timing pencils, like the British commandos use. And I need to see the target facility with my own eyes. I need to study the layout. Otherwise, I have no possible way to know where to place the charges."

"I am not yet in possession of the explosives," Captain Sebastian Grimm admitted.

"Tell me you are joking."

"When I went south on the bayou road to recover the explosives from the moored rowboat, sheriff's police were everywhere. A body had been discovered near the drop-off site. I could not get in close enough that day without being seen. I was going to return there to the bay tonight when things had hopefully quieted down."

Captain Kronenhauer shook his head in disgust. "Show me. Show me on a map."

"Come inside."

The two men left the porch of the old hotel and moved into a large interior dining room. Grimm dug into his valise and drew out a large, rolled map of the area. He unrolled it on the largest table, then weighted down the corners with four casebound books from a nearby bookcase.

The map was laid out with gridlines. Drawn on the map were shorelines, roads, rivers, bridges, and streams, all with approximate distances between. His finger moved down to the shoreline of Bay St. Louis, where he traced out an imaginary route in his mind. He located Cedar Bayou, then Grassy Point. Then he found the small X he had marked on the map with a thick, graphite pencil. The mark was on the north shore of Bay St. Louis, east of a finger of land.

"Here." Sebastian Grimm pointed. "This is where I told the men to anchor the rowboat. The blocks of W-Salt should be onboard, along with several rolls of detonation cord and a box of blasting caps."

"Okay," Kronenhauer said. "We go tonight. But first show me where I can work. I need a large vacant space, several tables, and plenty of windows I can open to keep the air fresh."

"Yes, this way. There is a large room in the back of the hotel."

"Could you have found a more out of the way dump? This building is barely standing."

"It is better than the place where Kesselring and I first met. Here at least we have electricity. But it isn't much, I admit. The South has never fully recovered from the Great Depression. This little half-dead village is referred to locally as Kiln. But in these parts, they do not pronounce the 'n'. The 'n' is silent. So it is pronounced more like Kill."

"A kiln is an oven, yes?"

"Yes. Kiln takes its name from the many kiln ovens once found in this area. They served the lumber industry, where they apparently dried freshly-cut timber. During the boom years, Kiln was home to any number of timber mills. There was also this hotel and a hospital. The first mill burned to the ground thirty years ago. It was rebuilt the next year. The second mill was dismantled for good during the Depression. Now all that remains of the town is a few farmhouses, that Catholic Church we passed up the road, this old hotel, and a small grocery store. No one will bother us here."

"Are you sure?"

Captain Kronenhauer suddenly turned. He thought he heard something coming up the gravel road.

Captain Grimm turned as well. He placed his first finger against his lips. The two men crept to the window and looked out. There was a cloud of dust rising from the road perhaps three-quarters of a mile away.

"I think it is an automobile," Kronenhauer said.

"If not two or three."

"Are you expecting anyone?"

"No."

"What are your perimeter defenses?" Kronenhauer asked, suddenly quite soldier-like. "*Schnell. Perimeterschutz?*"

"You are kidding, right? We are in the middle of fucking nowhere. Who would think to set up perimeter defenses in a place like this?"

"I would think of it," Kronenhauer snapped. The line of cars was drawing nearer. "It looks to me as if this hotel is about to become a battlefield."

Sebastian Grimm ticked off his limited resources on the fingers of one hand. "My armory consists of an infantry knife, two handguns, a rifle, a couple satchel charges, a length of detcord, and a matching pair of hand grenades. That is about it. Oh, and a mess kit. One fork, one spoon, one knife."

"*Wo sind die handgranaten und sprengladungen?* Where are the hand grenades and satchel charges?"

Grimm pointed to the opposite corner of the room. "In that footlocker. Detonation cord too."

"Hand grenade *und bündelladung* it is," Captain Kronenhauer decided. "I will wire the entranceway. You take the guns. Move left out the back door into that line of trees. Take out as many of them as you can when they move away from the cover of their automobiles. Go. Now. *Schnell.* Quickly."

Grimm reached for the closer of the two handguns on the table, pocketed a handful of shells and bolted toward the rear door of the hotel lobby. He exited along the back driveway at a run.

Just as quickly, Kronenhauer set to work, booby trapping the front door to blow when it was pulled open from outside. He knotted a length of thin steel wire, looped the wire over the handle of the door and strung the other end to the pin on a hand grenade. Then he anchored the hand grenade between a chair and a table leg and placed some heavy books on the chair so it could not easily move. When the front door opened, the wire would pull out the pin. Finally, he placed a satchel charge and a length of detonation cord beside the hand grenade. Touchy stuff, that. But explosives were his area of expertise, and he was good at it. He grabbed up the map from off the table and moved toward the back of the hotel.

Three cars pulled up in front of the old hotel, spinning up gravel in their haste, one to the left, one to the right, one directly in front of the hotel.

Twelve car doors snapped open as if on cue. Nine men got out. Three from each car. The drivers stayed put, doors open.

The men had weapons, three Tommy guns between them. The others held sawed-off shotguns in their hands. Eight of the nine men cautiously fanned out and tried to slowly encircle the big, old hotel. One man held back, remained close to the cars. This was Luca, Nico's closest confidante. He was obviously in charge. His Colt was drawn and in his right hand.

Luca signaled for Vittorio and one other man to approach the Packard. It was parked in the graveled drive. The two men approached the vehicle, glanced at the license plate on the rear, and nodded to Luca that, yes, this was indeed the automobile they had come looking for. If everything went according to plan, they were to kill the man inside, recover the car keys, then drive the Packard back to New Orleans. Nico wanted the car for his own.

By now, Grimm had found his spot near the base of a large tree in the nearby grove and begun to open fire. But his targets were still too far away to effectively hit with a handgun.

Two men with Tommy guns swung in his direction. They were energized and advanced quickly on his position, firing short bursts into the clump of trees where Grimm was partially hidden.

Grimm returned fire as the two men drew closer. But then the chamber clicked empty and he had to stop firing to reload.

The other men continued to advance in his direction, still firing short bursts into the clump of trees.

Then Grimm was hit by one of their bullets and went down. The pain was intense. Blood poured from the wound. The unloaded weapon fell from his hand.

Once Grimm was down, he was at the mercy of the other men. The gun had fallen from his hand and was now out of his reach.

Nico Carolla's men closed the distance quickly, still firing. They finished him off at close range.

Now that the man was dead, they signaled to Luca. Throughout the short battle, he had remained near the automobiles in the parking lot.

Luca cautiously approached the spot where Sebastian Grimm had fallen, bent over the body and looked carefully at the dead man's face.

"Yes, this is the man," he said. "This is the man who killed Hector and nearly broke my ribs. *Brutto figlio di puttana.* Ugly son of a bitch. Frisk him. Check every pocket. When you are finished frisking him, take your camera and snap a picture of the dead man for Nico. He will want proof that the man is dead. Then meet me out front by the cars."

The two men began to rifle through Sebastian Grimm's pockets. They found the signet ring in no time at all, followed quickly by the codebook containing the daily security passkeys presented as anagrams. Nico already had possession of Henry Brock's surveillance notebook. Though no one knew it yet, Brock's little book laid out the entire plot.

Meanwhile, three of the men still slinging shotguns advanced up the stairs of the large front porch and towards the front door of the once beautiful Jordan River Lumber Company

Hotel. The old hotel's front door was two doors, actually. An outer screen door, plus an inner solid door.

Ever so quietly, the first man pried open the outer screen door. He waited a moment then jerked open the inner solid door, expecting the other men to advance inside guns blazing.

But as soon as the first man crossed the threshold into the room, the entire front end of the hotel was blown into the parking lot by a violent explosion. The opening of the door had pulled the pin from the grenade. It blew first.

But the devastation was not yet complete. A millisecond later, the satchel charge planted by Kronenhauer exploded in a giant fireball. The concussion from the exploding grenade carried ample energy to detonate the RDX mix inside the satchel charge.

All three men were blown clean off the porch. One man lost a leg, the other an arm. Had they been conscious, the men would surely have screamed out in pain. But their cries were cut short. Major arteries had been severed by the blast, organs crushed, bones shattered. Their anguish would be short-lived. The man closest to the point of detonation was little more than splintered bone in a soup of pink mist, a nasty mix in the damp, humid air.

Luca fell to the ground of his own accord. He was unharmed but peed his pants. The remaining men rushed to his side.

"What the fuck?" Vittorio asked. *"Che minchia?"*

The front porch collapsed upon itself and the second floor of the dilapidated hotel collapsed onto the first. A blast of dust, bits of wood, and broken glass blanketed them all.

"Check inside for survivors," Luca ordered. "There must have been a second man, maybe a third." Even as he spoke, a fire broke out inside the hotel and began to consume what was left of the frame of the old wooden building.

"If there was a second man, Luca, he is quite dead now," Vittorio said. "No one inside survived that blast, I assure you. No one."

"But someone must have wired that door to blow. *Cazzo!* That was no ordinary — how you say? — *trappola.*"

Vittorio gave Luca a blank stare.

"Trappola esplosiva. Tranello. Trabocchetto."

"Ah, you mean booby trap," Vittorio finally said.

"Yes, booby trap! That was no ordinary booby trap. Whoever wired that door to blow must have had military training," Luca said.

"That may be true.   But he is most assuredly dead now. Let's go before this fire begins to attract attention.   We'll go home now and come back later with a flatbed truck for the Packard.   We couldn't find the keys.   Probably lost in the explosion."

Luca got to his feet, brushed himself off, picked up his weapon.   One of the men saw the wet spot on his trousers.

"*Bacha ma culo!* You want to make something of it?"   Luca dared.

"No, boss.   At first I thought it was blood.   I am sure it will dry before we get back to the city."

"Damn straight.   Now shut the fuck up and let's get moving."

WEDNESDAY
AUGUST 5, 1942
11 a.m.

New Orleans

"Last week my bank was visited by a financial auditor from the Cuban government, the Ministerio de Banco Nacional."

"Yes? And what of it?" Nico was still unnerved by the events of last evening. He had almost lost his life in a place where he once thought he was safe.

"These government officials are entirely corrupt, you must know that. This man was questioning me about the volume of my bank's cash deposits."

Martina Amerada was a beautiful woman; but one with nerves of steel. Very little could shake the woman. But today, Nico Carolla could see the tension in her eyes. He could see it in the way she carried herself. This normally calm woman was worried.

"I think what you mean to say is that he is questioning you about the volume of *my* bank deposits." Nico tried to state it in a quiet, calm voice.

"Your deposits, my deposits. What the hell is the difference? This man comes into my office. He closes the door, sits down, and starts to question me. My job is on the line here. You see that, right? Perhaps even my freedom."

They were once again in Nico's apartment. It was located upstairs, in a quiet corner of the city, near the heart of his operations, not far from Storyville. After hearing back from Aldo Carolla in Sicily, Martina had dispatched an urgent message to Nico with the last courier, asking him for this morning's meeting. Luca stood watch in the corridor outside the apartment door. Vittorio stood beside him. Nico was worried she might have been followed here from the ferry terminal.

Nico reached out his hand to calm her. "When a corrupt government official comes into your office and asks you a question, he is not looking for information. He is looking to get paid. He is judging whether or not he can intimidate you sufficiently to extract a bribe."

"You believe this to be true?"

"I do. With all my heart. Let me ask you this, Martina. Did he ask to meet with you again?"

"Yes."

"And did he ask that this second meeting take place at his office? Or did he say he would return to yours?"

"Yes, Nico, I see what you are driving at. Had he demanded I come to his office, then I would truly be in trouble. But if he can keep our meetings off-book, then the door remains open to a bribe. But what if my offer of payola leads him to arrest me for attempting to bribe a public official?"

"If you try to bribe an honest man, he will place you in shackles. But if you try to bribe a dishonest man, he will laugh and ask how big a bribe you are offering. So you have to ask yourself, Martina. Is this man a corrupt government official? Or is he an honest man?"

Martina turned away, went to the window. The apartment was on the third floor. The street below was busy, as it always was this time of day.

"You want I should have this man killed?" Nico asked.

"I think that would draw attention, make things worse. If out-of-the-blue you up and suddenly murder this nosey government auditor, the authorities will almost certainly suspect me. I will become guilty of a lot more than just simple racketeering."

"The killing would not have to be done by my people. Why not reach out to your friends at British Intelligence? Why not ask them to take out this — how you say? — pesky man for you?"

Martina answered that question with utter dead silence.

Finally, after a minute, she spoke. "You know about that?"

"I do now."

"I see. You had me followed?"

"Of course I did. It is how I must do business."

"You have to understand, Nico. I had no choice."

"I am not angry with you, Martina. *Madre di Dio.* We all do what we must to survive. The Sicilians help the Allies because we hate the Nazis, not because we wish to obey the law. The United States Navy looks the other way on the docks of New Orleans because they need landing craft more than they need more mobsters behind bars. The British play all three sides because they want to keep their empire. They hate the French. But they hate the Nazis more. So they cooperate with those they loathe, the

Frogs. No, I am not angry with you, Martina. I just want us — you and me — to lie together on the same side of the same mattress. MI6 is the controlling shareholder of the very bank you work for. I know that for certain now. How else could your *tentacoli* possibly reach so far, from New Orleans to Havana to Lisbon to Palermo?"

"*Tentacoli?*"

"Ah, yes. What does that mean in English? — tentacles. That's how it translates. Your tentacles stretch far, like a *polpo*, an octopus. Many long arms."

"But this man, this greedy man who wants me to offer him a bribe to keep quiet. He is not MI6. He is not *Mafioso*. He is not Cuban army. He is simply a corrupt politician."

"So we pay him however much he needs to keep quiet and be done with it," Nico said.

"Just like that?"

"Yes, just like that. Remember, Martina. Once this man accepts your hush money, he too has broken the law. You now have something to hold over his head, not the other way around. You control him. He no longer controls you."

Now, for the first time, Martina smiled. "Your confidence is infectious."

"The war complicates things greatly for all of us," Nico said.

"In more ways than you can possibly imagine," Martina replied, considering her next words carefully. "Can you keep a secret?"

"You are kidding, right?"

"In my line of work, strange things sometimes cross my desk."

"By your line of work, you mean as a spy?" he said.

"Yes, as a spy. But also as a banker. Strange things sometimes cross my desk."

"Okay," Nico said. "You have my full attention."

"I have a photograph."

"Okay."

"If I show you this photograph, can you promise me that you will not ask me where or how I got it? Do you and I have an understanding?"

Nico nodded his head in the affirmative.

Martina reached into her valise and drew out a small manila envelope. At one time the envelope had been taped tightly shut. But no longer. The tape had been cut and the envelope was now unsealed. From it she removed a photograph, a photograph of a man in a German uniform, Captain Wilhelm Kronenhauer of the Waffen-SS.

She handed the photograph to Nico. He looked at it briefly with wondering eyes.

"This man." She paused to gather herself, drew a deep breath. "This man is a Nazi."

"Ah, spy meets spy."

"Yes, something like that. This man is a Nazi, a demolitions expert sent here to the United States from Germany. He means to blow up an American factory, maybe an oil refinery, perhaps a weapons depot. At this juncture, the location of the true target remains unknown."

"*Madre di Dio.* You are certain there is to be a bombing?"

"Nico, there are no absolutes in the espionage business. But yes, much of this information comes from reliable sources and is known with a high degree of certainty."

"How, exactly, did you come to know all this, may I ask?"

"This, I cannot tell you," Martina answered.

"Can't? . . . . Or won't?"

"Our deal was, you don't ask, I don't tell. But, on the subject of this man . . . "

"This man means to blow up a factory? My factory? The City Park Avenue boat factory where so many of my people work? Is that what you are trying to say to me here, that one of the many Higgins' plants is going to be blown up by this lunatic? You realize that Higgins has more than one assembly plant, several in fact. All in or around New Orleans."

Martina shook her head. "I do not know this man Higgins, and I certainly do not know anything about his business affairs. You have to understand, Nico. I do not know what the actual target is. I do not even know if there is an actual target. If MI6 knows anything specific about the target, they certainly are not sharing that information with me. They may not even know it for certain themselves. That is how espionage works. Shadows inside of clouds behind waterfalls in the dark."

"They call this a metaphor, yes?"

"Yes, a metaphor."

"Then why the *cazzo* hand me this photograph? If you are unsure of the details, of what possible use is it to me?"

"Because the man in this photograph boarded a ship in Havana. I was there. I saw him board. The ship sailed and he later disembarked here, in New Orleans, down by the docks. Our local contact, a Marine Colonel named Peter Morgan, did his best to follow the man from the seaport when he disembarked. But Colonel Morgan lost the man somewhere in the bayous. So far as I have been told, neither the Americans nor MI6 have any idea where the man went after that or what his true agenda may ultimately be."

"None of which is my concern," Nico said. He did his best to hide his surprise upon hearing Peter Morgan's name come out of Martina Amerada's mouth. This was a man Nico had already met. Clearly, there was more to this Marine Colonel than he first suspected.

Nico continued without missing a beat. "I work neither for the American military nor for the British secret service. So I ask you again, Martina. Why give me this photograph?"

Now tears came to her eyes.

Were these crocodile tears? Nico wondered. *Or were they genuine?*

"I feel my life may be in danger. If they do not catch up with this man, this Nazi who got off the boat, someone may come looking for this picture. I need an insurance policy. If I should be killed, perhaps suffer an accident or be shot down in the street, then it is likely that MI6 sold me out. In which case, you must give this photograph to the Americans, the Navy perhaps, or the FBI or the Marines. Colonel Peter Morgan. This is who you must find should I meet an untimely end. Colonel Peter Morgan."

"You have this all worked out, don't you?"

"Not at all," she cried. "Not at all."

"Okay, as you wish. I will take possession of the photograph. But please, whatever else you do, please do not go out and die on me. You know my life would never be the same without you."

"We are a curious pair, aren't we?"

"In more ways than you know."

"Is there something you are not telling me?" Martina asked.

"You are going to hear about it anyway. So you might as well hear it from me."

"Yes?"

"There was a shoot-out last night at the *Taverna Monreal.*"

"Angel's place?"

"You know the place?"

"Of course I know the place. It's your Tuesday night game," Martina said.

"Yes, well someone tried to have me killed there last night."

"Oh, my god, Nico! I had no idea. Are you okay?"

"It was not the first time; it will not be the last. *Nonno* saved my life. He and I are to meet later this morning to discuss the ambush over lunch at the *trattoria*."

Martina shook her head angrily. "It was not the first time; it will not be the last. Brave talk for an idiot. You must be more careful, Nico. Your grandfather won't always be there to watch your back."

"Indeed."

Nico paused, then quickly moved to change the subject. "You haven't told me yet what Aldo had to say. Have they found the *pompinara* who assaulted my Josepha? Have they been able to assemble the information the Allies have asked for?"

"I could not say. Perhaps this envelope holds the answers you seek. It came for you in the diplomatic pouch. I haven't opened it. No one has seen the contents or read the message."

She handed Nico the unopened envelope. He judged the weight in his hand, considered its contents.

"Thank you, Martina," he said. "Now please do not be angry with me. I promised *Nonno* that he and I would meet today for lunch. I am late already. I really must go."

"He suspects, doesn't he?"

"My grandfather did not get where he is by being a stupid man."

WEDNESDAY
AUGUST 5, 1942
12:30 p.m.

"Little Palermo," French Quarter, New Orleans

"Nico. *Mio nipote.* My grandson. I am so happy you are here at the *trattoria* safe and sound after last night. Come in. Sit down. Have something warm to eat."

The Carolla supper club *Trattoria Sicilia* was not open to the public for lunch. The staff arrived only at 4p.m. Now, just after noon, it was quiet and dark.

Inside the *trattoria*, along one wall, was a long elegant bar, polished oak top, brass rail, tall barstools with padded backs. Rows of tall, slender wine glasses hung by their stems from a long overhead rack that ran practically the full length of the bar.

On the wall behind the bar was an ornate gilt-edged mirror. Also, row upon row of liquor bottles, some of which were filled with colorful liquors; plus linen napkins, toothpicks, and jars of olives; also a utility sink and a small stove with an oven underneath.

"You worry too much, *Nonno,*" Nico said as he crossed the threshold into the supper club from the street. The cool darkness indoors felt good compared with the midday heat and humidity outside.

The old man stood behind the bar, looked at his grandson across the wide counter, and smiled broadly. He was gray at the temples, with thinning hair on top. His accent was still heavy, his English far from textbook.

"You are future of the Carolla family here in America, you know that, yes?"

The old man brought a pot of steaming hot soup from the stove behind the bar to a table out front, set out two bowls, and a loaf of warm bread. The smell of warm bread and steaming soup was mouthwatering. Silver Dollar Sam, as some in the outside world called him, loved to cook for himself and to occasionally share his meal with one or two others. Within these four walls, he was known to customers simply as Sylvestro or sometimes as Sam. To family, he was known as *Nonno.*

"*Nonno*, you are scaring me," Nico said, placing his pistol on the table within easy reach. "What is this about? Why am I here?"

The restaurant, small and intimate, had sixteen dinner tables, with four straight-backed chairs at each table, a small paraffin lamp on each as a centerpiece, linen tablecloths and napkins, fancy table settings.

"After last night, you must ask?"

"No, I suppose not," Nico answered.

"Nico, my grandson. You are my flesh and blood. I practically raised you ever since . . . ever since . . . "

"Grandfather?"

"Ever since Michael, your father, my son, was killed in that robbery gone bad. Ever since your mother — *Dio, riposare la sua anima* — God rest her soul — abandoned family and took your older brother along with her. Then she suddenly became ill and died of consumption and your brother was raised in foster home by those . . . those . . . people."

Nico patiently sipped his soup broth, broke off a bit of warm bread, and chewed it slowly. "I do not want to disappoint you, *Nonno* — not ever."

The grandfather now spoke slowly and firmly. "This woman you are sleeping with. You know this cannot continue."

"*Madre di Dio*. You know about her?"

"Of course I do."

"She means nothing to me."

"I see way you look at her. Everyone does. Luca. Vittorio. Your wife. Everyone."

"Everyone?" Nico's face drooped. "*Che cazzo!* May we please talk about something else, anything else? Your words trouble me greatly."

"As you wish," *Nonno* said. "You rather we talk about that business at Jordan River Company Hotel earlier today?" He walked the soup pot back to the stove, placed it back on the burner.

"Not much left to tell. The men we were chasing blew up the place before we could corner and capture or kill them. The explosion killed two of our boys. One of the men we were after got away. We killed the other. In a day or two, perhaps as early as this afternoon, Vittorio will take some of the boys and drive back up there with a flatbed and tow the Packard back to the garage."

"Yes, yes, yes. You want that automobile so very badly; everyone knows that. But enough about car. I want to talk to you about your brother."

Nico was taken aback. The spoonful of soup he held in his hand and was about to bring to his lips and swallow, now stopped well short of the mark. "Why today of all days? Why should the subject of Earl Ray suddenly come up today?"

"That not his real name, you know."

"No, I did not know."

"His birth name was Roberto, my father's name. His foster family gave him that . . . that other name. Earl Ray Mackerel. Just sound of it make me ill."

"Roberto, eh?"

"Nico, when I am dead and gone, you will become head of family. You will become godfather to entire *famigghia*. Then everyone must answer to you and to you alone. But before I pass, something must be done about your brother."

"Are you dying?"

"No, I am not."

"What then? *Che cazzo*. Tell me what in the world this is all about. And how in the hell does my brother figure in?"

"Your brother helped set you up to be ambushed last night."

"Roberto was at Angelo's place last night? I thought as much. But what are you saying? That my brother was in on the hit? I thought you said Angelo was the one who had turned. Or did I misunderstand you, *Nonno*? I thought you said Angelo was the one who was in cahoots with the Provenzanos, not Earl Ray."

"Vittorio found your brother hiding behind dumpster at the *taverna* last night after raid. Luca beat truth out of him."

"I saw both Luca and Vittorio this morning and neither one said a word to me about that."

"Those were my instructions. I wanted you to hear it from me."

"I see. Have you already killed him then, *Nonno*? Or have you left Roberto for me to deal with? I will kill the man myself, if you sanction it."

"You realize, don't you, that I may be sent away from this country at any time? My — how you say? — *deportazion* order has already been issued by federal government. The war between America and Nazis is only thing that stands between me and being sent back home."

"*Madre di Dio*. Mother of God. Have we now changed the subject? Are we no longer talking about Roberto's treachery?

What could be more important at this moment to the *famigghia* than the attempt on my life last night?"

"Indulge me, *mio nipote*. Indulge me."

Nico shook his head with great reluctance. "Your deportation should no longer be a concern. We now have an arrangement with the military. We now also have a congressman on the payroll. He has promised to put a stop to your deportation order. In any case, the government needs us now. They need the *Mafiosi*. They need our manpower. The Allies cannot win the war without us. In this country, America, our people assemble nearly all their landing craft."

"I have no faith in government, nor should you."

Nico nodded as if he agreed. "But may we please return to the subject at hand? Tell me how you intend to handle this matter with Earl Ray? If the man tried to have me gunned down, he must not go unpunished."

"Nor will he."

"But why? Why would he suddenly turn on the family like that? Why would he turn on me? I have done nothing to harm him that I can remember."

Nonno pushed back from the table, got up, went behind the counter to the stove, poured himself more soup. Now he stood at the counter and sipped the soup directly from the bowl, no spoon.

"Maybe it is time you knew truth," *Nonno* said.

"What truth?"

"There are many truths, not just one."

"One truth at a time, *Nonno*. One truth at a time. What is the history between you and Earl Ray that you are not telling me? You could have invited him back into the fold at any time these past fifteen years. But you never did. Why not?"

"Back then, I had my reasons."

"Perhaps now that my brother has turned against us, I ought to know those reasons."

"At time when it happened, my reasons were good. Earl Ray got that — how you say? — mulatto girl pregnant. He wanted to marry her. He came to me, asked for my blessings. But I refused. I would not give him my blessings."

"So I have been told. But why not?"

"I had my reasons. But I was not at liberty to share those reasons with him at the time. He became angry. Then he did the unforgivable. *Madre di Dio*. He raised hand to strike me, his own grandfather. This was act of disrespect I could not let go unanswered. A son must never raise hand to his father, nor a grandson to his grandfather. It is never right thing to do, never! That level of disrespect angered me very badly."

"And now you are no longer angry?"

"I am old. There is difference. Anger soften with time."

"But this! An attempt on my life? This is inexcusable. You must know that. Roberto must die."

"And die he will. But your mother would never forgive me if I sanctioned you to kill your own brother. Nor would your grandmother. This is something I must do myself."

"My mother? *Cazzo!* My mother is long dead and buried. She gets no voice in this. Why would you say such a thing? Mother abandoned us, remember?"

Nonno shook his head. "The woman you knew as your mother did not abandon us — she abandoned you. And you are still angry about that. And you have right to still be angry about that. Hell, I would be angry too, if my mother abandoned me like that. But you blame your brother for your mother's disappearance, and that is plainly wrong. The boy had nothing whatsoever to say in the matter. Your mother just walked out of the house and took Roberto with her over my loud objections."

"*Nonna* would disagree with you."

"I hardly think so, Nico. I was married to the woman for thirty years. To this day I never understood Caterina, my love, my wife. It is same with all women. What they think — how they think — these are mysteries no man can ever solve. But what we must face today, you and me, right now, this instant, is much more complicated than all that."

"How so? You speak in riddles and I do not understand."

"Nico, I said before. There are many truths, not just one. The one I am about to tell you will be even more difficult to hear."

"More difficult than learning my own flesh and blood brother tried to have me killed?"

"Not your flesh and blood."

"Roberto is illegitimate?"

"Yes. And so are you."

After a long painful pause, Nico spoke. "What are you saying, *Nonno*?"

"Not *Nonno*. *Patri*. You are my son, not my grandson."

"*Che cazzo*. If you are my father, who is my mother?"

"Angelo's mother had sister. Thirty years ago sister was pretty woman. Roberto tried to have you killed because Angelo's mother recently spoke out of turn. He learned truth from a woman who can no longer keep secrets. She told Roberto that you were *illegittimo,* a *bastardo.*"

Nico's head was reeling. "If you are my father, who lies in that cemetery vault I visit each week on my walk? Who is Michael Carolla?"

"Also my son. When the woman who gave birth to you threatened to make a fuss if I did not pay her, my son Michael agreed to take you in, raise you as his own, give you family name, grant you legitimacy. Earl Ray is no relation of yours — nor of mine."

"And that is why you could not give him your blessings."

Nonno nodded.

"And that is why he now must die."

"Yes."

"And that is why I must be the one to put him down," Nico said.

"No, cannot be you. I already have murder charge against me. If your *Nonna* were alive today, she would not want one of her grandsons to kill the other, not if I could prevent it. She would say that killing Roberto was my responsibility; that his blood should be on my hands, not yours. It is my mistake to fix. Your brother will be dealt with and body disposed of where it will never be found."

"But it would not be one grandson killing another. He and I are unrelated; you said so yourself."

"That is not how world will see it. World not know you not related."

Nico turned away from his grandfather, tried to dispel his anger. "You ask too much of me!"

"Yes, perhaps I do. But that is role of a grandfather, is it not?"

"Or is it just to make trouble?"

"Yes, that too. But this must remain our secret, Nico, just between us two. Should truth ever become known, it would weaken us both. What I have said to you can go no further than four walls of this room. To the world you are my grandson and I am your grandfather. Yes?"

"Yes."

"Now enough business for one day. It is time you and I shared drink of our finest wine and savored the good life that we have. Grandfathers are good for that too."

The old man reached up and removed two wine glasses from the overhead rack and set them on the bar counter. Then he reached for an unopened bottle of wine from the special cabinet.

Nico didn't have the heart to ask him, but he suspected the truth might be more complex yet. His birth mother threatened to make a fuss. *Did Nonno have her killed? Is that how Nico came to be raised by his brother Michael? And why would Angelo's mother come forward now with the truth, after all these years? Was there another player in the mix that Nico knew nothing about?*

Nico would soon have to dig much deeper.

WEDNESDAY
AUGUST 5, 1942
7 p.m.

Bletchley Park, England

"Could we please just forget about work for one night and just simply have sex?" Constance McCallister asked breathlessly.

She raised her hips and slid her naked, sweat-soaked body from atop Shaun Yardley's. He had asked her a work-related question just as she was about to climax. It had ruined the moment and made her angry.

Yardley didn't seem to notice. "I can't stop thinking about it," he said. "It's not like throwing a light switch, you know. My mind isn't able to turn on and off on command."

Yardley's brilliance was often overshadowed by his obsessive-compulsive disorder. Anyway, her love-making was formulaic. Sex with this woman barely kept his attention on a good day.

"You have nothing to prove, you know," she said, covering up her breasts with the bedsheet. It was a hot August night and they had been at it awhile.

"Oh, but I do have something to prove," he said, getting up from the bed. His pants were clear on the opposite side of the room.

"Your father?" There was irritation in her voice. There seemed to be only two sorts of men in the world, those who treated women like playthings and those who seemed to always be crying out for attention.

Yardley nodded.

"Tell me about it. Then you better fuck me good."

"He may not even be my father."

"This again?" She shook her head. "Is that why you live in Great Britain instead of the United States?"

"Father sent me here to attend university. Cambridge. Where you and I first met. You were shagging someone from the maths department, if I remember correctly. But it's more than that. Dad stirred up a spot of trouble with that book of his."

"*The American Black Chamber?*"

"Have you read it?"

"Bletchley has a rather complete library. Yes, of course, I have read it."

"Too many people here at Bletchley have. Plus, there was that movie. Seven or eight years ago. It was a complete embarrassment," Yardley said with chagrin.

"Worse than the book?" she asked.

"The movie was pure fiction. Dad helped write the screenplay. Something about a German spy ring. The group was stealing U.S. government diplomatic codes during World War I. A second storyline told of efforts by the U.S. Army to crack German codes."

"Based on the work we are presently doing here at Station X, that doesn't sound like much of a fiction."

"Perhaps you have a point. Maybe father was onto something after all."

"By all accounts, the man was brilliant, still is. Just like his son."

Yardley smiled. "My father learned to use the telegraph from my grandfather. Grandpa worked as a telegrapher for a railroad company in Indiana. He taught his son Morse code. After my father's first year in college, he dropped out and went to work as a telegrapher, same as Grandpa. But Father spent every minute of free time learning how to play poker."

"Your father's other true love."

"His first love was not my mother, if that is what you mean," Shaun Yardley said with some disdain. "There were two things my father liked to do, play poker and drink alcohol. On a good day, he did both. The man was a fixture at any number of local taverns. He mastered the game in no time at all, a natural poker player if ever there was one. The game taught him how to bluff. More importantly, it taught him how to call a bluff. My father has a knack for games. He has a mind for games, numbers, and deception. He passed the civil service examination with high marks at a young age. Then he moved to Washington, D.C., where he began his career as a code clerk in the State Department. He set about teaching himself codebreaking, mostly by trial and error. The man was entirely self-taught. He honed his skills by reading coded telegrams he wasn't even supposed to see."

"Oh, I do love a juicy tale. Go on."

"There was this one night he told me about. I think the year was 1915. Dad was listening in on a line between New York and the White House."

"The White House is where the American President lives, yes?"

"Yes. The White House in Washington, D.C. Father was listening in. He copied down a telegram intended for President Woodrow Wilson. The cable had come from a bloke in Europe named Edward House. House was one of President Wilson's most trusted advisors. Thinking back on it now, I should imagine that was one of the first times an American cryptographer had ever eavesdropped on his own President of the United States. Dad said he solved their code in under two hours. He was aghast at the schoolboy techniques used to encode communications with someone as important as the President of the United States. Before long, Dad was reading details of Edward House's report to the President. House had met with Kaiser Wilhelm II, the emperor of Germany at the time, to discuss the prospects for peace."

"This is on the level?" Constance asked. "You are not making this whole thing up just to demonstrate how gullible I can be?"

"Scout's honor. I am telling you the truth. Dad burned any evidence of his eavesdropping. But he later presented a detailed report on America's easy-to-crack diplomatic codes."

"This was before the War?" she asked.

"Not before the Archduke of Austria was shot and killed and war broke out in Europe in 1914. But definitely before the Americans jumped into the fray, which was in '17. During World War I, my father left his job as a code clerk and joined the Signal Corps as a cryptologic officer."

"When did they stop calling it the Great War?" she asked somberly.

"Now they have decided to number them. I guess the leaders of the free world expect there will be other world wars down the road, number III, number IV, and so on. The Americans don't call it the Great War. They call it the First World War or, more usually, World War I."

"God forbid the high-muckety-mucks start numbering them. The first one was bad enough."

"Don't blame Bletchley Park. We had no say in the matter. But, like I said, back in those days American military codes were pathetically easy to break. Everyone was reading their mail, and the Americans didn't even know it. America was naïve about secure communications."

"When you say everyone was reading their mail, you mean us as well?"

"Oh, yes. In those days, the U.K.'s Room 40 was quite busy. They were reading the President's telegrams and much more. So were the Germans."

"How is that even possible?" she asked, throwing off the bedsheets and making a beeline for the lavatory. Yardley watched her from behind as she walked. Her breasts were too small and her bottom too large. But she would do in a pinch.

"A rather simple and elegant workaround. Our code unit made copies of every message that went over America's trans-Atlantic telegraph cable. The boys in Room 40 did this by tapping into all cable traffic that passed through a relay station on the western edge of England before the messages travelled across the ocean. The station at Porthcurno."

"We did this? To the Americans? Without them even knowing?" Constance McCallister was stunned by the revelation.

"Yes. But in the end, it worked to both our advantages, America's and Britain's."

"How so?"

"Hah!" Shaun Yardley exclaimed. "Another one of those brilliant stories from the first war that no one knows anything about. Before America ever came into the war, Room 40 intercepted a coded telegram sent by the German foreign secretary, Arthur Zimmermann. In the telegram, Zimmermann invited Mexico to join the war against the United States as a German ally. In return, the Kaiser would help finance Mexico's war and help it recover the territories it lost in an earlier war with the U.S. — Texas, New Mexico, and Arizona."

"Let me see if I have this straight. The Germans felt secure enough to send a hostile telegram over America's own communications lines and not worry about it being found out by the Americans? Is that what you are telling me?"

Yardley nodded. They switched places, he in the loo, she looking for her clothes on the floor.

"But the British intercepted the telegram?"

"The telegram was safe from American eyes, but not from the prying eyes in Room 40. British officials handed the Zimmermann telegram over to the Americans, ponying up some cover story as to how it fell into their hands. From there, the telegram made its way to President Wilson, who released the Zimmermann initiative to the newspapers in America. Publication of the telegram caused a national furor. At about the same time, Germany resumed unrestricted submarine warfare in the Atlantic. After seven U.S. merchant ships were sunk, the Yanks were finally jolted out of their neutrality and into the war. April 1917."

"And this telegram business was exactly the sort of weakness in American intelligence that your father was trying to point out."

"Exactly. Even before the Yanks jumped into the war, father began building a case for a military office devoted solely to intercepting and decoding enemy messages. He went so far as to suggest himself for the job."

"Ah, that trademark Yardley arrogance," she said.

"I will take that as a compliment. Dad parlayed his arrogance into a career. The ease with which he broke the American codes also got him thinking about the codes of other countries.

"Dad knew that codebreakers would be needed for the war. He persuaded the head of American military intelligence to admit him to the army for the purpose of setting up a new cryptographic section, what came to be known as MI-8. They made him a 2nd Lieutenant in the Signal Corps as well as chief of this newly created eighth section of military intelligence.

"When Dad founded MI-8, he had not a single cryptographer on the payroll. Everything code-related was being outsourced by the government to a private group tasked with looking for hidden messages in the plays of William Shakespeare. These blokes were trying to prove that Francis Bacon was the actual author of Shakespeare's many plays. That is where Dad first came in contact with the man who eventually undercut him, William Friedman. Friedman was the brightest of the bunch, a brilliant cryptographer in his own right."

"Silly buggers. Francis Bacon?"

"Oh, everyone loves a conspiracy, you know that. Dad's MI-8 began as a primitive, hands-on operation bogged down by methods of trial and error. They never moved much beyond searching for patterns in letters and numbers by eye, and trying to match sequences that appeared frequently with commonly used phrases. Even so, Dad had some early successes. More thorough searches of suspicious-looking individuals crossing the border into the United States led to a fortuitous discovery.

"I remember him telling me about it. In 1918, a lengthy cryptogram was found sewn into the sleeve of a suspected German spy as he attempted to cross the Mexican border carrying a Russian passport. I think the fellow's name was Lothar. Yes, that's what it was. Lothar Witzke. The evidence linked Witzke to two acts of sabotage against the United States, demolition of munitions at a San Francisco navy shipyard in 1917, and a massive and deadly explosion of a munitions depot in New York in July, 1916."

"Big catch, if you ask me," she said. "Cornering a German spy at the Mexican border."

"Oh, yes, big catch indeed. Father's unit performed well enough during the war that the American Army and the State Department decided to jointly fund his MI-8 after the war came to an end. Dad continued as head of the Cipher Bureau, what soon came to be known in the trade as the Black Chamber."

"So that's where it got its name."

"Yes, and by then Japan was a rising military power. Cracking Jap codes became a priority for the Bureau. Dad did not know even a single word of Japanese at the time, though that seems not to have bothered him. Japan's belligerence toward China jeopardized American policy. Its emigrants exacerbated American racism. Its naval growth menaced American power in the western Pacific. Its commercial expansion threatened American dominance of Far Eastern markets."

"Darling, it's no secret that the Japanese and the Americans are natural enemies. Xenophobia runs wild in both countries."

"An overstatement perhaps, but one I can live with. To break the Jap codes, Dad had a deputy of his study the Japanese language forward and backwards. They took a chance and correctly guessed that distinctive words in the newspaper or on the newsreels might also appear in their diplomatic dispatches. So they solved the problem by brute force, trial and error. After months and months of such work and tedium, as well as a fair amount of brainpower and intuition, they managed to piece together a fairly accurate picture of Japan's complex cipher code. They were still reading Japanese diplomatic traffic in 1921 when Washington hosted the naval disarmament conference."

"Yes, I learned about that conference in middle school. It changed the course of history, probably delayed the current war by several years at least."

"Who can say? All that is known for certain is that the American and British delegations to the conference hoped to hold the size of Japan's navy to six battleships for every ten in their respective fleets, a 5:3 ratio instead of the 10:7 ratio the Imperial Japanese Navy wanted. The American negotiators were kept abreast of Japanese bargaining strategy by Dad's Black Chamber decryption team. A telegram the team intercepted spelled out the Jap strategy. If pushed, the Japanese delegation was to give in to the Allies' preferred ratio, whatever it took to avoid a direct clash with the United States and Great Britain.

"It was a coup for the U.S., which got the armament deal it wanted. Dad was an instant hero. The win at the bargaining table would earn him the army's Distinguished Service Medal the following year. I remember his comment at the time — *Stud poker isn't a very difficult game once you've seen your opponent's hole card.* It was the height of Dad's cryptanalytic career."

"But there was trouble on the horizon, yes?" she asked.

Yardley nodded. "The trouble arrived on several fronts. William Friedman, that early protégé, became a rival. Then too, the flow of diplomatic telegrams began to dry up. Western Union and the other telegram companies began to balk at handing over copies of all their cable traffic without a warrant. After the war, telecom companies became less willing to break the law to help the government. The Cipher Bureau was becoming irrelevant.

"In the end, though, it was moral indignation that finally doomed the Bureau. When the incoming Secretary of State, Henry Stimson, learned of the Black Chamber and what it did, he deemed the whole business unethical and quite un-American. He was an arrogant lout. Stimson is supposed to have said something to the effect that *Gentlemen do not read each other's mail.* A high-minded statement, to be sure. The way Father tells it, Stimson was most offended when Father bragged he could read every stitch of cable traffic coming into or out of the Vatican. After this remark, Stimson turned and left the room. Dad was out of a job."

"Just like that?"

"Just like that. MI-8 closed its doors for good just two days after Black Tuesday, the stock market crash in late October, 1929. With Dad suddenly out of work and his cryptographic skills in very low demand, he took to writing about his experiences in codebreaking to support his family. Two years later, out came his book — *The American Black Chamber.* The book outlined the history of signals intelligence in the United States. It described the activities of MI-8 during World War I and the American Black Chamber in the 1920s. It went on to illustrate the basic principles of signals security."

"But the book was popular."

"Oh, yes, instantly popular. Thousands of copies were sold in the U.S. Thousands more were sold in the U.K. It was translated into French, Swedish, Japanese, and Chinese. The Japanese version sold thirty thousand copies.

"But, as I understand it, people in government were not happy."

"To put it mildly. The book was an embarrassment to the U.S. government, a shocking exposé. Dad had disclosed methods of surveillance and subterfuge. He had described a clandestine world, a world of pilfered telegrams, forged wax seals, and invisible inks. He had revealed that telecommunications companies cooperated secretly with the Cipher Bureau. He had compromised sources, alerted nations that their codes had been broken, and revealed methods and motives."

"But why would your father publish such a thing?" she asked. "Doesn't that make him a traitor? It would surely violate our Official Secrets Act."

"Dad believed that by publishing his book he would force the U.S. government to reestablish a signals intelligence program."

"But it had the opposite effect."

"Indeed it did. The U.S. considered prosecuting him. But he hadn't actually broken any laws. Laws regarding the protection of government records came later. The Espionage Act was amended to prohibit the disclosure of foreign code or anything sent in code. Dad's second book about Japanese diplomatic codes was seized by U.S. marshals and to this day has never been cleared for publication."

"But your father's first book was a blockbuster."

"He became a celebrity, toured the country, gave speeches. There was the film, like I said. He was free to work for the highest bidder and foreign governments were willing to pay. In 1938 he went to China for an amazing salary, where he worked to form a Chinese Black Chamber for Chiang Kai-shek and his Nationalists. The Chinese were at war with Japan's occupying forces. They wanted the famous breaker of Japanese codes on the payroll, working for them. More recently, he was hired by the Canadians to help set up their wartime codebreaking operation."

By this time, Constance was dressed again and had forgotten all about sex.

"That story you told me earlier about Lothar Witzke got me to thinking. What if this whole anagram business is like what happened in the Great War? What if it is also about uncovering a sabotage plot? Maybe we ought to be looking at munitions depots in the South as possible targets?"

"The same thought had occurred to me. Heh, why the hell did you put your clothes back on? I thought we were going to have sex after we talked?"

"Same time, same place, tomorrow. But mention one word tomorrow about business or the office while we are fucking and that will be our last time together."

"Mum's the word, I promise."

THURSDAY
AUGUST 6, 1942
5 a.m.

South Pacific

LST 15 slowed to a crawl. In a few moments, the ship's bell would ring. Then every man onboard would be set in motion. Boats in the water. Men in the boats. Engines on. Make for shore.

For the men, the signal to attack would come almost as a relief. An LST or Landing Ship Tank was no cruise ship. Conditions onboard such a vessel was seriously rough, the most cramped, primitive and noisy environment imaginable.

During the long trip over from the launch point, there had been no place to sleep. The interior of an LST was mostly a large open space. But today that space was filled to overflowing with half-tracks, Higgins boats, artillery shells, armored vehicles, tri-pod machine guns, equipment, and of course the men plus their gear.

PFC Russell Brock hunkered down with the rest of his squad, closed his eyes, tried to get some shut-eye. The men were heavily armed. Satchel charges. Explosive mortars. Machine guns. Bandoleers and spare clips of ammunition. Entrenching tool. Two days' rations. Medical kit. Bandages. Sulfa powder. Morphine syrette.

Then there was the stuff a man did not need but had to have with him anyway. Cigarettes. Photographs of loved ones. Newspaper clippings. Dime novels. The random lucky rabbit's foot.

The officers and corpsmen embedded with the young Marines carried other things as well. Walkie-talkies. Extra bandages on their web belt. Full medical kits. Extra syrettes.

The morphine syrette was a true battlefield innovation, a simple device for injecting precious fluid into the body through a needle. A syrette was like a syringe, with one big difference. Rather than a rigid tube armed with a piston as in a standard hospital syringe, a syrette had a flexible tube that could be squeezed between one's fingers like a tube of toothpaste.

On a battlefield, the use of a syrette was simple and straightforward. Break the seal. Remove wire loop pin. Insert hollow needle under patient's skin at a shallow angle, not too deep. Flatten flexible tube between one's finger and thumb, then squeeze. The squeezing action pushed the morphine out through the flexible tube and into the wounded soldier's body.

Finally, as a safety measure against an accidental morphine overdose, any man administering first-aid was to fasten the empty morphine tube to the wounded soldier's collar using the wire loop pin. This marker served to inform others of the dose already administered. Too much morphine could lead to respiratory arrest and kill a wounded man.

Brock was at the edge of sleep when a sudden noise on deck woke him. This was perhaps the fifth time in ten minutes that his sleep had been disturbed.

Woods sat next to him rubbing something round as if it were a sacred stone or good luck charm.

"What you got there?" Brock asked his friend. Woods was usually not the talkative kind. But now, as the sun rose above the horizon, he began to open up.

"Challenge Coin. It was my uncle's from the Great War. He gave it to me when I enlisted. Here, take a look."

Woods handed the oversized coin to Brock, who turned the heavy bronze medallion over in his fingers. It was tarnished and badly scarred. Engraved on one side was a vintage aircraft, maybe a Sopwith Camel or similar aircraft; on the other side, a fancy insignia with the number 17 inscribed in the center.

"What exactly is this thing?" Brock asked. "I never heard of a Challenge Coin before."

"Truth is: the coin didn't actually belong to my uncle. He won it in a poker game from its original owner, an American aviator of the time."

"Boy, you must be scared. I never heard you use such a big word before. Aviator?"

"Pound sand, you motherfucker. Want to hear my story or not?"

"Spill."

"As the story goes, when the United States came into the First World War, boys from wealthier families formed their own aero squadrons. They often enlisted together as a group, much like members of a club. But it was an exclusive club, and they often had a sort of membership card which came in the form of one of these medallions. The leader of the group had the squadron insignia struck on a medallion of solid bronze like this one and gave each member of the squadron an identical medallion."

The ship heaved suddenly to one side as the sea became choppier. Brock was a Marine, not a sailor. He was comfortable around guns and explosives and infantry knives, not around boats and rolling seas.

"That's what this coin is, one of those limited-edition medallions?"

"Yes. One of the pilots from that squadron was shot down behind enemy lines. He avoided being captured by the German patrols but lost his personal identification in the process. To avoid the enemy, he dumped his uniform and put on civilian clothes. Then he pushed west toward the French lines. He crossed no-man's land at great risk and stumbled onto a French outpost on the front line."

Woods continued. "The French soldiers were about to execute the American pilot when he produced the medallion. It was the one thing he kept when he dumped his uniform and personal effects. One of the Frogs recognized either the plane or the squadron insignia on the medallion and the pilot's life was spared."

Brock chuckled and turned away. "You actually expect me to believe that cockamamie story? It sounds completely made-up to me."

"God's honest truth, Brock. I'm telling it to you just the way my uncle told it to me. Not a word has been changed. Once the story made the rounds back in England, where the American squadron was headquartered, coins like this one became a tradition among flyers and later with certain infantry units. Like I said, my uncle won it in a poker game. He gave it to me later, along with the story I just told you. Consider it yours to keep if I don't make it through this thing alive."

"That's morbid. We are all going to come out of this thing okay. Padre said so himself. Have some faith, Woods."

"What does the Padre know? What does any Padre know? They all tell us the same thing, what we want to hear." Woods seemed disgusted.

"Maybe some of the men need to hear it. You know, to stiffen their resolve. Lots of boys are scared. Hell, I'm scared. Aren't you?"

"I guess so," Woods admitted. "But if the Church doesn't believe in war, why send a priest to the front lines?"

"I'm too tired to think. Let me go to sleep already."

The two fell quiet and Brock began to nod off again. It was early morning and the night just ended had passed quietly and without incident. After their LST 15 was loaded and moved out to anchorage, all they could do was wait while the other transport ships did the same. Ship after ship was loaded with men and equipment. Once loaded, each ship moved away from shore where it joined the growing line of boats at anchorage.

What's a man to do while he waits? Russell wondered. Check and recheck your ammo. Recheck your weapon. Make sure it is clean. Make sure you have with you everything the sergeant said to carry. Bandages, syrette, knife. Check the combat knife. *Is it sharp?* Once they were in their landing craft and headed for shore there would be no time for such things.

Before long, fine-toothed metal files began to surface on deck and make the rounds. When his turn came, Brock took the metal file and sharpened his bayonet. Then he sharpened the cutting edge on his entrenching tool. Then he passed the file on to the next guy and again cleaned his weapon. *No misfiring carbine was going to get him killed.*

The men discussed the upcoming beach assault. How many Jap defenders would there be? How dug-in would they be? Could the Coasties safely land their boats? Could the Marines storm the beach, take the island? How many of them would die trying? At the end of the day, would there be joyful shouts of Semper Fi? Would they see the Bravo Zulu flags hoisted and flying from the signal masts? Those Bravo Zulu flags were the Navy's way of saying that a job had been "Well Done."

It wasn't so much that the men were untrained, for they surely were not. They had all been to basic. They had all been to machine-gun school. They knew how to scale a wall. They had studied the terrain maps of the three islands. Each coxswain knew where to aim his boat, towards what side of which beach.

But how hard was the coming fight likely to be?

Now the men began to reminisce. They were tired of waiting, so they began to think of things past. The days of preparation on the island of Fiji, just departed. The arduous training at Parris Island and San Diego. The Drill Sergeant that kicked their asses. The little whiney guy who washed out of boot camp.

They reminisced about home, now so very far away. They reminisced about this or that girlfriend, this or that wife, the one that got away, the fight they had with their mother or father, the roads not taken.

A few men found solace in their prayerbooks. Some men carried Bibles. Other men had short novels to read, the odd pocketbook to skim. The men traded them off for others they had not yet read or wished to read again.

Favorite pastimes began to pop up. Card games like pinochle. Dice. Craps. The moment would be soon. Then they would go. Morale was high. The motto of the 1st Marine Division was voiced loudly. *No Better Friend, No Worse Enemy.* Talk of that furlough to Hawaii once this job was done. Would they be able to go home afterward?

God, how they missed their mother's cooking, their father's steely gaze.

•

•

Now nerves were on edge. They had been at anchorage for hours. The deck of the LST was beginning to take on the dimensions of an over-crowded prison, one with limited toilet facilities.

Constantly checking and rechecking one's weapon and equipment had kept the men occupied for a while. But now the novelty had worn off and the men were rapidly becoming bored. Nerves were on edge. Tempers were beginning to fray. The occasional scuffle broke out. All that pent-up adrenaline would soon have to be burnt off.

What Private Brock would not have given, right about then, for a rough and tumble game of touch football. Or a run around the park. Or thirty minutes of vigorous calisthenics. A swim in the ocean. A bicycle ride in the country. Something, anything, to burn off some of this nervous energy.

But there was no room on deck for such shenanigans. The men were sandwiched together like slices of bread in a breadbox. But old bread, wet and damp and moldy and smelling of mildew.

Fatigue, not boredom, helped a man sleep. Without proper exercise, it was physically impossible for a fit, young man to tire himself out sufficiently to fall soundly asleep. The 1st Marine Division battle cry — so fervent and loud an hour ago — had now diminished in volume, no longer a war cry, a mere statement of frustration.

These men, highly trained all, were ready to go. To a man, they were mentally prepared to get it over with, no matter what "it" turned out to be.

Even if spoken only in whispers, each man was certain he would come through it unscathed, "it" being what lay ahead. If anybody got hit, surely it would not be him; it would be the other guy.

A Marine had to think that way. He had no choice. Not if he didn't want to lose his mind. The other guy might lose a limb. — But not him.

Faces darkened. Some men talked to God, a God who up until now was rarely in their thoughts. These men — these Marines — were primed to kill or be killed.

Is that such a callous thing to say?

No, not really, not if a man thinks about it. The Marine Corps drills that thought into a man's head every waking moment. What Drill Instructor hasn't yelled it at his men during bayonet training? *Jarheads, there are only two kinds of bayonet fighters in this world — the quick and the dead.* It was the mission of the Marines of 1st Division, to seek out and destroy the enemy. Not dawdle about listlessly, waiting for something to happen. Dithering was not part of their Code.

Consider an athlete. After years of intense practice and training, years of trial by fire, he has suddenly been benched without explanation. Now he has to sit there on that cold bench night after night, heart pumping, mind racing, body ready to jump into the fray on a moment's notice — but never being tapped nor told when his turn at bat was coming. Frustrating.

Finally, late in the day, they slipped anchor and sailed toward destiny. Darkness was soon upon them. The men curled up in whatever small space they had to themselves and drifted off into restless slumber.

But, for most of the men, sleep was fractured. Night brought its own demons. The sea was rough. Some men threw up. Other men wandered the deck aimlessly. One man could be heard crying, the sort of crying only a grown man could do.

Even those who were at ease with themselves could hear the lapping sounds of nearby boats. But the boats themselves were ghosts, dark shapes upon the water. Every ship was running without lights.

•

•

A chaplain on a battlefield has but two duties to perform, both sacred. He must attend to dying soldiers, giving them comfort and absolution in their final minutes. And he must instill enough faith in the living ones to ensure they stand firm with their buddies and carry the day.

No army dare go into battle without a man of the cloth in the ranks. He carried with him Goodness and Right and Honor and Duty. The pharaohs of Egypt, the kings of Greece, the Emperors of Rome; they all had their divinities. The Ancient Greeks had their oracles and their Mount Olympus. The American Indian, his medicine man or shaman. The Egyptians and Aztecs, their sun gods. The representatives of God in the twentieth century were no different, whether they be chaplains or ministers, rabbis or priests, vicars or parsons. Protect the souls of men in battle; hurry the spirits of the fallen to a better place.

At one time or other, all such men were called upon to minister to men of other faiths. The dying want to be certain God will throw open His heavenly doors at the right moment and grant entrance to their souls. The living want to be sure that they are not purchasing a one-way ticket to Hell when they haul back on the triggers of their machine guns or pull the pins from their hand grenades and kill the enemy in an explosion of blood and tears.

Father Roman was such a man. In times of peace he might be found in a tribal village, Java or Borneo, or in the far northern reaches of Inuit Canada, ministering to a small but growing flock, spreading the Gospel.

But in times of war, he wanted to be at the front lines. Bald head. Long, white flowing beard. Slender build. Deaf in one ear, scar on his cheek. A joyful man.

Father Roman had been at the water's edge in Pearl Harbor on the day of the attack. He had been in silent mediation with his eyes closed, preparing for the day's duties when he heard the thundering roar of an aircraft engine and the high-pitched whine of an incoming shell. The explosion knocked him off his feet, cracked two ribs, shattered the eardrum in his left ear. Now he could no longer hear sound on that side of his head.

The attack by the Japanese on Father Roman's beloved America engendered a crisis of faith. Roman Yanukovych had come to America from The Ukraine a decade earlier, during the Great Depression. The Bolsheviks had declared war on reason and on religion in his homeland after the revolution. As a Greek Orthodox monk priest, he suffered depravation at their hands and witnessed despotism as it brought fear and hunger to the streets of Kiev. Roman became an outcast in the land of his birth, a pariah. When he saw a chance to escape, he did.

As a young man in the Ukraine, before the revolution, Roman apprenticed at a lumber mill. He learned about harvesting trees, how to slice them into planks for lumber. For a time, he attended the District School of Forestry, where he studied wildlife management and learned about the larger mammals of Northern Europe and Asia. He spent a summer in the Ural Mountains, living off the land, making notes, studying the habits of wolves and bears and other carnivores in the wild as they hunted and took down their prey.

But becoming expert in such things was not what Roman Yanukovych wanted from life. He took no pleasure from seeing trees cut down or from watching entire hillsides denuded of growth. The rains would come, the topsoil would wash away, the animals would leave and the forests would never recover. No, Roman Yanukovych wanted something else. He wanted what his uncle had. Roman wanted to join the priesthood.

The fly in the ointment was that Roman Yanukovych came from a poor family. His mother wanted grandchildren. His father insisted he learn a trade. So he did. He went to work in that deplorable lumber mill and learned about forestry.

Then everything changed. The Bolsheviks came. They murdered his father and his uncle, butchered their neighbors, raped the girl next door. His mother forgot about grandchildren. Roman joined the Order.

America beckoned. It offered opportunity, a chance to practice his faith without threat of persecution. He boarded a freighter in the Black Sea and left the Old World forever. When war came to America in the Pacific, he felt it his patriotic duty to enlist. Now, here he was, in the Pacific, onboard an overcrowded troop ship about to make landfall on an island held hostage by a violent enemy. He was surrounded by men much younger than himself, young frightened men, men he had ministered to onboard the troop ship only one hour before.

The impromptu service had gone as well as could be expected. Then the questions began. "Why do the men call you Padre?" one man asked. "Aren't you a priest?"

This was a question Father Roman was prepared for. "In the United States military, men like me are called chaplain or padre, regardless of what faith we represent."

Roman didn't say it outloud, but the truth was that soldiers and sailors fought harder and with more confidence when they knew a representative of God was beside them on the battlefield. If the soldier died, he would die with the belief that someone nearby would guide their soul to the afterlife once it left his body.

"But I'm not Catholic," another man said. "What good are you to me should I meet my maker?"

This was another question Father Roman was prepared for. "I'm not Catholic either, son. Greek Orthodox. But in the eyes of God we are all the same, soldiers fighting bravely against an implacable enemy."

"Are you yanking my chain?"

"Not at all. If your time comes, I will kneel down beside your body and pray. If you are Catholic, I will give you the Last Rites. If you are Jewish, I will say a traditional Hebrew prayer for you. If you are Protestant, I will pray for your soul just as your hometown pastor would."

"What if there is no God?" a worried man asked. He couldn't be more than twenty years old.

Sometimes Father Roman Yanukovych had to remind himself that not everyone was a believer. This was one of those times. Not everyone had faith. Still, it was Roman's job, his proud duty, to help instill faith. Even at great peril to himself, even as the dead and the dying lay wounded in the mud or the sand or the freezing snow, with shells bursting around them and bullets flying just above their heads, he had to give the men comfort.

"Son, even if you do not believe in God, allow Him to be there beside you on the battlefield, for surely He will be. You can take comfort in that."

"But what about you, Padre? Are you coming ashore with us? Or are you staying behind where you'll remain safe from harm?" The question was framed like a wisecrack or a dare, something Roman was not prepared for.

"Priests don't fight," another man said. "It's not in their nature."

"Perhaps not with a knife or a gun," Roman retorted sternly. "But mark my words. Priests do fight. And we fight hard. Only, our weapons are different from yours. We fight with words and prayers. We fight to keep you alive, to lift your spirits, to keep you clean in mind and body, to get your soul safely to heaven if need be. And yes, we do come ashore. I will land on that island beach right alongside you, and I will be right beside you every step of the way."

"But, Father, why are you even here?" The young man was insistent. "Every padre I ever knew as a boy growing up was a pacifist."

"As am I. The very thought of war I find to be loathsome. War is utterly futile and senseless. But I love America. God loves America. Do I think that this war will make for a better world? No, not really. But if we stand by and allow the Nazi and the Fascist and the men of great evil to run wild in our world, the darkness will become deeper and the night longer."

Many of the gathered men nodded their heads somberly. They understood what was at stake. Father Roman continued.

"God does not bless war, son. But he does bless you and the soldiers and marines like you, who, in good conscience, are willing to place yourselves in harm's way in order to brighten the world and shove evil back into the box from whence it came."

Father Roman gave the men absolution and the service ended. This was an hour ago. But now came the same man as before, the one who questioned during the service whether there even was a God. He sat down beside Roman.

"Bless me Father, for I have sinned," the man said.

Father Roman glanced sideways at the young Marine, who had tapped him on the right shoulder. He had seen that look many times before these last days, the look of men who were brave but feared death, men who did not wish to die in battle while still carrying the weight of some heavy burden.

"Father?" the young Marine asked again, when Roman did not quickly answer.

"Son, this is not a confessional booth." The boat was rocking from side to side, the soldiers spaced so tightly, they were practically sitting on top of one another. Privacy was a luxury they did not have.

"But Father, I had sex with another man's wife, a man in my platoon."

"And you thought this would be a good time to come clean about it?"

It was a harsh response, and Father Roman immediately regretted having answered the boy in such terse terms. He had already administered general absolution to the Marines before the ship set sail.

"Father, I need to be absolved of my sin. I need to be absolved of my sin before we hit that beach and go into battle. This you must do for me. I do not want to have some Tojo shoot me dead on the sand out there with this awful thing still hanging over my head."

"I understand, son. And what if that man, the man whose wife you have slept with, is suddenly called upon to save your life on the battlefield? What if at that moment in time he decides to treat you with the same reckless disregard you showed him when you slept with his wife? What then? How will my hearing your confession in this place, right here tonight, help you later on during that man's moment of doubt?"

"But Father! You must hear my confession!"

"I understand, son. My left ear then. Whisper your confession in my left ear."

The Marine did as Roman instructed and was happy for having done it. Father Roman smiled when the boy was done, gave him the sign of the cross, patted him gently on the head, and sent him on his way back to his seat. Roman was deaf in that ear. He had not heard a word the boy said.

Russell Brock had witnessed the exchange. When the young Marine moved away, Brock sidled up next to the monk priest.

"I was told you are deaf in that ear, Father."

Father Roman considered his answer. "I most certainly am."

"So you did not hear that Marine's confession?"

"Not one word."

"How does that not make you a hypocrite?"

"I never claimed different."

"What then?"

"There are two types of confessions in this world, son. Right-ear confessions and left-ear confessions. I save my right ear for those people who really mean it. That boy did not."

FRIDAY
AUGUST 7, 1942
6 a.m.

South Pacific

The ship's bell rang. It was time.

Private Brock realized he had fallen asleep. He propped himself up now on one elbow, tried to make sense of where he was and what was going on.

He sensed noises, unfamiliar sounds. *Where the hell was he anyway?*

"CRA-A-ACK!"

Aircraft from the carrier USS *Wasp* (CV-7) dive-bombed multiple Japanese installations on the neighboring islands of Tulagi and Gavutu-Tanambogo.

Now the big guns onboard the taskforce ships let go a salvo. The cruiser USS *San Juan* (CL-54), the destroyers *Monssen* and *Buchanan*. The sound blew away the last vestiges of sleep. Brock was instantly awake and alert.

Now came the deadly symphony of artillery. Booming cannon fire. Banks of deadly rockets. Shells launched from armored tanks on deck. All from a menagerie of Navy ships positioned in and around the LSTs in the sea.

"CRA-A-ACK!"

Again from the *San Juan*. Sixteen, five-inch guns. Sixteen, one-point-one-inch guns. The ship heeled over following each discharge from its big guns.

The thundering cannonade was deafening. Down on the deck of LST 15 it was next to impossible to make oneself heard over the din. Hand signals were now the order of the day.

The LCVPs were now off their davits and in the water, the men clambering down the cargo nets and aboard their boats. The motors running full-tilt in idle. The shore, a distant blur a mile or more away, cloaked in smoke and morning fog. The relentless thunder-like percussion of big guns pounding out volley after volley of artillery shells.

Brock's landing boat was now ready for its run, Coast Guard man at the helm. The tide was rising rapidly. Most underwater obstacles were now safely submerged. Earlier boats had cleared several "safe" lanes through the obstacles and onto shore. It was much like clearing a minefield. The only safe passageway was to follow closely in the wake of those who had gone before.

The thousand-yard run to shore was frightening. Bodies in the water. Splintered plywood. Backpacks. Boots. Blood. Sharks circling.

And not just in the water. On the beach too. Mostly on the beach. Wounded soldiers. Damaged boats. Discarded equipment. Shrapnel. Body parts. Blood.

Their Higgins boat was underway, bow slightly raised, water flashing along the gunwales. It was flanked on both sides by other such boats. All riding low in the water. All aimed for a shoreline blanketed by gunfire and volumes of smoke. Shells were raining down on the stretch of beach ahead. Ceaseless explosions. Distant outcries of pain. Their boat was supposed to aim for a seaplane ramp. But the seaplane ramp had already been blown to smithereens by enemy fire.

Saltwater tore at his eyes. Brock breathed hard.

Would they be struck from behind by friendly fire? Or would the big guns parked to their rear offshore cease firing in time?

Just as that thought crossed his mind, the pattern of shelling changed. No longer were the Navy gunners parked in the bay just offshore targeting the beach and shoreline in front of them. Now they had begun directing their fire inland, at suspected enemy positions.

The boat was rocking crazily. It had a shallow draft. The water was rough. Men got seasick. Puked all over themselves and their buddies.

Thick, acrid smoke hung along the shoreline, now nine hundred yards away. The yellow-green smoke was lit up here and again by booming flashes, the product of American shells detonating on the sand dunes and rocks beyond the beach. Now booming plumes of water sprouted from the sea as Japanese guns returned fire. The enemy blasted away at the beachfront and at the ocean, but did so blindly.

Their LCVP was less than half a mile out now. Other LCVPs had already landed ahead of them. Marines were moving from shore to the first line of dunes. The beach was actually the front line in the initial stages of battle.

From offshore, the destroyers unleashed bank after bank of deadly rockets on the enemy lines and known positions. Intell was constantly changing. The machine gunners onboard the landing boats began to lay down fire.

This was a critical moment. Close-in support fire had begun. Only a couple hundred yards, now, from "RAMP DOWN!"

Geysers erupted in the water around them.

The Nips are firing back, Russell thought nervously. *This is about to get hairy.* Support fire shifted up the bluffs. Return fire answered the threat.

Ping! Ping! Ping!

They were being bombarded by small-arms fire coming from somewhere up ahead onshore. Bullets were bouncing off their landing craft, sometimes splintering the plywood hull.

Instinctively, the men ducked. The incoming fire was sporadic and unsustained, not entirely lethal at this range, but fear-inducing nonetheless.

When the moment came, would he wilt? Or would he measure up?

Russell couldn't be sure of the answers himself. His courage had yet to be tested under fire.

Some men were already out of their boats, clawing their way up the beach under constant and heavy enemy fire. Soon, he would be too.

Dead bodies drifted past their boat. Everyone saw them. The boat sat so low in the water, their dead eyes were practically at sea-level. Young, broken bodies; all so recently killed; faces still warm and pink, but eyes quite dead.

Fuck! Could there be a harsher reality?

Suddenly they were there, at the shoreline, motor idling, people shouting orders, others screaming.

"RAMP DOWN! RAMP DOWN! RAMP DOWN!"

Now the men were on their feet. Now they were on the steel ramp. Now they were on the muddy sand. Bullets were peppering the water around them. Some men had already been hit and gone down.

Russell Brock suddenly realized something. He had been singing silently to himself. Trying to calm his nerves, perhaps. But singing nonetheless.

" . . . Mine eyes have seen the Glory of the Coming of the Lord. He is trampling out the vintage where the Grapes of Wrath are stored . . . "

The Battle Hymn of the Republic. His mother had taught it to him when he was a boy. They had sung it day after day in the boys' choir at Randolph-Macon Academy. He had to memorize every verse of it for English class. Now he was belting it out in full voice. Over and over again. First silently, then in quiet whispers, then aloud.

" . . . He hath loosed the fateful lightning of His terrible swift sword. His truth is marching on . . . "

Machine-gun fire danced all around them. Half the squad hit the dirt.

Gunnery Sergeant Forrester yelled at his men. He had told them time and time again during training.

Move directly off the beach. Keep moving. Never hit the dirt, no matter what.

But sometimes fear trumps training. Evolution teaches a man one thing; the military teaches him something else.

The Gunnery Sergeant bolted into action. He grabbed first one man, then a second, and propelled them both bodily across the rock and sand and up the sloped dune.

"Get on your feet, God damn it! Off your asses! Up the beach!"

Sometime during those first few moments, probably when they were exposed coming off the landing craft, Brock got creased by a bullet. It struck his upper arm, took out a measure of muscle.

But the funny thing was he never felt the damn thing hit, at least not right away. Too much adrenaline pumping through his veins. The body's natural defense mechanism. It turned off the pain, spurred a man to action.

Brock only discovered the gunshot wound moments later, when his right hand felt sticky as he went to grab hold of his carbine. He looked down, now, and saw the blood. It had run down his arm and onto his hand from the spot where the bullet dug into his flesh.

Once Brock reached a spot of relative safety, he dropped his web belt and his backpack to the ground, then removed his field jacket. He had his friend Woods cut open his shirt sleeve, sprinkle sulfa powder into the wound, and apply a bandage. That would have to do for now.

Brock slipped his field jacket back on, as well as his backpack. He and Woods moved to catch up with the rest of their boat team. The team's walkie-talkie had been pierced by a bullet and was now useless. The squad leader discarded it in the sand.

PFC Brock looked back across the short section of beach they had just crossed. Ugly business. Blood mixed with sand. Dead mixed with wounded. Sand dyed dark brown by blood.

A battlefield possesses a sick smell all its own. Burnt gunpowder. Warm, spilt blood. Seared flesh. Smoldering oil. Vomit. Urine. Feces.

For the longest moment, Brock could smell nothing else. The stench hung thick in the stagnant morning air, unmoving, unyielding, the whole lousy revolting sickening smell. He hated his mother. But now he missed her dearly.

The smells violated his nostrils in a way that few things could, an unholy alliance of smells these men were not likely to soon forget. Some men would soon add their own vomit and urine to the mix.

What an awful bloody horror.

FRIDAY
AUGUST 7, 1942
Near Dusk

South Pacific

Late in the day, 7 August 1942, Marines of the 2nd Battalion, 5th Marine Regiment secured the northwest end of the island of Tulagi without opposition.

The 2/5 joined Edson's Raiders, the 1st Raider Battalion, who were already advancing towards the southeastern end of the island where the Japanese were dug-in on Hill 281. The Japanese defenses included dozens of tunneled caves dug into the hill's limestone cliffs, as well as machine-gun pits protected by mounds of sandbags. The advancing Marines reached these defensive lines near dusk. It was a terrible time to begin a full-scale assault. Daylight was fading fast. They decided to go to ground for the night.

Once the sun went down, things got nasty. The Japanese attacked the Marine lines five separate times, beginning at about 2230 hours. The attacks consisted of frontal charges, along with individual and small-group infiltration efforts towards Edson's command post. At times this resulted in hand-to-hand combat with the dug-in Marines.

Just after midnight, the Japanese broke through the Marine lines. They captured a machine-gun post, but were soon thrown back. The Japanese were not smart in the way they attacked and suffered heavy losses as a result. By 0200 hours the Marine lines held for good.

Brock's unit was not part of this initial action. But it was described to him afterwards by one of his buddies from another squad when they both lay wounded in the hospital ship after the fighting was over.

" . . . Full darkness set in. There was movement to the front. You could hear the Tojos jabbering. Then the Nips found a gap and began running through the opening. The gap was sealed shut when another one of our squads closed the gate. Some butterheads had crawled to within twenty yards of Bosco's squad. Bosco began lobbing grenades from a prone position. But he was throwing blind. His grenades were going off mere yards from our own position. We had to duck every time the fucking things exploded. The enemy was all around us. It was brutal and deadly. We were so close to one another we had to be careful not to kill our own boys. We were tired. But if we fell asleep, we would surely be killed . . . "

Later that morning, the Marines landed reinforcements in the form of the 2nd Battalion, 2nd Marines. They surrounded Hill 281 and the adjoining ravine and proceeded to pound both locations with heavy mortar fire.

Then the offensive assault commenced. The Marines attacked the two positions using improvised explosive charges to kill the Japanese defenders. The enemy was trying to take cover in the many caves and fighting positions spread throughout the hill and ravine. By mid-afternoon, the Marines had overrun the Jap positions and significant resistance ceased. In the battle for Tulagi, 307 Japanese defenders died, along with 45 American troops.

What happened next would not go so easily.

The nearby islets of Gavutu and Tanambogo housed the Japanese seaplane base as well as more than 500 Japanese naval personnel from the Yokohama Air Group. Also the 3rd Kure Special Naval Landing Force, as well as Korean and Japanese civilian technicians and laborers from the 14th Construction Unit. These were the forces that Brock and his cohorts were about to go up against.

The two islets were basically large ugly mounds of coral sticking out of the sea. Each was less than one-hundred-and-fifty-feet high and they were connected to one another by a sixteen-hundred-foot-long manmade causeway. The hills on Gavutu and Tanambogo were called, respectively, Hills 148 and 121 by the Americans, the number designating their height in feet above sea-level.

When Brock and the Marines from his regiment arrived on the scene, the Japanese who were bivouacked on each islet were well entrenched in bunkers and caves constructed on and within the two hills. This was a double challenge for the Marines because the two islets were mutually supportive. Each was in machine gun range of the other. There was trouble from the get-go because the U.S. military mistakenly believed the islets to be garrisoned by only two hundred naval troops and construction workers.

At noon on 7 August, Brock's Marine unit assaulted the coral reef island of Gavutu by boat from the open sea. The approach to the narrow strip of beach was harrowing and before long the terrifying experience gave Brock profound respect for the skills of their Coast Guard coxswain and his boatcrew.

It was nothing short of amazing for Brock to watch the coxswain work, a brave young man once attached to a Coast Guard unit stationed near San Diego. The man made it look easy as he deftly maneuvered their heavily-loaded Higgins boat through enemy fire. They danced with strong ocean currents, past hazardous reef outcroppings, around — sometimes over — treacherous sandbars, bow crashing through rolling surf.

Brock didn't have time to reflect upon the man's heroism just now. But the Coast Guard boatcrews had a grueling and frequently dangerous job. Everywhere the war took them in the Pacific, the Coasties unloaded their craft on foreign beaches while under fire from Japanese snipers. The coxswains and crews worked long hours, sometimes for days on end, never leaving their boats to sleep or even eat. Coffee and food were lowered down to them on lines that dangled over the side of a troop or supply ship. They slept on their cargo while anchored in some lagoon with sharks circling their boat, the sun blazing overhead, their sleep constantly interrupted by the sounds of intermittent gunfire emanating from shore.

Coral reefs were treacherous. They vastly complicated landings. So did changing tides. Yet, Brock's Marine unit somehow made it ashore, where they almost instantly ran into trouble.

Aerial support was nil. The invasion force lacked sufficient numbers of aircraft to provide cover for all three landings at the same time, Guadalcanal, Tulagi, and Gavutu. The earlier naval bombardment had damaged the seaplane ramp. The destruction of the ramp forced the landing craft to deposit the Marines in an exposed location on a nearby beach. This is where Brock and his boatcrew had first come ashore. This is where Brock was creased by that bullet.

Now they were on the beach and being hit by Japanese machine-gun fire from all sides, left and right. Casualties were heavy. But Brock was lucky. Of the Marines that made it to shore, one in ten was either killed or wounded on that open patch of pebble and sand. Now, those that could walk or run scrambled inland for cover to escape the deadly crossfire. It was coming from Jap positions on both islets.

"Fuck!"

Brock heard the cry from his friend, Leonard Woods. Woods had been hit and was bleeding badly from a gut wound.

Brock broke cover and turned to help his friend. Woods was in great pain and could not feel his legs. "I'll get you help," Brock said.

"Leave him!" Sergeant Forrester yelled. "We need to get these Brownings in place and start returning fire. Brock! Get your ass over here this very instant and help me! Woods will have to wait!"

The Browning machine gun, model M1918A2. Chambered for the .30-06 Springfield rifle cartridge. A medium machine gun, sometimes referred to as a Browning Automatic Rifle, or BAR for short. Tripod stand. Weight of thirty-one pounds. Twenty-four-inch-long barrel. Rate of fire between 440 and 600 rounds per minute. Muzzle velocity — 2800 feet per second. Effective firing range — 1500 yards. Used a 250-round cartridge belt. Air-cooled. Simply the most lethal portable weapon of its time.

"Aim the fucking thing at those goddamn caves! That is where the butterheads are hiding." Forrester pointed and yelled. By now the Marines had become scattered and badly pinned down.

Jolted by a rush of adrenaline, Brock promptly forgot his training. Slow, short bursts. That is what he was supposed to do.

Instead he went wild with the Browning, not letting go of the trigger, not hitting much of anything with the bullets.

Overhead could be heard the scream of incoming bombs. American dive bombers were now dropping bombs on neighboring Tanambogo, diminishing the volume of fire from that direction.

But the explosion of bombs only served to amp up Brock's adrenaline level further. His finger remained on the trigger. Spent cartridges were spewing everywhere.

"Ease up, boy! Hand off the trigger!" This was Gunnery Sergeant Forrester yelling at him now.

Brock ignored the order and kept on firing blindly at the caves above their position on Gavutu.

Because the gun was air-cooled, uncontrollable firing could lead to a dangerous cook-off. Earlier models had been water-cooled. But to save on weight, the newest versions used a different technology. It had to be fired differently from the earlier models.

If the gun became extremely hot from prolonged firing, the cartridge next in line to be fired could find itself coming to rest in a red hot barrel. This would likely cause the propellant in that next cartridge to heat up to the point where it would ignite on its own without warning. With each succeeding shot heating the barrel further, the gun would continue to fire and become uncontrollable until the belt of ammunition was spent.

In this situation the trigger would no longer be what was causing the gun to fire. This is classic cook-off. It was the reason gunners were taught to cock the gun with the palm facing up, so that in the event of a cook-off, their thumb would not be dislocated by the reciprocating charge handle. Gunners were trained to manage the barrel heat by firing the weapon in short, measured bursts. Three to five rounds at a time, with a delay between bursts to forestall its overheating.

"Gunny, take control of that weapon from this horse's ass of a Marine," Forrester yelled. "Private, let loose of that gun and get your ass up that hill. Kill me some fucking Tojos."

Now Brock stopped firing. The gun was hot but not quite hot enough to cook-off. The gunnery sergeant pushed him away from the gun and propelled him in the direction of his squad leader.

The squad started up Hill 148. But Brock held back to check on his friend. Woods was near death. No medic was in sight.

"Take it," he said, coughing up blood. "Take the coin. Give it back to my family, if you can."

Brock nodded his understanding, removed the Challenge Coin from Woods' pocket, and then started up the hill with the rest of his squad. This was a day he would not soon forget.

The hillside was riddled with caves and manmade bunkers, a living nightmare for a small group of American fighters trying to make their way uphill. Much of it was like island hopping. Capture an enemy bunker, then use it as cover to launch an attack on the next one up the hill, and so on.

But each bunker taken cost American lives. The sun was still up. No one was going to be taken by surprise out here. Toss in some grenades, hope you hit something, advance across open ground under enemy fire, flush the bunker and jump in. Take cover.

Now it was late afternoon. There was a bunker about twenty-five yards ahead of them. Their unit was taking small arms fire from that location. Brock dropped into the nearest foxhole. It was already occupied. The man sitting there was leaning quietly against the side of the foxhole half-asleep. He looked tired. Brock said something to the man. That is when he realized the man had already breathed his last.

From his current position, Brock fired several rounds from his carbine at a Jap he caught a glimpse of disappearing into the next bunker up the hill. He noticed beside him in the foxhole the dead Marine's M1 Garand rifle and he decided to use it to fire into the enemy bunker. The weapon appeared rusted in the afternoon light.

Was it safe to fire? Brock wondered. *Or might it rupture in my face?*

But, in the end, the decision was easy to make. Brock was low on ammunition in his own rifle, so it seemed a small risk to take.

Brock fired the dead man's Garand several times in succession. Then, on his right, about twenty feet away, he heard an explosion. Sensed it more than heard it. Bright flash of light. Sharp sound of thunder.

Too close for comfort, he thought grimly. His arm was throbbing badly from where the bullet had creased him earlier in the day.

A moment later, a sizzling sound and a plume of white smoke.

Damn! Brock thought. *White phosphorous shell.*

A moment later, another explosion, this time on his left. Same white smoke. This time it was accompanied by the horrific screams of one of his buddies. The man was running to the rear, his combat pack smoldering on his back, parts of his jungle fatigues on fire.

Now Brock was seriously scared. This injury was likely the result of friendly fire. The U.S. Navy used mortar shells of the white phosphorous variety, perhaps 60 or 81 mm, fired from the rear.

Lousy way to go. Brock thought, shoving the Challenge Coin deeper in his pocket. *Burned nearly half to death by one of your own.*

The advance continued slowly uphill. But nightfall would soon be upon them and everything would change again. The Marines methodically dynamited caves one by one, as they emptied them of their occupants and slaughtered them.

Bloody work. Bloody awful work.

SATURDAY
AUGUST 8, 1942
Daybreak

South Pacific

Artillery shells crashed in the water beside the two men as they came ashore on the Pacific island of Gavutu. Sergeant Boggins and Corporal "Stosh" Whitehorse.

The beach had already been cleared of the enemy. Earlier waves of Marines had seen to that. But that did not mean the enemy could not continue to fire blindly from over the next ridge or the neighboring islet of Tanambogo. Even blind guns were bound to hit something every now and again.

After completing their training at the Camp Elliott Navajo Communication School, the nearly three dozen men of 382 Platoon were broken into groups. Thirteen graduates of Camp Elliott were now assigned to 1st Marine Division; sixteen to various companies of the 2nd Marine Division; and three were retained stateside to recruit and train two hundred additional Navajo as code-talkers to be attached to various Marine units scattered throughout the Pacific.

The larger group would go ashore at Guadalcanal in about three weeks' time. But first, the islands of Gavutu and Tanambogo had to be cleared of the enemy, two small islands connected by a causeway. This small group of Navajo was an advance party to test out their methods in the field, their first actual test under fire. At its core, the code was still straight-up letter and word substitution. What made it unbreakable was the use of Navajo words to represent English letters and words.

Each code-talker was accompanied ashore by a second Marine. Code-talkers were valuable military assets. They had to be protected. More importantly, the code itself had to be protected. This second Marine was an experienced Marine, usually a sergeant who had already seen action. His job was to keep his charge alive, protect him in the field, and shield him from enemy fire.

But it was also this Marine's job to perhaps kill his charge. If the code-talker was at risk of being captured alive, then this unfortunate protocol would have to be invoked. The Navajo code was too valuable an asset to risk having a soldier break under harsh interrogation or torture and give up the code's secrets.

"Quick! Find a place where we can set up," Sergeant Boggins said, looking nervously about.

Corporal Whitehorse, a Navajo code-talker nodded. He was lugging with him on his back a large hand-crank radio set. It was the size of an overgrown shoebox and weighed in at about thirty pounds.

Stosh found a spot behind a rock outcropping, dropped his backpack, and began to turn the hand-crank to power-up the set. The hand-crank charged a generator which powered the transmitter.

Half a minute later, Whitehorse was ready to broadcast and receive. He grabbed hold of the mic and held one of the earphones to his head.

"Remember, Stosh. You must stay low and out of sight," Sergeant Boggins said, keeping his carbine at the ready. "I need you alive and in one piece. You need to be in constant contact with those guns of ours up on the ridge. Also with the deck of that destroyer out there." Boggins turned and pointed offshore. "Now get to work."

The radio crackled to life, and Whitehorse began to direct fire orders to a nearby artillery unit. The position reports came in rapid-fire from the field.

"We are getting hit by machine-gun fire. Big gook nest due west of our position. Map coordinates 7H," a breathless Marine radioed in from his position below Hill 148. "Shell that position, God damnit! Can anybody out there hear me? Shell that fuckin' machine-gun nest! Map-square 7H. Hurry up! We are getting creamed like corn out here."

Corporal Whitehorse rapidly converted those grid coordinates to Navajo code and transmitted. In the radio room of the destroyer offshore, a second Navajo code-talker received the code, transcribed it back to English and handed the coordinates to the Gunnery Sergeant. He radioed the gun team and then the ship heeled over as the big guns took aim and fired.

Moments later, a barrage of shells rained down on Hill 148 as ordered. But the shells fell short of the target and a bit west.

"Short of target, damnit! Elevate two degrees," came the new instruction from that desperate Marine in the field. "Grid 7H.

Short of target and fifty yards due west. Elevate two degrees. Swing right three. Repeat. Up two, right three."

Whitehorse encrypted the new instructions in Navajo code. Then, rapidly speaking his native language into the mouthpiece of the field phone, he transmitted the new coordinates.

"Dzeh dibeh-yazzi dzeh a-keh-di-glini wol-la-chee than-zie dzeh . . . "

Thirty seconds later, a new rain of fire from the ship offshore.

"Bang on!" Sergeant Boggins exclaimed, as the second round of shells took out the machine-gun nest. "Bang on, Semper Fi!"

All day long it would be that way, and well into the night. Directing fire. Calling up reinforcements. Evacuating the wounded. Warning of enemy movements.

Back at Camp Elliott, countless hours had gone into perfecting and memorizing the code, countless more hours of concentration and practice. Each letter of the alphabet could be represented by one or more Navajo words. The letter A might translate into Navajo one of three ways, as ant, apple, or axe. Common military terms had words all their own. A fighter plane was a hummingbird (da-he-tih-hi). A battleship was a whale (lo-tso). A destroyer was a shark (ca-lo). A hand grenade was a potato. A tank was a tortoise. And so on.

Once the words were translated into Navajo before being coded and sent, only another Navajo could decode the message. The letter A, when represented by the word Ant would be transmitted Wol-la-chee. The letter B, often represented by the word Bear, would be transmitted as the Navajo word Shush. C was Cat was Moasi. And so on.

But no matter how complicated, Stosh was determined to get it right. He stayed at it, now, hour after hour. Though hoarse, tired, thirsty, often under enemy fire himself, he stayed at it. And all the while, Sergeant Boggins maintained watch, keeping an eye out for trouble.

At one point an enemy patrol slipped past the Marine line and worked its way down onto the beach where Whitehorse and Boggins were holed up manning the radio.

Sergeant Boggins charged the enemy patrol as if his life depended on it, for it surely did. Corporal Whitehorse hunkered down and radioed for air support. Then he put down his field phone and picked up his own carbine, firing at the advancing commandoes. The firefight was short. Minutes later, a single Navy aircraft strafed the beach. What was left of the rogue enemy patrol scattered.

•

•

About dusk, Russell Brock's squad moved to a ridge that overlooked the causeway that ran between Gavutu and Tanambogo, about sixteen hundred yards in length. No landings had occurred yet on the second islet. The ridge where they were now bivouacked sloped steeply upward into a terrain of rocky hills, caves, and ravines. Their new position afforded them a better view of their objective, Hill 148. Word spread that the enemy planned a counterattack for some time during the coming night. So, the Marines dug-in and prepared themselves on high alert for a *banzai* attack in the next few hours.

The *banzai* charge was already something of a legend from earlier days in the war when the Philippines fell. Twenty or thirty Japs would come yelling out of the landscape shouting a blood-curdling "Marine you die!" while firing their weapons at the enemy and hurling grenades. To mount a blind charge in this fashion was a form of ritualized suicide, the sick product of a society that romanticized death in battle and considered suicide an honorable final accomplishment to one's life.

In anticipation of the attack, the Marines were instructed to fix their bayonets on their rifles and wait. It was a long and scary wait. Each minute felt like an hour.

Positioned as they were on the ridge, they listened for any telltale sound of movement in front of them or to either side. If the enemy came, they might charge up the ridge or perhaps descend down the slope from higher up. Who knew?

But to hear anything with clarity was damn near impossible. Once the sun went down, an artillery duel erupted between opposing sides. Brock's squad sat square in the middle, along with most of the other Marines holed up on Gavutu.

Incoming and outgoing artillery rounds hissed overhead. The hot, screaming shells passed perilously close to their position on the exposed ridge. The contest continued back and forth for several hours. And all throughout, the same thought corralled every man's brain. Some men stated it outloud.

What if a short round falls directly on us?

Sergeant Forrester answered. "Don't sweat it, boys. I guarantee you will never hear the one that takes you out."

Somehow that logic did not sit well with Private Brock, and he again began to sing. The <u>Battle Hymn of the Republic</u>.

" . . . I have seen Him in the watch-fires of a hundred circling camps. They have builded Him an altar in the evening dews and damps . . . "

" . . . I can read His righteous sentence by the dim and flaring lamps: His day is marching on . . . "

With their listening ability sharply impaired by the din of artillery fire, the men had to rely solely on their night vision. It helped that the moon overhead was bright.

But even that distant light was obscured intermittently by thick clouds. Plus, there were jungle plants and overgrowth. The Marines would likely have only seconds of notice before the enemy overran their position. Not much of a margin for safety.

Unexpected help came from Marine mortar platoons to their rear and on the beachhead. Throughout the night, the mortar platoons fired round after round of flares into the night sky. The flares helped illuminate a large area in front of Brock's squad. This made it more difficult for the enemy to approach their position unobserved.

At two or three-minute intervals, they would hear the hissing sound of a mortar round sending up flares. The phosphorescent flares were bright, so bright the men could see almost 100 yards in front of them. It was enough apparently to deter the enemy from crossing the illuminated ground. There would be no *banzai* assault tonight.

A little before daylight they repositioned themselves a few hundred yards downslope and to the rear. Another squad took their place on the exposed ridge. Brock's squad stopped in an area with scattered foxholes that had been dug by the previous unit. All each man had to do was choose a safe-looking foxhole and jump in.

Russell was relieved. He was tired and hungry and dehydrated. Not being forced to dig yet another foxhole today would be a blessing.

But the blessing was short-lived. He jumped in an existing foxhole beside another man. At first he thought the other man was quietly sleeping. Then he realized the terrible truth. It was just like before. The other man was dead.

But Brock really had no choice but to stay put. The foxhole was shallow, yet it was better than nothing. In some places the loose lava gravel was ankle-deep, which made it impossible to dig even a shallow foxhole.

Here the dirt and gravel were loose enough to dig the shallow foxhole deeper. Brock unsheathed his entrenching tool and set to work. A deeper foxhole offered added protection against artillery and mortar rounds. Other men had begun digging much deeper holes, spider holes, one-man fighting holes, deep enough for a single man to stand in and fight from, yet small enough that the surrounding dirt became a form of body armor against incoming shells.

Brock kept digging. All the while, he kept a close eye on the dead Marine, as if the dead man might reach out in a haunting way and touch him with his ghostly presence.

Digging down further with his entrenching tool he struck "hot dirt." This startled him and he fell backward with a yell.

How the fuck could the ground beneath his feet be on fire? Had a hot flare become buried in the ground somehow? Was it still smoldering beneath the soil?

"What the hell?" he muttered. "The dirt's burning hot."

"Hot dirt everywhere," a Marine said from the next foxhole over.

"Hot dirt?"

"Volcanic," the other Marine replied.

Brock shook his head as if he understood. But he didn't, not really. Some Pacific islands were little more than granite caps perched on top of a semi-active volcano far below. While the volcano was unlikely to erupt any time soon, hot lava lurked beneath the surface. If a man didn't want his buttocks to become badly blistered by the heat, he needed some form of insulation between his bottom and the hot ground — a blanket, a spare uniform, perhaps a block of wood. Brock frantically searched the ground around him for something to shield his ass and sit on but found nothing.

Brock choked back a wave of panic. Noise. Lack of sleep. Dehydration. The everpresent smell of death. Bugs. Flies. Snakes. — They were all taking their toll.

Suddenly, the foxhole seemed uncomfortably small and crowded. Brock's upper arm was throbbing where he had been hit, almost as if it were on fire. Russell Brock suddenly felt sorry for himself.

How in blazes had life dealt him such a crummy hand? Whereas he once thought he held four aces, now he couldn't even muster a low pair. Could the game already be over for him? Was he to be nothing more than a cigarette butt discarded on the floor after a losing hand? Was there no longer any way for him to get out of this godforsaken rat hole alive?

Brock's entry into the war only months before had begun with such high hopes. He had been an adventurous lad. His reasons for joining up had been simple enough.

Go off to war, kick the crap out of the enemy, come home a hero, become someone important.

December 1941. The Japanese attack Pearl Harbor. Thousands of American boys join up to fight the enemy.

May 1942. The Battle of the Coral Sea. First Allied victory at sea. Later that same month, Russell Brock graduates high school.

Two weeks later, on a train to Parris Island, South Carolina. Boot camp. It didn't matter that he could not yet drive a car, did not have a steady girl, had never smoked a cigarette, had never once shared a beer with his buddies, was not yet even old enough to shave.

The day Brock left home for the war began in a railway station in New Jersey. He and his mother sat on one of the dozen or so hard wooden benches in the center of the waiting room. A fan turned overhead, trying feebly to push around the hot air. But it didn't help much. The summer heat had become trapped in the high-ceilinged room, along with more than a few flies.

Mother and son sat in absolute silence, not exchanging a word. This was not unusual. They hardly ever spoke. The large wall clock ticked the minutes loudly by.

They were not alone in that waiting room. Other soldiers. Wives. Mothers. A few daughters.

As the train approached the station from the north, his mother handed him a small paper bag she had brought with her from home. Russell thanked her for the gift but did not open the bag. *Why bother?* It would be lunch. He would open it later as the train pushed south. Probably a stick of gum. A small apple. Two crackers with three sardines sandwiched between them.

Brock got up from his mother's side to leave. She told him to be careful. He nodded and walked away. No heartfelt goodbyes, no tears, no "I love you," no kiss on the cheek. They parted stoically, as they had lived.

He switched trains in Washington, D.C., boarded a second train for Beaufort, South Carolina. Then onto a cattle truck along with twenty other rooks. A slow and bumpy ride. Holding onto the wooden staves. Motored over the causeway, across the swamp, then onto Parris Island.

By the time they arrived on the island, the setting sun was low in the sky. It was orange, nearly red. The men jumped off the truck and were soon among the other boots.

But now where the fuck was he? Knee deep in the brown, sucking mud of a foxhole keeping company with a dead man covered in maggots, while holding his breath and expecting a *banzai* attack at any moment. *Could there be a better formula for guaranteeing a sleepless night sweating it out on an enemy ridge?* Brock was exhausted. His eyes were drooping and he nodded off.

His nap was short.

A few minutes later, Sergeant Forrester came through with Father Roman not far behind. The order had been given. They were pulling back further for hot coffee and sandwiches.

Exhaustion turned to exhilaration. Sleep was no longer a priority or even a concern. Brock bounded to his feet and nearly leapt out of the foxhole. Food and drink were exactly what the doctor ordered, exactly what Brock needed to raise his spirits, if only a little.

Forrester's orders were explicit. *Move fast. Go for coffee on the double. Grab a couple sandwiches. Get your ass back in your foxhole.*

Forrester instructed them not to congregate around the coffee containers, not to remain out in the open long. Enemy snipers had been taking potshots at Marines all morning long. No use giving them an easy kill shot.

Brock waited patiently in his foxhole for his turn to grab some chow. By his estimation, the coffee containers and table with sandwiches had been placed in a dangerously exposed space. There were caves and tunnels everywhere. *Who the hell knew where a sniper might be holed up?* Several Marines had already been killed or wounded that morning by sniper fire.

"Go in one or two at a time," Forrester barked again. "Grab your coffee and your grub and get back out of sight, back to your foxholes."

When Brock's turn came, he jumped out of his foxhole like a jackrabbit and headed for the coffee containers, clutching his empty canteen cup in one hand, rifle slung over his good shoulder.

He scooped up his coffee, grabbed a sandwich, and ran back toward his foxhole. Coffee sloshed from his cup as he ran.

Suddenly he was out of breath. So he slowed from a trot to a walk about ten yards from his foxhole. He took several more steps, then sensed movement on his right side.

Out of the corner of one eye, Brock spied an extended arm and a hand pointing down to a slender stick directly in front of him. Looped around the stick was a thin length of tripwire that disappeared into the ground.

Russell stopped dead in his tracks, not daring to breathe.

Fuck! A landmine!

He looked straight down at his boots, head swiveling rapidly from left to right and left again. Had he not seen that extended arm, that pointing finger, his right foot would have passed right through the trigger line. He would now be badly maimed or worse.

Brock slowly began to breathe again. He stepped over the line rather than through it. By the time he could turn to thank the Marine who had just saved his life, the extended arm had disappeared back into the foliage. It was as if that arm had never even been there. Brock had no idea who had saved his life.

Brock hurried on to his foxhole, choked down several gulps of coffee and tried to relax. The sandwich was in his mouth and the coffee had just hit his stomach when it happened, an explosion near his foxhole.

The next guy in line behind him hadn't been as lucky as he. No extended hand to point out the lethal danger.

The explosion knocked PFC Brock back and off his feet. A plume of yellow smoke. The acrid smell of enemy explosives. A panicked call for a corpsman.

It did not sink in right away. Brock had come perilously close to sharing the identical fate as the infantryman behind him.

A second later, when it dawned on him how close he had come to dying or being horribly maimed, he gagged at the thought. The coffee he had just swallowed surged up into his throat, now, from his stomach and gushed from his mouth onto the ground at his feet. It was a visceral reaction. The mind controlled the body, not the other way around.

The wounded man cried out in pain, his foot and part of his leg gone, evaporated, destroyed. The injury called for a tourniquet. But this far from a hospital ship there might be no saving the man, no matter what was done for him.

Brock stood frozen as the horribly wounded Marine was given morphine and loaded on a stretcher still screaming. Two men carried the wounded Marine down the hill on the stretcher, down toward the aid station on the beach. If he made it that far alive, he would receive preliminary medical treatment at the aid station. Later, if he could be stabilized, they would place him onboard an amphibious tractor and he would be taken to the hospital ship offshore.

But Brock's day was not yet done. Hill 148 still had not been taken.

The Captain in charge gathered his men. Two squads were to work their way up the hill from the left, two more from the right. One squad was to hold their current position and a second was to proceed up the hill from the center. First squad to the top would get a warm dinner.

Gunnery Sergeant Forrester and his men got what they believed was the easiest assignment, to hold their current position.

But no sooner had the other squads set out to the left and to the right and straight up the middle than trouble began. It came in the form of sustained shelling from the neighboring islet, Tanambogo. Enemy troops were still moving unimpeded back and forth across the causeway, artillery as well as mechanized equipment.

Brock was unable to see what sort of gun was lobbing shells in their direction. But it must have been a good-sized gun, 50mm or larger. The butterheads likely had spotters on the opposite Hill 121, because the incoming mortar shells were now landing uncomfortably close to their position.

One of the men bounded out of his foxhole looking desperately for better cover, panic in his eyes, when an incoming shell struck him practically head-on. A moment later, there was a large report and a pink mist hung in the air where his body had been moments before.

Brock cringed and began an immediate conversation with his Lord above. He was barely one sentence into that plea when "Bang!" his world changed forever.

An incoming mortar struck near his foxhole. The explosion buried him along with two other men. Everything went dark. But before he lost consciousness, Brock recalled the foxhole collapsing on top of him. Then his life was over.

Minutes passed. Eventually someone pulled his lifeless body from the rubble by his legs, along with the bodies of the two other dead men.

Brock was bloody and unconscious and not moving, not breathing, presumed dead. No medic was called. No treatment was initiated.

The officer responsible for keeping tabs on such things, pulled one of Brock's dog tags from his neck and counted him among that day's dead. Then the officer moved on to the next casualty. Grisly work, but someone had to do it.

Sometime later, maybe five minutes, maybe longer, Father Roman was called to perform the Sacrament of Last Rites over the three dead men. Brock's dead body was carted away along with the two others.

Then Russell stirred.

"Oh, my God, the man is still alive," the monk priest shouted. He wet himself and dropped to his knees, begging God to forgive his mistake. In his haste and state of utter exhaustion, he had declared a living man dead.

"Medic! Medic! Medic!" he yelled. "This man is still alive! Hurry! Hurry! Hurry!"

The white-faced medics rushed Russell down the hill and to an aid station on the beach. He would be transported as quickly as possible onboard a waiting Higgins boat to a hospital ship moored in the outer lagoon. The United States Marine Corps would shortly win the day, and the Battle of Guadalcanal — of which Gavutu and Tanambogo were a part — would soon be one for the history books.

In the meantime, Brock had a long period of recovery ahead of him.

**SATURDAY
AUGUST 8, 1942
12:30 p.m.**

Kiln, Mississippi

"What the hell kind of shit storm have you dragged us into?" Günter Kesselring screamed at Captain Wilhelm Kronenhauer in the parking lot of the demolished Jordan River Lumber Company Hotel. Broken timbers lay everywhere, a product of the improvised explosives he had attached to the front door when he and Captain Grimm were trying to escape three days ago.

"You dare lay blame for this royal *gesudel* at my door?" Kronenhauer barked. "This whole mess is Sebastian Grimm's fault. Now Grimm is dead and you yourself are to blame for much of this *schmiererei*."

"How dare you!"

"What a cock-up, what a royal cock-up. *Verpfuschen*. This has been botched since the beginning. That fancy car you have been driving around in is what led those Sicilian pigs to our doorstep in the first place. That automobile is attracting unwanted attention everywhere you drive it."

"Fine. You take the damn thing," Kesselring barked right back. "On these poorly built American roads, it handles like a piece of broken farm machinery. Not a finely engineered automobile at all."

"Then leave the damn thing parked in a garage somewhere, where it can't be seen. Or give it back to Pfingsten. I had to hide it that day after the hotel was blown up and the Sicilians left to tend to their wounded. They came back later with a truck looking to take it home with them, but then gave up quickly when it wasn't parked in the lot where they left it. They probably meant to sell it on the black market. New automobiles bring a lot of money on the black market these days. They are no longer being manufactured in the United States. That's how short the Americans are on war materials. They will never be able to win the war."

Kesselring shook his head, as if in disdain. "Göring and Himmler are depending on us. My father too. We need to take out that Higgins boat plant, and we need to do it very soon. Our intelligence services report that the Allies are about to move against North Africa, maybe within the month. Plus, we have now learned that the Tucker gun turrets they use on many of their bombers are manufactured here in New Orleans as well. Only we don't yet know in which of their facilities."

"*Mein Gott.* This Higgins company has more than one manufacturing facility?" Kronenhauer asked angrily. "Why have I not been told this before? *Mein Gott.* This demolitions job is becoming more difficult with each passing day, not at all what I signed on for, nearly impossible for just one man to handle alone."

Günter Kesselring calmly pulled his meerschaum pipe out of his pocket, stuffed it with tobacco, struck a wooden match against the heel of his boot, and lit a fire in the bowl. He took a satisfied puff before he spoke.

"Detailed information about each facility is part of the intelligence we lost when Henry Brock went missing. Three boat assembly plants that I am aware of. City Park Avenue, Michoud, and St. Charles Street. There may be a fourth on Industrial Canal."

"Back up a second," Captain Kronenhauer said. "Did you say you have been in contact with Herr Himmler?"

"Oh, yes. I wired him two days ago. I told him that because of your royal cock-up, the Americans now have Brock's ring, most likely his notebook, as well as Sebastian Grimm's codebook containing the daily passkey . . . "

"*Mein Gott.* What the hell?" Kronenhauer interrupted. "If Grimm's codebook is in the wind, exactly what cipher did you use to encode your message when you sent your wire to Himmler? Don't tell me you sent a top secret communication in the clear, uncoded?"

"Well . . . " Günter Kesselring stuttered, the smoke rising from the bowl of his lit pipe. "I . . . "

"What a fool you are, Kesselring! Any man in his right mind would shoot you dead where you stand."

"Well then, go ahead and shoot."

"Don't think I won't. You do not belong here. You would not even be here if not for the influence of your fucking father. What a numbskull you are, Günter. *Dummkopf.* You have to be the stupidest man alive. Sending a top secret communiqué in the clear uncoded? *Gesudel.*"

"I had no choice," Kesselring said. "In any case, Himmler replied in open code as well. He said the plan needs to be accelerated. Within the next few days at the latest."

"Cannot be done," Kronenhauer said. "Absolutely cannot be done. And now I find myself working with the comedy team of Laurel and Hardy."

"I will let that last remark slide, Captain. Now tell me. Why can't this be done sooner?"

"What does that silly question make you? Laurel? Or Hardy? Think about it, Kesselring. I only just now recovered the detonation cord and the *plastiksprengstoff* from that rowboat. I haven't even had the opportunity to surveill the boat plant. Now you go and tell me that there are three, maybe four manufacturing locations I need to concern myself with. Are you out of your mind? This job requires an entire commando team, not just one man."

"We go tonight. You and me together."

"Go where?"

"We go see what we can learn about these facilities; learn how to gain entrance to them."

Kronenhauer laughed, a good solid belly laugh. "We do three months' work in one long night? You and me together? Laurel and Hardy?"

"And why not?"

"What the hell do you know about espionage, Kesselring? Have you even completed basic training, much less infantry school? You are little more than a glorified paper pusher, *ein papierschieber*. Be happy I tolerate your presence."

Günter Kesselring's face burned red with anger. "We go tonight. You and me together . . . And that is final."

"I do not take orders from you, Kesselring. You are not in my chain-of-command."

"But I am your ticket home, Captain. And in case you have forgotten, my father has final say in pretty much everything military. So unless you want to spend the rest of your natural life as a fugitive here in America, you will absolutely obey my orders. And if you think this job is more than the two of us can handle alone, I know just the man we can call to lend us a hand."

"I do not work with outsiders. You are trouble enough."

"Rudyard Pfingsten is not an outsider. He is one of us. Always has been."

SATURDAY
AUGUST 8, 1942
10 p.m.

Cuba

The air over Casilda Bay was pregnant with tropical humidity. But that was not unusual for this time of year. A crescent moon was the central fixture in the night sky, with great swatches of the Milky Way obscured by a bank of low-hanging clouds.

The open-air cantina was crowded, nearly a carnival atmosphere. The music was loud, the patrons happy and carefree, the sweet-smelling alcohol flowing freely. A man and a woman sat at a small round table near the encircling hedge. They sat close to one another and spoke in whispers. But their body language did not define them as lovers, more like business associates attending an important meeting.

The woman spoke first. She was crisply dressed with impeccable manners. She was a banker. Her name was Martina Amerada.

"This arrived two days ago in the diplomatic pouch from Lisbon. It is from Aldo Carolla," she said, holding tight to the sealed envelope.

Peter Morgan peered at her through the haze of the dimly lit garden restaurant. Smudge pots around the perimeter were practically the only source of light: smudge pots, a crescent moon, and a single flickering candle on each table.

"Martina, since when does a private bank like yours receive confidential items from overseas in a diplomatic pouch? Under international law, aren't such pouches reserved only for embassy communications and the like?" Colonel Peter Morgan was a good looking man, in or out of uniform, and Martina had noticed.

"I sit here with a drink in my hand, band playing calypso music, and you wish to quote me international law? Is that actually what the two of us are here for?"

"That is not really my point. I am just setting the ground rules. Either we choose to obey the law. Or we choose to ignore it.

But if we choose to ignore it, there may be consequences. A diplomatic bag is a container that carries with it certain legal protections. It is used to transport official correspondence or other items between a diplomatic mission and its home government or other consular office. So long as the bag, which is usually locked, is externally marked to show its status, the bag has diplomatic immunity from search or seizure, as does the diplomatic courier, who is similarly immune from arrest and detention. I don't want to spend the rest of my life at hard labor breaking rocks after a court martial."

"You really are such a sweet man. Must we worry about such things tonight?"

Martina stared at him with longing in her eyes. Casilda Bay and the small village of Playa Ancón was, for her, a two-hour rail trip over the highlands from Havana, a bit further for him by Army jeep from Guantanamo Bay, the American enclave at the southeast corner of the island. Casilda Bay was filled with tropical fish, white sand beaches, and sandbars that stretched for miles. Idyllic in every way.

"I want a straight answer," Morgan said firmly.

Martina stared back at him, laughed, and sipped her rum. "Colonel, let's leave aside for a moment the why and how of the diplomatic pouch. Let's concentrate instead on the what. I have not opened it. But inside this latest pouch from Aldo Carolla is likely to be maps and other intell regarding the island of Sicily. Your bosses, that Admiral you work for, will be gloriously happy to have whatever information is in this pouch. I promise you. He will not question you or concern himself — not even for a moment — about such niceties as to whether this information arrived by legal means or whether it did not. The only question that needs answering at this time is this: Do you have the money? And is it enough? The money goes back to Aldo the same way as the information arrived here, in the pouch."

"Of course, I have the money," Morgan said, undoing his money belt. "Do you want it now? It's all black money, washed and untraceable. My people don't want to advertise the fact that the government of the United States of America is underwriting the Sicilian mob. That kind of press we can do without."

"I got that. My people are very discreet."

"And who exactly are your people?"

"You want to see my credentials?"

"You haven't given me a straight answer since we sat down, Martina. You know you are playing a very dangerous game, don't you?"

"Again, I find your concern touching, Colonel. But honestly, for a military man, aren't you being overly dramatic? Besides, it's none of your damn business. When are you going to get that through your head?"

"Woman, you are running money for the Carolla crime family. You got that, right?"

"Keep your voice down!" Martina ordered, looking around to see if anyone was paying them undue attention.

"Yes, I will keep my voice down. But running money for the Carolla crime family is a very dangerous place for a woman to be."

"Seriously? This whole make-believe put-up-job of you pretending to care about my well-being is actually about sex, about me being a woman? I should be in the kitchen with an apron busy making babies? You don't know much about women, do you, Colonel?"

"I am not married, if that is what you mean."

"No surprise there."

Morgan looked Martina straight in the eye. "Women like you, classy women, do not crawl into a mobster's bed as a cure for loneliness. Women like you must have a reason."

Martina Amerada put down her drink and scowled. "You have been spying on me?"

"I don't have pictures of you and Nico Carolla in bed together, if that is what you mean. But yes, my people have been spying on you two. The War Department has a lot riding on this love connection between you and the Carolla family. But mark my words, Martina. If you are not careful, this spy business is going to get you killed. Like I said — absolutely no place for a woman."

She laughed it off. "My family has been in the intelligence business since before the Spanish-American War. My grandfather worked in the embassy, where he was recruited into the British Intelligence Service near the turn of the century. My father followed in his footsteps and so did I."

"Well, my family has been in the ship-boarding business since the first days of the Republic, even before that in the colonies."

"Ship-boarding?"

"First as pirates. Later as marines."

"Ah, yes, ship-boarding."   She smiled.   "Now tell me. Whatever happened to that man I asked you to follow the middle of last week?"

"Wilhelm Kronenhauer?   Not much to tell.   I followed him from the pier that day after his ship docked, like you asked.   Later, I lost him in the swamps northeast of New Orleans.   I have yet to learn what he was after or who he met with after I lost him."

"Shame.   It seems that he is into something quite nefarious. I don't have all the details."

Just about then, a man in a dark hat passed closely beside their table and seemed to stop and listen to their conversation. Peter Morgan immediately switched gears.

"Do you care to dance?" he asked Martina.

"I thought you would never ask.   Let's."

SUNDAY
AUGUST 9, 1942
2 p.m.

French Quarter, New Orleans

"Certainly you must know how unusual it is for a U.S. Marshal to break bread with a member of a major crime family," Duncan Baxter said. He was not quite ready to get comfortable in the chair that had been offered him.

The two men, Nico Carolla and Duncan Baxter, faced one another from across a large table in the small tavern. It was an old building, centuries old, one-story tall, square and squat, with a steep roof-line. Lafitte's Blacksmith Shop. In the French Quarter of New Orleans, on the corner of Bourbon Street and St. Philip Street.

Baxter was flanked by his junior partner, Marshal Nolan Greeley; Nico, by his two closest lieutenants, Luca and Vittorio. Otherwise, the tavern was deserted. The atmosphere was tense, each man rightfully suspicious of the other.

"We couldn't exactly meet at the family *trattoria*, now could we?" Nico said. "But this place Lafitte's is different. They tell me pirates once operated out of this place."

"Some say they still do," Duncan Baxter replied darkly.

"You trying to say something, Officer?" Nico retorted.

"Marshal," Baxter replied. "Not Officer. Marshal."

"Okay, Marshal," Nico said. "What is it that you want?"

"I knew your father, Nico, when you were still just a boy. Michael Carolla. Sylvestro's eldest, if I remember correctly. And I know Silver Dollar Sam himself. First met the man fifteen or more years ago. Since then, we have crossed paths more than once, him and me."

"My grandfather has good things to say about you as well, Marshal. But even you must know that I cannot be seen as cooperating with law enforcement," Nico said. "If word were to ever get out about this cozy little meeting of ours, it might call my leadership into question."

"And I cannot be seen as coddling a criminal," Duncan Baxter said. "There would be repercussions for me as well."

"Good, then we both have something to lose," Nico said. "Anyway, I think we are safe from observation here. Can you vouch for your man?"

"Who? Greeley? Yes, of course. The man is above reproach."

"Is that so?" Luca said. "Heard your new man has a problem with — how you say? — *alcol*."

"Alcohol," Nico corrected.

"Yes, alcohol," Luca said.

Marshal Nolan Greeley stiffened. "Had a problem. Past tense. I quit drinking months ago." Then, very much ill at ease, he quickly changed the subject. "What kind of place is this anyway?" he asked.

"Out-of-towner?" Nico asked.

"Yes. Way out of town," Greeley answered. "Denver, Colorado, was my last posting. Now what were you saying about this place being a home to pirates?"

"You want to know about this place? *Cazzo!* Let me run it down for you," Nico said. "I know the local history. Lafitte's Blacksmith Shop. But not a blacksmith shop at all, a tavern. Built by pirates nearly two hundred years ago."

"Pirates? Seriously? Black Beard and all that?"

"That is the story. Jean and Pierre Lafitte. Notorious privateers. Illicit dealers in so-called black ivory."

"Ivory? Like from whales?" Greeley asked.

"Not whales. Slaves. Black African slaves. The Lafitte pirates posed as blacksmiths to mask their nefarious trade. This building was once their clubhouse, a grog-soaked home base. They called it a tavern. It was more like a private club."

"Built to last, that is for sure," Nolan Greeley said, properly impressed as he looked around. "You say this place is two hundred years old?"

"Creole French have a fancy name for this kind of construction," Nico said. "Briquete-entre-poteaux. I have no idea what those words mean, or even if I pronounced them correctly. But the place is rock solid. Framing timbers of cypress. Soft, porous clay bricks inbetween. Exterior covered with a thick coat of lime plaster to protect the supporting walls from the rain — bricks and timber alike. The roof is covered with tile. This type roofing came into general use in New Orleans after the Great Fires of the late 1700s."

"Okay, history lesson is over," Duncan Baxter said. "Time for us to do what we came here to this musty old place to do."

Nico nodded, got more comfortable in his chair, placed his *Bernardelli* .25 on the table where it was clearly visible. He was done taking chances. "Please tell me what it is you want, Marshal."

"There have been several suspicious deaths across the river in Hancock County, Mississippi. I am not here to accuse you of anything, so please do not get your back up. I am only here to learn whether you know anything at all about these deaths."

"The only way this is going to work, Marshal, is if you show me your hand before I show you mine," Nico said. "No hole cards."

"Fair enough. Bay St. Louis. Death number one. An older white man. Heavyset. Found naked. No visible wounds on the body. His tongue had been cut out, probably postmortem. Perhaps the killer meant for us to think in terms of certain Old World methods for dealing with a miscreant who had ratted out his brothers."

Nico Carolla remained nonplussed.

"Death number two. Scrawny black man. Fully clothed. Shot twice. Once with a rifle, once with a shotgun. Face unrecognizable."

Nico Carolla twitched imperceptibly.

Baxter continued. "Death number three. This was a violent death. It happened onshore. Near the little town of Kiln. A white man. Very fit. Seems there was a shootout, perhaps accompanied by the detonation of military-grade explosives. The gunman — or gunmen — likely left the scene in a hurry by car. There were multiple tire tracks in the gravel road outside."

Now Nico spoke. "And you have no suspects for these deaths?"

"No, we do not."

"And you are not here at Lafitte's today looking to finger a suspect or arrest anyone for these crimes?"

"No sir, we are not."

"In that case, we may have some things that might help you in your investigation." Nico motioned to Luca who produced three items, all of which he handed to Nico.

"*Madre di Dio.* That first man, the white man whose tongue had been cut out, I am told he died of natural causes in a local cathouse of some repute. I am not at liberty to tell you who put this book in my hands. But I do know that this book is said to have once belonged to that dead white man you just spoke of."

Nico handed Duncan Baxter the small notebook that once belonged to Henry Brock, the one Hector had stolen and later died for. Baxter palmed the notebook, looked briefly at its contents, then handed it on to Marshal Greeley.

Greeley opened the book.

"I think it is German," Nico said.

"Indeed it is," Greeley said. "And I can read it. My parents were German immigrants. Came here after the First World War. Spoke it at home all the time."

"So is it a Travel Guidebook, like one of my people thought?" Nico asked, looking in Vittorio's direction.

"No, it is not," Nolan Greeley answered stone-faced.

"What is it, Greeley?" Duncan Baxter asked.

"If I didn't know better, I would say that an experienced intelligence officer collected much of this information. What is in this book is clearly the result of many hours of surveillance. All hand entries. Detailed maps. Bus schedules. Shipping manifests. Numbers of staff at factory gates. The comings and goings of trucks, people, water vessels, train cars."

"What exactly is the intelligence officer surveilling?" Nico Carolla and Duncan Baxter asked the same question at practically the same moment.

"The Naval Air Station at the foot of Elysian Fields Avenue. The Eureka Tug-Boat Company facilities beside Lake Pontchartrain and along Industrial Canal. There is something here about City Park Avenue in Mid-City. Also, Bayou St. John."

"Then there is this." Nico handed Greeley the signet ring that had already caused so much trouble. "Have you ever seen anything like this before?"

Greeley turned it over in his hand. "A signet ring. Rather old, I would say. A baronet ring, I believe they call it, for minor noblemen. There are compendiums on such things, reference books. All the old duchies and baronies of Europe had family shields. Each semi-royal family had one. The family crests are all registered, or at least they once were. That royalty stuff has been outlawed in Germany since the Treaty of Versailles."

"Versailles?" Luca asked.

"The treaty that ended the First World War," Greeley answered. "Nineteen-nineteen, I believe. Versailles is a city in France."

"And what about this?" Nico handed him the second small book. "This second book and the signet ring both came from that third dead body, the one found near Kiln."

"Ah, the mystery deepens," Greeley said as he paged through the second book. "I think these are codewords for some kind of cipher. Anagrams maybe, for some keyword or key phrase. I think this book of ciphers is worth a great deal to whoever lost it. Certainly something he might kill for, something he would rather not have fall into the wrong hands."

"A German book filled with maps, a foreign signet ring, and a book of ciphers. I am not sure I like the sounds of this one little bit," Baxter said.

"You will get no argument from me there," Greeley said. "We may have stumbled onto some sort of spy-novel espionage plot here. Maybe the Nazis are planning to take out the Naval Air Station or the tugboat company. What else does that company manufacture?"

Nico nodded. "Many of my people work there. We also provide security. The Eureka Tug-Boat Company builds landing craft for the Marine Corps and for the U.S. Army, what you people call Higgins boats. They also build high-speed PT boats and machine-gun turrets. Last I heard they were working on a motorized lifeboat that can be dropped into the water by parachute from the air."

Duncan Baxter suddenly became absolutely quiet. He looked at Greeley whose mind was also churning.

Finally, Marshal Baxter got slowly to his feet and looked around the poorly-lit room. "Thank you for your time, Mr. Carolla. You may consider our investigation of these three deaths officially closed. Your involvement in these matters is no longer required, and I would prefer if this entire conversation remained forever confined within the four walls of this room."

"*Cazzo*. This is serious, isn't it?" Nico asked.

"Yes. Very." Baxter answered.

"Someone official must be told," Nico said. "The army? The *polizia*? Someone in government?"

"Yes, I agree with your assessment, Nico. But you must not be the someone who does the telling. I must be the one."

"Looking for headlines? A bit of front-page glory?"

"You don't know me at all, do you?"

"Perhaps not. But exactly who will you tell, Marshal?"

"I am not yet sure. The FBI? Perhaps the top man at the Naval Air Station. Perhaps Higgins himself. On this, Marshal Greeley and I must reflect, consider our options. But I repeat — your involvement in this matter is now officially closed."

"I do know the name of one Marine Colonel that is stationed here locally. I have reason to believe that this man can be trusted with such things. Colonel Peter Morgan. You might reach out to him."

"Morgan, eh? Perhaps we will do that."

"Well then, there is one more thing you must know before you go," Nico said.

"Yes?"

"I have this photograph."

Now Nico pulled from his vest pocket the photograph Martina Amerada had given him in their previous rendezvous, the photograph of a severe looking man wearing a German uniform with SS insignia. He handed Baxter the photograph of Wilhelm Kronenhauer.

"Who is this man?" Marshal Baxter demanded to know.

"I do not know. But I think this may be the man you are looking for, the man who is involved in your espionage plot."

"Where can I find this man? What is his name?"

"All questions I cannot answer."

"Who gave you this picture?"

"Yet one more question I cannot answer."

"Is there any god damn thing you can tell me?"

"All I can tell you is this, Marshal. I have it on good authority that the man you are looking for may be driving a flash Packard."

"That is not much to go on," Marshal Baxter said.

"A Custom Super Eight Packard. With Mississippi plates and an 'X' gasoline ration sticker. A big letter H in the upper left-hand corner of the plate. The H stands for Hancock County. Hancock County, Mississippi."

"Yes? And how did you come to know this?"

"It was parked at crime scene number three, the one outside Kiln. When my men went back to the crime scene to retrieve that automobile with one of our flatbed trucks, it was gone, poof."

"What possessed you to retrieve a parked car with a flatbed truck?"

"I have always wanted to drive a fancy car like that custom coupe. I am telling you. You find that Packard, you find your bad guy. I think the man in the photograph is the man you will find behind the wheel. *Capiche?*"

"Yes. I *capiche.*"

MONDAY
AUGUST 10, 1942
9 a.m.

German Coast near New Orleans

"Greeley, promise me you won't say anything to these people about the codebooks Nico Carolla gave us," Marshal Baxter said. He and his partner were seated in the older model, four-door Chevrolet driving west along the south shore of Lake Pontchartrain. The square, boxy car had wide running boards on each side and large rounded fenders over all four wheels. "Odds are that one or more of their number may well be Nazi sympathizers."

"I understand the stakes here, Duncan. It is the signet ring we need help with, not the notebooks. My rough translation of the contents of these books should be more than sufficient to get the attention of the Navy brass at the N.A.S. That is our next stop after this one, right? Colonel Peter Morgan's office?"

"Yes, absolutely. We need to turn these materials over to the military just as soon as we possibly can."

Lake Pontchartrain was on their right, now, as they drove west. They would shortly turn south and make their way across the Mississippi River.

"What do you make of this photograph?" Duncan Baxter asked.

"It isn't much to go on. Perhaps Morgan or one of the other Navy boys can make a positive identification," Greeley said as he slowed to make the turn. "But before we get to our first stop, let me give you a little background on these people. I have lived among them long enough to know that the Germans of southern Louisiana are a rather tight-knit community. Some have married into the French, others into the Creole and colored communities. But most still live apart. They call their enclave the *Côte des Allemands*, the German Coast."

The two men were driving almost due south now. The bridge across the Mississippi River revealed a broad body of water almost the color of mud, slow-moving and heavy with barge traffic. There was a vehicle on the same road not far behind them.

"Are we being followed?" Baxter asked, turning his head.

"Maybe." Greeley looked in the rearview mirror. "But to be fair, this is the only thoroughfare south. We shouldn't get ahead of ourselves. Let me slow down, pull over, and see if they pass."

"Fair enough," Duncan Baxter said. "Now tell me again. Who exactly are these people you are taking us to see?"

"We are almost there. Ten more minutes. The sign is just up ahead."

Greeley slowed the car and pulled briefly off the road. A moment later, the car that had been following them drove past without slowing. Greeley waited a minute longer and then pulled back onto the road and continued driving south. He picked up his story where he left off.

"Like I said, the sign is just ahead. *Des Allemands*. The German Coast. We follow the highway south, then west until the bayou bridge. We turn left this side of the bridge, just before we cross the bayou. They call it *Bayou des Allemands*, the German Bayou. Then we follow the bayou road south to Schaubhut Lane. That is where he lives, up the lane in a big two-story house."

"Who? What is the man's name?"

"Rudyard Pfingsten. He is a sort of district mayor. In the Old World, he might have been called a burgher."

"Can you vouch for this man?"

"Not in the way that you probably mean," Nolan Greeley said. "He and I belong to the same Lutheran church; that is about the size of it. We have met just the once. He probably doesn't even remember me."

"Great. Just great."

"That is how it is around here. Surely you must know that. Rudyard Pfingsten is the big fish in the local pond. I am but a minnow. The minnow always knows who the big fish are. But it is hardly ever true the other way around."

"So why are we even bothering with this fellow?"

By now they were on the bayou road. It ran parallel to the water of *Bayou des Allemands*.

"Because he knows damn near everyone in these parts. And damn near everything about them. Oh, here it is now. Schaubhut Lane. We have to motor up this lane a short distance."

Within minutes, Greeley pulled into the driveway of a large, white, clapboard house and parked. The house had a large covered porch that extended around the exterior on three sides. Open, airy space.

"This is it. Number Twelve. I hope to hell the man is home."

"It looks like we are in luck," Baxter said. "Someone must have heard us coming up the drive. We have a welcoming party on the porch, complete with shotgun and snarling guard dog."

The man yelled down at them from the steps of his porch. "And who might you two turds be?"

"At least he called us by name," Marshal Baxter grumbled quietly.

"United States Marshals," Greeley yelled back at the man. Duncan Baxter produced his shield.

"I ain't broken no laws."

"No one said that you have."

"What then?"

"We just want to ask you a couple questions," Duncan Baxter said, slowly approaching the porch. The dog growled menacingly.

"I ain't answering nobody's questions, not lessin' you turds gots yourself a warrant," the man with the shotgun said.

"These aren't those kinds of questions," Baxter said, standing his ground.

"You have one minute to 'splain yourself or else I gets the real law out here on this porch." He cocked his gun.

"Are you Rudyard Pfingsten?" Nolan Greeley asked, producing his shield as well.

"Who be askin'?"

"I rent a house from a woman up the road a bit," Greeley answered, pointing vaguely in that direction.

"That make us friends?"

"We met once in church, you and me."

"That still don't make us friends. Thirty seconds left on your minute, bub. What is your business with me?"

"People at church tell me you are one very smart man. They tell me that you know a little something about German history? Is that true?"

"I know certain things, yes."

Greeley reached into his pocket. "Have you ever seen a ring like this before?"

"Cain't see it from here. Bring it on up. Real slow now."

United States Marshal Nolan Greeley advanced slowly, holding the ring out on front of him like an offering at church. Pfingsten reached out and took it from him, held it up to the light.

"This is a family heirloom, a signet ring," Pfingsten said, dropping some of his southern Louisiana accent.

"You know about such things?" Marshal Baxter asked, approaching as well.

"To a degree. German nobility is a bit of a thing with me." Pfingsten lowered his weapon and chained up his dog. "Please come in, you two. I have some reference books on the shelf in my library that may be able to help shed some light on this thing."

"You have a library of reference books?"

"What? You think I am too fucking stupid to read?"

"That is not really what I meant."

"Yes, that is exactly what you meant. And yes, I do in fact have a library of reference books," Rudyard Pfingsten said, advancing across the room to a bookshelf weighted down by a dozen or more heavy volumes. "Family crests. Royal seals. That kind of thing."

"Germany has a king?" Duncan Baxter asked.

"It did once. But no longer. The Great War ended imperial rule. And yet, many of the once noble families still adhere to the old practices, the old ways."

"I could never quite understand quite why a modern nation would still want to pledge allegiance to royalty, a king and queen," Baxter said.

"It is rather simple really," Rudyard Pfingsten said, rummaging through the books on the shelf. "Ordinary people are dumb. They cannot decide for themselves."

"Is that so?" Greeley snapped. "Pity us poor ordinary folk."

"Ah, here it is, my reference book — the Registry," Pfingsten said, his hand upon the thick spine of a leather-bound book. "Americans do not understand royalty. They think it a useless affectation. But royal lines have long served a useful purpose in Europe and especially the British Isles."

Rudyard Pfingsten spoke now as though his rough-edged southern accent had magically disappeared. "Dukes and duchesses, barons and earls. The kings granted fiefdoms and the fief holders kept the local peasants in line. Loyalty was rewarded with protection. Marriage cemented alliances."

Pfingsten continued. "But such arrangements also made for nearly constant warfare. Every fief holder jockeying for position against every other fief holder. Shifting alliances. Competing foreign interests. Treaties and lies and double-crossings."

"Geez," Greeley said. "Sounds like the Sicilian mob to me. One family pitted against every other."

"You are not far off the mark, Marshal. Some families trace back their heritage hundreds of years. My own family is an indirect descendant of the Thienen clan. Thienen are — or at least were — a noble family, part of the German Uradel."

"Your-a-what?" Marshal Greeley stumbled over the words.

"Uradel. Translates roughly as 'ancient nobility.' The Thienen family belongs to the *Equites Originarii.*"

"Another magic word?"

"Original Knights. That is how those two words translate. Original Knights. The oldest families of Schleswig-Holstein, the noble families. These families can trace their ancestry back more than ten centuries, back to the time of Charlemagne, back to the days of the Holy Roman Empire, the Second Reich. Baron von Thienen."

"Von?"

"All the knightly families of the Holy Roman Empire were distinguished by one of two prefixes, either *von* or *zu.* Any family with Uradel status was heraldically entitled to a three-pointed coronet. They were also recognized as being of baronial rank. This is where your signet ring was born."

"I don't think I understand," Greeley said.

"You don't understand much, do you boy? All the legitimate males of a German baronial family inherit the title of Baron or Freiherr from birth. Likewise for the legitimate daughters. Baroness or Freiin."

"But, like you said, the Great War, the First World War, changed everything," Marshal Duncan Baxter said.

"It did indeed. After the Great War ended and the Armistice was signed, there was no longer any legal privilege associated with hereditary titles. From that moment forward, Baron was no longer spelled with a capital B. But the Registry still exists. And I happen to have a complete copy of it."

Rudyard Pfingsten hefted a large, leather-bound book in his hand. He brushed off the layers of dust, carried the aged tome to a nearby table and opened it ever so gently, taking great care not to crack the spine worse than it had already been. A musty smell lingered over the yellowed pages.

"You are looking at history here, gentlemen. These materials date to Charles the Great. A written record of the Original Knights, the *Equites Originarii.* Their colors. Their family crests. Their lineage. Their official seals. A detailed record of the boundaries of each fief. Fences. Landmarks. Roads. Rivers. Rock formations. That kind of thing. If the signet ring is genuine — and mind you, that is a big if — the design on this ring may match one of those in this compendium."

Rudyard Pfingsten flipped through the pages of the book until he came to a section entitled *Familienwappen.*

"Here it is," he said. "Family Crests." Then he started slowly paging through that section, comparing the drawings and sketches to the engraved artwork on the ring.

"Hand me that magnifying glass," Pfingsten said. "This may take some time." He continued to speak as he slowly turned the pages.

"Germans have a long history here in Louisiana. Most settled right here, in these parts, on the east side of the Mississippi River. This area came to be known as the German Coast. Local names still reflect our German heritage, even if they are sometimes written in French. *Bayou des Allemands*, for example, means Bayou of the Germans, that kind of thing. Our intermixing with the French goes back several hundred years, back to the influx of immigrants during the Mississippi Bubble. Early 1700s."

"Mississippi Bubble?"

"The financial bubble that changed a nation. It began two hundred years ago, in the first or second decade of the 1700s. John Law. Convicted murderer. Millionaire gambler. Law purchased the Mississippi Company armed with nothing more than a satchel-full of outrageous promises. His goal was to help grow the French colony right here in Louisiana.

"The King of France, Louis XV, had grand visions of his own. He granted Law's company a trade monopoly to North America and to what we now call the West Indies. At about the same time, the King underwrote a private bank with capital composed of government bills. He renamed it Banque Royale, or Royal Bank. The bank's notes were guaranteed by the King himself."

Here Pfingsten stopped his explanation, looked very closely at a given page in the Registry, compared it to the design on the ring, then decided they did not match and moved on.

"The Mississippi Company absorbed rival trading companies and soon the King granted it a monopoly for commerce on all the seas. Meanwhile, the King's bank began to issue more notes than it could possibly backstop in coinage. This led to economic inflation, which was followed shortly thereafter by a bank run. The value of new paper currency was cut in half.

"Ever the gambler, ever the swindler. Law exaggerated the wealth of Louisiana. In no time at all, the public squandered all its excess liquidity on wild speculation in the company's shares. The popularity of the company's shares was so great it sparked a need for the central bank to issue even more paper currency. Finally, in 1720, the King's bank merged with Law's company and John Law himself was made Comptroller General of France.

"But then the bubble burst. The French government was forced to concede that the face value of all the paper currency issued by Banque Royale was greater than the value of all the metal coinage it held. When investors attempted to convert their notes into specie *en masse,* the bank was forced to stop payment on its paper notes. Law had no choice but to flee the country."

Pfingsten again stopped flipping pages, this time for a much longer time. He picked up the ring, turned it into the light several times and finally said, "I think we have a winner. I think I have found a drawing that matches the design on your ring." He pointed to the page open before him.

"Seriously? To what family does the ring belong?"

"According to these entries, the last known remaining member of the family is Baron Heinrich von Brockdorff. He is listed here as having fought for the Kaiser in the Great War."

"That is all you have?"

"There is a little here on Brockdorff's father. His mother was also of Uradel lineage, Uradel blood. But that is about it. Do you mind telling me how you came to be in possession of this rather special ring?"

Marshal Baxter was about to deliver a made-up explanation for how he came to be in possession of the ring, when an automobile pulled up outside the house. Two men were seated inside.

"Are you expecting anyone?" Greeley asked, peering out through the half-drawn drapery. "They drive a mighty fine car, I will give them that."

Something about the way Marshal Greeley said those words aroused Baxter's suspicion. He, too, looked out the front window. He saw one man, then a second man exit the automobile. That is when he realized he and Greeley were in trouble. The automobile was a Packard. Nico had warned them about a Packard. Now here it was.

It was at this moment that Marshals Baxter and Greeley heard the metallic sound of a gun being cocked behind them. Greeley instinctively reached for his own piece.

"Please do not make me shoot you," Rudyard Pfingsten said calmly. "Please take your hand away from your holster and place your hands upon your head. Both of you. Do it now."

The front door opened and Günter Kesselring stepped into the room. Captain Wilhelm Kronenhauer stepped in right behind him. Baxter and Greeley instantly recognized him as the man from the photograph.

"*Mein Gott.* What do we have here?" Kronenhauer asked, drawing his own weapon and training it on the two U.S. Marshals.

"What we have here are two prisoners of the Third Reich," Rudyard Pfingsten answered. "They came here asking about this." Pfingsten handed Captain Kronenhauer the signet ring that once belonged to Henry Brock.

"And you were actually telling them?" Captain Kronenhauer saw the opened Registry on the table beside the door.

"*Was zum teufel.* What the fuck did you expect me to do? I had to keep them busy somehow until the two of you showed up to save the day, didn't I?"

Kronenhauer nodded as if he understood.

Pfingsten continued. "I will wager you fifty dollars that if you search these two men carefully, you will find Brock's surveillance notebook on them and likely Grimm's book of daily passcodes as well. I suggest, however, that you first confiscate their weapons."

"Yes, of course," Kronenhauer said. "Gentlemen, we can do this the easy way or we can do this the hard way. But I am only going to ask you once. At this time, would you please surrender your weapons?"

"I suggest you do what the man says," Günter Kesselring chimed.

"Remove your weapon from its holster very slowly," Kronenhauer instructed. "Keep your fingers on the butt and away from the trigger. Then turn the gun over and hold it by the barrel. Bend down and place the gun flat on the floor. Then kick it across the floor to me with your left foot. Do it now. *Schnell.* You first."

Captain Kronenhauer motioned to Greeley, who did what he was told.

"Pick it up," Kronenhauer ordered Günter Kesselring. Kesselring growled. He wasn't accustomed to taking orders.

"Now you." He motioned to Duncan Baxter. But Baxter refused to comply.

"Let's say I tell you to go fuck yourself," Baxter said. "What then?"

Kronenhauer raised his weapon and fired it, missing Greeley's head by inches. The bullet lodged in the wall behind him.

"If you fail to comply, I shoot your partner. Then I shoot you."

"You are going to kill us anyhow."

"There is a small chance that I do not. However, if you fail to comply with my instructions, then you are most assuredly a dead man."

Baxter acquiesced. He slowly extracted his weapon from its holster, set it on the floor the way Kronenhauer asked and kicked it away. Günter Kesselring picked up the weapon and handed it to Captain Wilhelm Kronenhauer. Both guns were now on the table behind him.

"Now what?" Kesselring asked.

"Now we kill them both."

Günter Kesselring shook his head furiously. "Then what the fuck are we going to do with the bodies? These two men are federal marshals for Christ sake. People will come looking for them."

Kronenhauer answered. "By the time their bodies are found, we will have completed our job here and be out of the country. If Pfingsten is right, and these two clowns are actually in possession of Brock's notes, my work becomes that much easier. Search them."

Pfingsten raised his hand to object. "Even if we have to take them out later, they first must be interrogated. We need to know who beside these two know of our plans."

"I don't believe they told anyone. Otherwise, why would they even be here? We get the book, we kill them, we get the hell out of here."

Baxter spoke. "Even a Nazi pig cannot be stupid enough to kill two United States Marshals on American soil. Tie us up, if you must. Hold us as hostages if it makes you feel powerful. But if you kill us now you will never get out of this country alive."

"Brave words for a man facing three loaded weapons. We don't need hostages. And you are wasting my time." Then Kronenhauer turned to Pfingsten. "Search them. Find those books. Then take care of these two after we leave. Dump their bodies downstream somewhere. Kesselring and I have much work to do before the day is out."

"*Ya voll*, Captain."

MONDAY
AUGUST 10, 1942
10:45 a.m.

German Coast near New Orleans

"Follow them. See where the bastards go. Whatever else happens, do not let the fuckers out of your sight."

Those were Nico Carolla's instructions to his lieutenants, Luca and Vittorio, following the meeting yesterday afternoon between Nico and the two U.S. marshals at Lafitte's.

The two Sicilians sat parked outside Duncan Baxter's apartment the entire night. He never once left the building, not to take a walk, not to obtain something warm to eat. By early this morning, their wait was over. At approximately 8 a.m., Marshal Greeley arrived on the scene. Minutes later, he and Baxter climbed into the Chevrolet "Stovepipe" and made preparations to leave.

Greeley and Baxter worked their way west out of the French Quarter, then south across the Mississippi River into the German Coast. Luca and Vittorio followed them in their car to the foot of Schaubhut Lane. Then they parked as close as they could along *Bayou des Allemands* Road, remaining careful to stay out of sight. From this vantage point they could keep an eye on the big white house up the lane, as well as any comings or goings, of which one in particular caught their attention.

Half an hour after they arrived, they witnessed the Packard come down *Bayou des Allemands* Road from the main highway and turn up Schaubhut Lane. Both men recognized the car right off. It was the same Packard from the street outside the Mahogany Hall brothel, the same car from the parking lot at the old Jordan River Lumber Company Hotel. An unfamiliar man was at the wheel, another unfamiliar man in the passenger seat. The angle of the sun made it difficult for them to make a positive ID. But the Packard's sudden appearance set the nerves of the two Sicilian men on edge.

After a further half-hour wait, the Packard left again, the same unfamiliar man at the wheel, the same unknown passenger.

"Do we follow the Packard?" Vittorio asked anxiously asked. "Or do we stay with the marshals? We haven't seen either of them come or go for more than an hour now."

Luca shook his head. "Nico was quite specific. He said to stay with the marshals. So we wait. *Capiche?*"

Yet another half-hour slipped by and the two Sicilians were beginning to grow concerned. The sun was almost directly overhead. "I think we should go in," Vittorio said. "The marshals may have gotten in over their heads, as the Americans say."

"Two U.S. marshals? In over their heads? I find that hard to believe," Luca said. "They have badges. They have guns. What kind of man is going to mess with the *polizia*, with two armed officers of the law?"

Then, after two more minutes of waiting, Luca changed his mind. "Okay, get in the car. We are going in."

Rudyard Pfingsten met the two men on the front porch of his home, just as he had met the two marshals earlier in the day, with a shotgun in one hand and an angry dog at his side. Once again, his rough-edged Southern accent was on display.

But the two Sicilians answered in kind, with guns and voices raised. "*Che minchia?* Where the fuck is Marshal Baxter?"

"I don't know what you pair'a wop bastards be talkin' about. I be the only one here and you be trespassin' on private property. I would be within my rights if I shot you pair'a ginzos dead where you stand."

"If you think you can manage it old man, then by all means let's have a go," Luca said, cocking his gun. The Colt .38 was loaded and aimed directly at Pfingsten's belly. "Otherwise, step aside. Give us any further trouble and we will put you in the dirt right along with that ugly dog of yours. Now I will ask you one last time. What have you done with the two U.S. marshals that arrived here an hour ago? Their 'Stovebolt' is still parked out front." Luca pointed to the automobile they had followed to this location under Nico's orders. It had a distinctive shape with high ground clearance, and was easily recognizable, even at a distance.

"I am going to summon the sheriff," Pfingsten said, dog tugging at his leash.

"*Fongoul.* I would like to see you try."

"Who are you people, anyway?"

"Step aside, old man. This is the last time I ask you politely."

When Rudyard Pfingsten did not budge, Luca let loose a round from his .38 directly into the dog's brain. There was a single pathetic yelp and an explosion of blood. The tension on the leash slackened as the carcass fell to one side.

Now Vittorio yelled. "Drop your weapon old man, or you will be next."

Vittorio took the man's weapon and pushed Pfingsten roughly aside. Luca brushed past him and into the house.

As soon as Luca stepped inside, he drew a sharp breath. Marshal Greeley had been shot dead. Marshal Baxter was still alive but just barely. Luca recognized them both from Lafitte's.

Baxter tried to speak. "The Higgins boat plant . . . these people are Nazis . . . they are going to blow it up . . . warn Nico . . . get help . . . " Then Duncan Baxter breathed his last.

"Into the car." Luca ordered Rudyard Pfingsten at the tip of a gun.

"I am not going anywhere with you," Pfingsten said, hand deep in his pants pocket.

Luca punched Pfingsten in the head with the butt of his shotgun. Blood surged from the wound. Pfingsten dropped to one knee, cried out in pain. Whatever he had been fishing for in his pocket was now in his mouth.

"On your feet, *brutto figlio di puttana*, ugly son of a bitch Nazi swine! Into the car!"

"Guinea pig! I go nowhere with you."

Luca hit him again.

"Stop it, Luca!" Vittorio yelled. "You are killing him."

Luca hit Pfingsten yet again. This time the man began to become cooperative. Vittorio half carried, half walked him out the door and down to the car. Luca kept his gun trained on him the entire way.

"Bind his hands and legs," Luca said, instructing Vittorio to use the quarter-inch rope in the trunk.

"Okay, Nazi asshole. Start talking. We saw the Packard leave your house, this house. There were two men in the car. Who were those men and where were they headed?"

"Go to hell."

"Here is the deal, friend. You either talk to us here or Nico will make you talk to him later. But that might require the loss of a finger or two, maybe an eye. You will be happier later if you talk to us now."

"Go to hell," Pfingsten said, biting down hard on the cyanide pill. Such tablets, cyanide enclosed in rubber, were distributed to all German operatives. Death ensued inside of three minutes.

"Okay, let's toss this *pezzo di merda* in the trunk of the car. Next stop, Nico Carolla and the *trattorria.*"

But before either man could move, Rudyard Pfingsten started to shake and foam at the mouth.

"*Che cazzo?*" Vittorio said. "He is like a rabid dog."

Then it was over. Pfingsten was dead.

"Shit! Nico needs to be told what has happened right away. *Rapido.*"

MONDAY
AUGUST 10, 1942
4 p.m.

Western Mediterranean

The HMS *Fidelity* was built in 1920. She served first as the French merchant vessel *La Rhin*, then was later recommissioned by the Royal Navy to serve Her Majesty as a special service vessel during World War II. *Fidelity* measured 265 feet from bow to stern, with a beam that exceeded forty-one feet. She had a crew complement that numbered just under three hundred.

Though she was powered by a large, triple expansion steam engine, HMS *Fidelity* was not a fast-moving ship. Even equipped with that big motor, she could barely make ten knots. Much of the reason had to do with displacement. *Fidelity* was a heavy ship. It weighed in at the better part of twenty-five hundred tons. Plus, she carried with her onboard two catapult-launched Kingfisher floatplanes, one Motor Torpedo Boat, and two Landing Craft of the Higgins variety. She was armed with four, four-inch guns and four deck-mounted torpedo tubes.

For more than a year now, *Fidelity*'s portfolio had been to troll the waters off the coast of southern France conducting secret missions. She operated under the direction of the Special Operations Executive, landing agents on the French or Spanish coast and picking up from those same places Allied POWs who had escaped German prisoner-of-war camps.

But today, and for the last week, her assignment had been different. *Fidelity* was to play host to a high-level secret meeting in advance of Operation Torch. Four men, one woman. Each foreign national had been picked up on shore and brought onboard *Fidelity* by one of her two landing craft.

Commander Ian Fleming. Director of 30 AU and MI6's liaison to the Admiralty. Fleming did not fight in the field along with the 30 Assault Unit. But he did select targets and he did direct operations from behind the lines. At its formation the unit was but thirty-men strong. Under Fleming's watch, it grew to five times that number.

Aldo Carolla. Nico Carolla's great-uncle and senior *Don* of the Palermo Mafia families on the island of Sicily. His network was now providing maps and other valuable intelligence to the Allies ahead of the impending North Africa landings, Tunis and Algiers in particular.

Colonel Daniel Morrison. U.S. Office of Strategic Services, liaison to Wild Bill Donovan, acting chief of OP-20-G's codebreaking unit. Morrison had only just recently arrived in London after a long dangerous trip east that began in the Pacific. First stop, San Diego. Then the Naval Air Station in New Orleans, where he met first with Marine Colonel Peter Morgan, then later that same day with MI6's Havana connection, Martina Amerada. He and Fleming had crossed paths before. Theirs was an uncomfortable alliance.

Mieczyslaw Zygfryd Slowikowski. Polish operative. Staunch British ally. Codename Rygor. Head of Agency Africa, perhaps the single-most successful intelligence operation of the war, now headquartered in Algiers.

Madeleine Barclay. Former French agent. Once known as Madeleine Bayard, now First Officer of the ship and member of the Women's Royal Naval Service. In a testament to her skills as an operative, she was permitted to serve as an officer onboard a British naval vessel, rare even for a Wren. Her rank of First Officer was the equivalent of Lieutenant Commander.

Once the five got settled around the galley table and the boat was safely away from shore, Commander Fleming was first to speak. By some measures he was the highest ranking intelligence officer at the table.

"Operation Torch is due to commence in about ninety days. Our job here today — this afternoon and this evening — is to review operational details as regards the amphibious landings of the Eastern Task Force. There are more meetings to come. But the first order of business today is for the five of us to make an assessment and report our findings to General Eisenhower in Gibraltar and Vice-Admiral Sir Bertram Ramsay. We need to assure them that our planning group has not overlooked recent changes in intelligence that may affect our timing or choice of landing spots."

Rygor spoke up. There was no hiding his heavy Polish accent. "As I have said from outset, Algiers is key to success in North Africa. If we fail to take Algiers, we fail to capture North Africa. Without North Africa as a — how you say *trampolina* in

English?" — Rygor paused to think. Then the word came to him. — "Yes, springboard. Without North Africa as springboard, any attempt to take Europe back from Nazis will be at cost of much blood and treasure."

"Do you even have a clue what the fuck you are talking about?" Colonel Morrison asked. There was disdain for the Polish officer in his voice. "We are going to win this war with or without Algiers, with or without North Africa, with or without the Poles. Just like we are winning it in the Pacific — on our own."

"*Mój Boże.* My God. I have never heard such foolish talk, and from an American no less," Rygor said. "Thanks goodness your President Roosevelt does not think the way you do. Everyone in chain-of-command, from highest ranking general down to lowliest private agrees. North Africa first. Then Europe. Algiers is key to both. If you believe different, you should not even sit at table."

"I am here on behalf of the OSS," Colonel Morrison said. "Bill Donovan wants to make sure you folks don't fuck this thing up."

"Fuck this thing up?" Madeleine Barclay said. Her penchant for foul language was legend. She was a woman in a man's world, not an easy place to be. "No one holds a monopoly on fucking things up, Morrison — and certainly not you Yanks. Bill Donovan can go fuck himself. If not for Commander Fleming and Admiral Godfrey, Wild Bill would not even have so much as a clue how to run a spy agency. The man has been at his desk how long? One week? Ten days? And you come barreling in here with accusations?"

"Madeleine is right," Rygor said to Morrison.

"It's First Officer Barclay to you, you little Polish prick — not Madeleine. You and me are not on a first-name basis, and don't you ever forget that."

"My apologies, First Officer," Rygor said gently. "I mean no disrespect."

"Do not patronize me, you fuck. I earned my bars fair and square, just like everyone else."

"You have made point," Rygor conceded. Sometimes his tenuous hold on English tripped him up. "As I was saying, no one hold monopoly on fucking things up. Why not ask Commander Fleming about that? I am confident he knows a bit more about real world than you do, Colonel. Go ahead. Ask him."

Fleming nodded. "Match point Rygor. He is right, you know. Not a week goes by in this bloody war that someone doesn't cock-up something. War is messy. Advance planning can turn to shit in the blink of an eye. Mistakes will be made. Men will die. The British Army has a saying. TARFU. I think it is *apropos* here. Barely one week from now, we are headed full-bore into the port of Dieppe. Do you know how many different ways this operation can go off the rails? I long ago lost count."

"And yet you plunge ahead blindly," Rygor said. "I have seen operational details of upcoming raid. I believe it to be poorly planned. Unless great many things go right, Dieppe action not likely to succeed as planned."

"*Scusami.* I know not of such things. What make you so smart?" Aldo Carolla wanted to know.

"For openers, there is not enough Allied fire support built into plan," Rygor said. "That is where TARFU really kick in, does it not Commander? How do your English country boys put it? — Things Are Really Fucked Up."

"It is not I who plunge blindly ahead," Fleming retorted. "Operation Jubilee is all Vice-Admiral Lord Mountbatten. Foolish old man. MI6's role in this undertaking is quite limited. My people — 30 Assault Unit — have but one small operation planned to coincide with the larger invasion force."

"But even your sideshow will fail if main event go off book," Rygor said.

Fleming shrugged. It was not that he didn't care; it was that he hadn't any choice in the matter. A soldier was in the business of carrying out orders, not questioning them. Fleming's intransigence on the matter had gotten him nowhere.

"*Mafankulo*, Rygor. You like it when other people fail. I think it is true. I see it in your eyes." Aldo Carolla criticized Mieczyslaw Zygfryd Slowikowski in his harsh, broken English with a Sicilian swear word thrown in for good measure. "What make you so very smart? *Suina Polacco.* Polish swine."

"You expect me to sit here quietly all night and be insulted by some *Mafiosi* scum?" Rygor got to his feet as if he meant to leave the meet. He turned to First Officer Barclay. "Take me home. I am leaving this very instant."

"Sit down and shut the fuck up," Barclay ordered. She was not one to mince words. "You are not going anywhere. Our two countries are allies. We five are going to have to find a way to get along even if it kills every last one of us. Poles with Brits. Brits with Yanks. Yanks with Frogs."

"And the *Italianos*? The *Siciliano*?" Aldo Carolla asked. "What about us? We on front lines of this war." Aldo was still hurt and heartbroken by what had so recently happened to his niece Josepha. He wasn't going to be happy until every last Fascist pig on the island was either dead or strung up by his hand.

"We are collectively all trying to save your Guinea asses, no help from the likes of Mussolini." Colonel Daniel Morrison was indignant.

"*Cazzo!* Sicily is little more to you people than stone to step on along way," Aldo said angrily. "You *Americani* do not give fig about us. All you and Churchill want is Hitler's head on pike."

"Stepping stone, you Guinea," Morrison retorted. "Not stone to step on — stepping stone."

"Enough already!" Barclay shouted. "Both of you, shut the fuck up."

"I have been at this longer than most," Rygor said calmly.

"Not longer than I," Fleming retorted.

"Do not be silly, Commander. I joined *Wojsko Polskie* — Polish Army — in 1918. You were barely out of diapers at time."

"Actually, I was ten years old in 1918. Born May 1908."

"In the Mayfair district of London, according to your dossier," Morrison chimed.

"You trying to say something, Colonel?" Fleming's bullshit radar was set to high. "Trust me when I tell you — I am getting plenty fucking tired of your mouth. Maybe you and I should step outside. Better still, maybe I should have a sit-down with your boss. His offices are but one floor above our own in New York City. Room 3603. Principal operations center for Allied Intelligence."

"All I am saying is that you come from money. I do not."

"Yes, I will keep that in mind for your next performance review," Fleming snapped in anger. "And while we are at it. Do not be so hard on Mieczyslaw. He is absolutely right, you know, about the Dieppe Raid. It may yet turn out to be a total disaster. — But it will not be MI6's disaster. Our operation is a sideshow to the main event, just as Rygor said. 30 Assault Unit. We see a chance to snag an Enigma machine. We cannot pass up that chance."

"So Commander, why don't you give those of us not born in Mayfair a rundown on what might go wrong," Colonel Daniel Morrison said. "We certainly do not want a repeat of those blunders when our boys hit the beaches of North Africa."

"Fair enough," Fleming said. "We all have clearance. The Dieppe Raid. Imminent Allied attack on the port of Dieppe. Northern coast of France. Planned for nine days from now, August 19. The assault is scheduled to begin at 0500 hours that day. Six thousand infantrymen, predominantly Canadian. Primary objective is to seize and hold a major enemy-held port for a short period of time."

"But why take such a risk? The Germans will be expecting you. Why go in without adequate air support?"

"First, to prove that it can be done. Second, to gather intelligence."

"So this assault on Dieppe is little more than a pissing contest?" Morrison asked in disdain.

"I would not use those exact words, but maybe in part," Fleming answered.

"Are you limeys pissing for distance? Or for accuracy?"

Fleming smiled. "I would say accuracy. In addition to the raid, the Allies also want to destroy German coastal defenses, as well as port structures and strategic buildings."

"But my read on this operation is that virtually none of those objectives will be achieved," Rygor said. "Allied fire support is grossly inadequate, like I said. Raiding force will become trapped on beach by manmade obstacles and by German fire. Instead of demonstration of British resolve, bloody fiasco will show world that Allies cannot possibly hope to invade France for very long time yet."

Fleming continued. "I am told that part of the plan is for the RAF to lure the Luftwaffe into open battle. But of course Lord Mountbatten's plan places many of our aircraft at risk, as well as the Royal Navy. SAFU, as they say."

"Do not know that one," Rygor said.

"Self-Adjusting Fuck-Up," Morrison interrupted. "Jarhead slang. United States Marine Corps. Refers to a screwed-up operation that will work itself out given time."

"That's not how it was explained to me," First Officer Barclay said. "I was told it meant — Situation All Fucked Up."

"Forget I even brought it up," Fleming said exasperated. "Now, about MI6's role in all this, the sideshow as you put it. My commando team will be sent in to pinch one of the new four-rotor Enigma code machines, along with the associated codebooks and rotor setting sheets. Bletchley Park is up shit-creek without a paddle. They are having one hell of a time cracking the secrets of the new four-rotor machine."

Fleming continued. "But whatever happens at Dieppe — good or bad — valuable lessons will be learned. Even if the Dieppe Raid fails, whatever mistakes are made will not be repeated in our upcoming landings at Casablanca, Algiers, and Oran."

There was now total quiet around the table as everyone in attendance digested the sobering news.

"Now, can we finally talk about Algiers?" Commander Fleming asked. "My 30 Assault Unit is programmed to land just west of the city. By the way, Aldo, thank you. My team owes you a great debt of gratitude. The detailed maps of the area that you provided us with have been indispensable."

"I wish to accept full credit. But I cannot. The man Rygor did all the — how you say? — legwork on those maps, not I," Aldo Carolla admitted in his fractured English. This, despite their earlier tiff. "We need more men like him, if you ask me."

"Thank you, sir. Agency Africa has been intelligence gathering success, if I say so myself. And I apologize to you for earlier outburst."

Carolla accepted the apology with a nod. "So tell me, Rygor. How does Polish soldier come to be in North Africa?"

"Joined Polish Army in 1918, like I said. Fought in Polish-Soviet War that began in winter of 1919. War last two years, two brutal years. Later, I complete course in advanced military studies — *strategia i taktyka*. Strategy and tactics. Then I work at Polish Ministry of Defense. In 1937 I was transferred to Ministry of Foreign Affairs, then appointed secretary of Polish Consulate in Kiev. My actual function in post was to collect intelligence in southern Russia. When current fight broke out and France — how you say *kapitulować* in English?"

"Capitulated," Fleming said.

"Yes, exactly. When France capitulate to Germany in June 1940, I organized clandestine evacuation of top Polish military personnel. I also establish intelligence service that began to report to military authorities in London. Bletchley Park would never have broken early Enigma codes without our help. A year later, I go to Algiers, where I become man by name of Rygor. My job since then has been to plan for this day. Like I try to explain earlier, Algiers is prize we simply must have before we can move onto Sicily and then Italy. Operation Torch. Allies' first large-scale amphibious landings in Algeria and Morocco. Torch commences three months from now."

Commander Ian Fleming liked and had great respect for this man Rygor. Rygor knew all the rules. — And he knew when to break them.

Never go near children. That was one of Rygor's cardinal rules. Yet, he used his own son, then in his early teens, as a watchman.

Never employ women, not on technical military tasks. That was another of his rules. Yet, his wife was his most trusted associate and helped him with his ciphering.

Never go near hostile security services. Yet, he befriended a disaffected senior police officer who kept him and his family supplied with all the false papers they needed.

The man Rygor was an enigma wrapped in a riddle. In the teeth of every sort of obstacle — some quite local, others in the shape of impractical instructions from exiled Poles in London — Rygor and his sub-agents provided great quantities of data of every sort. Military, economic, geographic, even political. MI6 thought him invaluable. Fleming could not agree more.

"So what is plan?" Rygor asked. "For your unit, I mean."

"On the day of the invasion, now scheduled for 8 November, my men are to land west of the city of Algiers. This will be at a place called *Sidi Ferruch*."

Fleming reached for a map and indicated a location. "Again, thanks to you and Aldo, we now have detailed maps and photographs of the landing area and of the surrounding countryside. Italian naval headquarters are on the outskirts of the city. My team's orders are to locate and pinch battle orders for the German and Italian fleets. That, plus current codebooks and any other documents we can put our hands on. Then get the whole kit-and-caboodle back to London."

Colonel Daniel Morrison interrupted. "As long as we are on the subject of codebooks and the like, get me up to speed on this anagram business, will you?"

Commander Fleming seemed genuinely surprised by the question. "How is it that this information should land on your desk?"

"You gave it to Donovan, remember? You told him of the possible threat to an American target, the one your decoders unearthed. Donovan shared that intell with me."

"Why would Colonel Donovan hand this information off to the likes of you?"

"The likes of me? I am one of the senior members of our decoding team. Or did you not know that? My department oversees several projects, including the Navajo code-talker program. We are working on cracking the anagram puzzle, same as you. Even as we speak, Colonel Donovan is building a database of possible American targets the Germans might try to go after. That list should be in the hands of Bletchley Park within a matter of days, perhaps sooner."

"I will tell Fieldstone to expect it. But tell me the truth. Has your team made any progress whatsoever in cracking the riddle yet?"

"No, not so far."

Now Aldo Carolla interrupted. "I find it — how you say? — *strano* — that our *discussione* should turn to subject of anagrams."

Fleming thought a second. He knew tidbits of Italian. "*Strano*. Strange. Peculiar."

"Yes, peculiar," Aldo said. "I find it peculiar that our discussion should turn now to subject of anagrams."

"How so?"

"This is a type of word play, yes? The game is to again mix letters of a word or phrase to generate new word or phrase, using all same letters exactly once. Yes?"

"That is correct, Aldo," Fleming said. "What about this do you find so peculiar? Do Sicilians not play this game?"

"Yes, I know of young people on the island who do. But that is not what I find so peculiar."

"What then?"

"My nephew Nico in America. We often exchange *telegrammi*. Not long ago, he told me in wire that just such a book had fallen into his hands. He said book was filled with page after page of anagrams. He turn book over to a United States Marshal. This is like policeman, yes?"

"Jesus God," Fleming said jumping to his feet. "I must have that marshal's name right away. That man may hold the very key to solving this puzzle and figuring out what the American target is. How soon can you reach your nephew, Aldo?"

"I could not say," Aldo replied. "War make communication difficult. Nico and I do not often have occasion to speak. We usually *corrispondere* through intermediary."

"Officer Barclay, please take this man down to the ship's wire room." Fleming said excitedly. "Aldo needs to send a priority message."

"Commander, you know I cannot do that," Madeleine replied. "We must maintain radio silence until well after this meeting is adjourned."

"To the contrary. This is a risk worth taking. Please. Talk to the captain. Take Aldo to the wire room. We absolutely need to track down that U.S. Marshal as soon as possible."

First Officer Madeleine Barclay nodded reluctantly. "Follow me," she said to Aldo Carolla, then led him down the narrow passageway toward the wireless room. The ship was rolling gently with the swell.

Rygor turned to Fleming. "You have piqued my interest, Commander. Can you share with me latest anagram you have decrypted? *Moja żona* has been known to work wonders with ciphers."

"*Moja żona?*"

"My wife, for goodness sake. It is Polish. It means 'my wife'."

Fleming nodded, as if he understood. "Thus far, I have three actually, all employing the same thirteen letters. In the order received, these are the three Bletchley Park has given me. Let me write them down for you:

BEAUT KRAUT EGO
BOA AUK TREE GUT
TAKEOUT EAR BUG

This latest one, which we just broke, could be an instruction of some kind. Or perhaps a warning. At MI6 we are experimenting with tiny listening devices. We call these devices bugs. The prominent use of the terms 'ear' and 'bug' in this message might be a synonym for listening or listening device."

Fleming continued. "Aside from that, the only other two words that have popped out so far from unscrambling these anagrams which might be applicable to the war is the word GREEK. Also the word ROUGE. Operation Rouge was a top-secret name MI6 once considered for an amphibious landing on Malta. But that particular operation was scrubbed, never funded, never executed."

Rygor already had a fresh piece of writing paper in his lap. He had written down the thirteen letters from the anagrams. Now, from the list, he struck out the letters G,R,E,E, and K. He studied the remaining letters, made a few notes, and then spelled out a new word, "U-BOAT."

"Oh, my God! A U-boat? Where?" Colonel Morrison shook with fear. "Are we under attack?"

"No, you ninny." Rygor exclaimed. "Look at remaining letters in anagram. Once you subtract GREEK from original thirteen letters, it is right there. U-BOAT."

"You are frigging brilliant," Fleming said. "I have had two Wrens working on this problem for more than two days. You crack it in less than twenty seconds. Is that even possible?"

"I hardly think it cracked," Rygor said. "I found one word. And still three letters remain. More to point, that word only fell out because we began by assuming that the word GREEK is correct. The whole thing hinges on that. It may be — what is word in English? — a mirage. There are yet thousands of combinations to consider."

"I don't believe in coincidence," Fleming said. "You have solved it."

"Sometimes working in language not your own make solve puzzle such as this one easier. But I lack your conviction that puzzle has been solved. May I hand puzzle to wife to work her magic on? She is genius in family when it come to ciphers."

"Why yes, of course."

Just about then the ship's bell began to ring. *This was the signal that they were under attack.*

"All Stations! All Stations! Possible bogey at seven o'clock. Smoke stack sighted. Enemy destroyer. Prepare to come about. I repeat. We are under attack. Enemy destroyer at seven o'clock. Man the guns! Battle Stations!"

The siren went off. An explosive shell landed in the water near the *Fidelity*. By now the first team was at the four-inch guns, loading shells.

"General Quarters! General Quarters!"

The XO's orders boomed out of the loudspeaker in rapid, shotgun fashion. "Launch Motor Torpedo Boat. *MTB 105* in the water. MTB in the water."

The gunnery teams launched flares over the target area. They lit up the night sky bright as day.

"Load torpedo tubes three and four. On my mark. Fire!"

"Possible snorkel at nine o'clock.   Depth charges in the water."

"Crew to the Kingfisher. Ready at the catapult. Engage, engage, engage!"

TUESDAY
AUGUST 11, 1942
10 a.m.

Bletchley Park, England

"We have intercepted yet another wire from Waffen-SS Headquarters in Bremen. We have strong reason to believe that Heinrich Himmler or someone close to him is the author of this wire. It is a frantically long transmission. Uncharacteristic of an SS communication. Something big is definitely afoot."

Shaun Yardley held the typed copy in his hand. He passed it over the top of his desk to Liam Fieldstone, his boss, who studied it closely. Copies had already been distributed to Ian Fleming's group at the Admiralty.

"How many does that make?" Fieldstone asked.

"Four, that I am aware of," Yardley said. "Four messages, four anagrams." Yardley displayed a nervous tic courtesy of his obsessive-compulsive disorder.

"There seems to be no logical end to this game," Fieldstone groused. "What is the anagram this time? For the last twelve hours we have been puzzling over the GREEK U-BOAT theory advanced by Commander Fleming. Ever since the attack on the *Fidelity*, where Fleming and the others barely escaped with their lives, he has become dug-in on the subject. Not even Rygor's unit has been able to make much of it. Rygor now believes Fleming's take on the whole thing is entirely wrong. If this series of messages has anything at all to do with North Africa, we are running out of time."

Shaun Yardley pointed to his chalkboard. There were thirteen capital letters written horizontally across the board in alphabetic order. The letters corresponding to the words GREEK and U-BOAT had been struck through with chalk leaving just three letters clear and legible: A-T-U.

"Does that mean anything to you?" Shaun Yardley asked. "Three letters. A-T-U."

"Constance and the birds in the Wren nest have been working on that," Fieldstone said. "Rygor too. Rearranged, the letters spell TAU. What might that mean, you ask? The relevance is unclear. TAU is the nineteenth letter of the Greek alphabet. Perhaps it stands for the nineteenth day of the month, or the nineteenth hour of the day."

"The nineteenth day of the month is one week from now."

"What is it with you, Yardley?" Fieldstone said with irritation. "Think outside the box. Beyond the obvious connotations, all we have thus far as a meaning for TAU is either a city in Romania or else a tiny island in the South Pacific, little more than an atoll really. Either location could be an Axis target, although for what reason is not entirely clear. Neither location holds much value militarily, certainly not enough to warrant such a sophisticated code."

"Maybe this latest message will help," Yardley said. "The anagram this time is: GATE OAK TUB RUE. Same thirteen letters. The possibilities are endless. Rue is French for street. Oak Street? Near the gate? What gate? My head is spinning."

Shaun Yardley continued. "There may, however, be one consolation prize. This time we may have something more to go on than just a riddle."

"You have my attention," Liam Fieldstone said, looking again at the typed copy of the long, convoluted message Bletchley Park had just deciphered from Himmler's office.

"We may have caught ourselves a break; two actually. First, take a look at line twelve. Do you see it? Do you see the word I am talking about?"

Liam Fieldstone peered at the paper. "Line twelve?"

Yardley nodded in the affirmative.

"Kesselring?"

"Yes, that is the word. Kesselring. General Field Marshall Albert Kesselring. One of the highest ranking officers in the *Luftwaffe*. The very man we may come up against in North Africa and Sicily."

"A name that prominent in a poorly coded message? That is suspicious on its face."

"Indeed. Now take a look at line four. Another unexpected word. The message-sender may have been in a rush. We think the word is Tucker."

Fieldstone was confused. "What is Tucker?"

"Not what. Who. Preston Tucker. An American inventor of some note. What makes that man important to our discussion today is the gun turret our Mr. Preston Tucker has invented."

"Should I know what that is?" Fieldstone asked in an impatient tone.

"No, probably not. But an American combat soldier would," Yardley said. "The Tucker gun turret. A swiveling ball turret that has been placed on nearly all of America's bombers, all her high-speed PT boats, all their landing craft. A simply astonishing piece of equipment, a game-changer when it comes to beating the Jerrys."

"Once again, you have my attention," Fieldstone said. "How does our Mister Tucker fit in with all this? Why would his name be so prominently mentioned in a Waffen-SS message sent by Himmler?"

"Why indeed! Tucker turrets are manufactured by the Eureka Tug-Boat Company."

"What of it?"

"Eureka Tug also manufactures the famous Higgins boat."

"Go on."

"Andrew Higgins has several manufacturing plants in and around the city of New Orleans. New Orleans is in the southern United States, on the north shore of the Gulf of Mexico."

"Ah, the noose tightens," Fieldstone said. "People make fun of you, Yardley. But you are a veritable walking encyclopedia. All lines of inquiry now point to New Orleans. First, Wilhelm Kronenhauer. Now this. Clearly, the target must be along the coast there somewhere."

"People make fun of me?" Like so many people with mental disorders of one form or another, they do not recognize the defect in themselves.

Fieldstone cocked his head to one side but said nothing.

Shaun Yardley continued. "If all lines of inquiry now point to New Orleans, I say we get the Yanks in on this thing bloody soon. We need to reconsider this series of anagrams in terms of every high-value target in or around the city of New Orleans, including the Higgins boat plant and any army or naval facilities."

Fielding nodded energetically. "Wire Donovan. Wire him right fucking now."

•
•

August 11, 1942, 11 a.m.
Bletchley Park, England

"Christ, where does a girl even begin with a list like this?" Constance McCallister asked. "I have only been here one week. But have you ever seen such a thing? The list runs on for pages. And the soddy thing is not even alphabetized, just helter-skelter. How in blazes did that bloody Yank put together a list like this on such short notice?"

Liam Fieldstone shared the woman's chagrin. "I am told he began compiling this list even before we requisitioned it. I think Commander Fleming had a hand in that."

"Has a hand in everything these days, doesn't he?"

"A question for another branch of the military perhaps. My question to you, Constance, is something quite different. Can you put two of your sharpest girls to work on this list right immediately now?"

"No, I do not see how. We do not perform magic tricks in Hut 4, you know that, right? No bunny rabbits to pull out of our hats. The countdown to Operation Torch has begun. Every spare body I have is on that."

"Two hours," Fieldstone said. "Two girls for two hours. If nothing shakes loose in two hours, bring the list back to my office and return to work on Operation Torch traffic. Agreed?"

Constance nodded her head in the affirmative. "Okay, tell me again what we are looking for here."

"Yes, quite. With the help of our MI6, the Yanks have formed a central intelligence agency they call the Office of Strategic Services, the OSS. Her Majesty's Secret Service has trained practically every single one of their people. Much of the physical training takes place in the backwoods of North America. The head of the agency is an American. Colonel Wild Bill Donovan, they call him. Some sort of a cowboy, or so I gather. What you have in front of you is a list this Donovan has prepared, a list of possible American targets a Jerry saboteur might wish to go after."

Constance chuckled. "Since when did we start working for the Americans, a cowboy no less?"

"Since one of your girls broke that Waffen-SS code that suggests the Nazis have targeted a U.S. facility," Fieldstone replied.

"It is always nice to be told that you are loved," Constance said severely. "So what actually is on this list? It runs on for pages."

"Yes, I can see that. Donovan has assembled on this list every U.S. coastal military asset he can think of, plus every U.S. corporation with a federal procurement contract, every railroad line, every munitions depot, every lock and dam on rivers in the Deep South."

"Goodness. Is there no way to narrow the list of possible targets?"

"Actually, it is worse than you think, Constance. A nearly impossible job, in my estimation. Even with this list in hand, we cannot be sure whether the German codename for the intended target is its legal name or some nickname or even an abbreviation."

"I absolutely do not follow," Constance said.

"Let me give you a for-instance. In some social circles, NOLA is American shorthand for New Orleans, Louisiana. Other Americans colloquially call it the Big Easy. Who can say how the Nazis refer to it? New York City is called the Big Apple. Chicago, the Windy City. The target may very well be on Donovan's list. But in their communications the Jerrys may be calling it by some other name entirely. We are wandering blind in the dark, I tell you. All we have for certain are the thirteen letters from the four anagrams and this list of possible targets. We need to find where these two data sets intersect. We need to make soup from Irish potatoes."

"Two girls for two hours is hardly enough."

"My original point."

"Then let me stir the pot a bit more for you," Constance said. "Since last we spoke, I dug further into the question of what TAU might stand for or what it might mean. I came up with two further meanings I would like to share with you."

"Go on."

Constance nodded. "Not only is Tau the nineteenth letter of the Greek alphabet as I have already said, but in the ancient Greek system of numerals Tau had a value of three hundred."

"Woman, you teach me something new every day."

"In your dreams," Constance snapped.

"I didn't mean it that way," Fieldstone replied.

"Of course you did, Liam. You are a slug. Once a slug, always a slug. Shall I go on?"

Fieldstone silently nodded.

"As I was saying: In the ancient Greek system of numerals Tau had a value of three hundred. Taken alone, the number three hundred tells us absolutely nothing. It could stand for any number of things, maybe a clue to the intended target. Three hundred could be a distance, three hundred miles perhaps, or three hundred kilometers. It could be a compass bearing, three hundred degrees. It could be a time of day, 0300 hours. It could even be the three hundredth day of the year, about two months from now."

"You are one brilliant woman. Did anyone ever tell you that? And pretty too." He put his hand on her shoulder in a very familiar way.

"If you want to make a pass at me, Fieldstone, think again. I already have a man."

"Shaun Yardley? That Lothario with a nervous tic hardly qualifies as a man."

"And you do?"

"Can we please get back to it?"

"Yes, Tau. Aside from its value of three hundred in the ancient Greek system of numbers, there is another possibility we might consider. The Franciscan orders consider Tau to be a symbol of their order. St. Francis of Assisi considered Tau to be a symbol of redemption and the Cross. Nearly every Franciscan church has painted a Tau with two crossing arms, both with stigmata, one of Jesus, the other of St. Francis."

"Stigmata?"

"Marks on the hands and feet resembling the wounds of crucifixion."

"Ah yes, I see. Distinctive marks painted on the two crossed arms, say on a stain-glass window."

"Precisely. And members of the Secular Franciscan Order wear a stylized wooden T — or Tau Cross — on a string with three knots around the loop."

"So what does all this spiritual mumbo-jumbo get us?"

"I really have no clue. The job of a Wren, even a pretty one, is to gather and process information. The job of a Wren's boss — even an annoying one — is to separate the wheat from the chaff. And while we are busy separating things, maybe it would help narrow down Colonel Donovan's list if I knew what kind of attack we are expecting. A bomb dropped from the sky? An explosive charge placed on the inside wall of a factory building? An artillery shell fired from the deck of a ship?"

Liam Fieldstone sighed. "It will probably not be a bomb dropped from the sky. Captain Kronenhauer is not an aeroplane pilot; he is an infantryman. But it might be a shell of some sort fired from the deck of a ship. One of our working theories includes the possibility of a U-BOAT. Aside from that, we haven't much to go on. This guy Kronenhauer. He is the key to the puzzle. We need to find the bastard."

"Needle in the haystack?"

"More like lizard in the bayou," Fieldstone quipped.

"So how does one capture a lizard?" Constance asked.

"I guess in the ordinary way," Fieldstone said. "Find out what a lizard likes to eat and use its favorite food as bait."

"Yes. Or lower the temperature in the room until they become stiff from the cold and stop moving."

"Or entice him into the open with a female of the species." His hand lingered on her shoulder.

"Ah, and what would you know about the female of the species?"

TUESDAY
AUGUST 11, 1942
11 p.m.

New Orleans

Captain Wilhelm Kronenhauer knew better than to walk in the front door of any place he wanted to be. His training had made it instinctual. The rules were the same no matter where he went: tavern, grocery store, or factory.

Always use the side door. Or, better still, the back door.

So, if he was going to use explosives to blow up an industrial plant, a facility surrounded by fences and protected by guards and guard dogs, he could not walk in the front gate. He could not scale the fence or shoot out the lights. He could not take out the guards. He could not outrun the dogs.

The only way in was from the water, either from the shores of Lake Pontchartrain or from the concrete banks of Industrial Canal. Every Higgins boat manufactured by the Eureka Tug-Boat Company, every fast-moving PT boat, every landing craft of any sort; they all had to leave the plant in the hold of a ship or on top of a flatcar. Supplies arrived the same way, either overland by railcar or across the water by barge. Captain Kronenhauer meant to gain access to the plant that same way — from the water.

Captain Kronenhauer sat low in the boat, dark cap angled down over his head. The boat was an earlier model Higgins boat, the sort booze smugglers used during Prohibition. Plywood frame, single rear engine, easy to run up on the banks of any lake or river, no machine-gun turret. He had with him in the boat individually wrapped satchels of *plastiksprengstoff*, rolls of detonation cord, and a supply of pencil detonators, a form of blasting cap. He had, in other words, everything he needed to destroy much of the boat assembly plant. On his person he carried a semi-automatic pistol in his shoulder holster and an infantry knife and flashlight on his web belt.

There were nine buildings in all on the grounds of the facility. Nine, relatively nondescript buildings. Most were small; one was immensely large.

Since Wilhelm Kronenhauer was working alone and had at most only a few hours until daylight, he could not hope to wire every last one of those buildings to blow. So Kronenhauer had to be choosy. He had sufficient time and materials to take out several targets — a section of rail line, both loading docks, and perhaps one or more of the hammerhead lifting cranes. He reasoned that if he could destroy these targets, that ought to inflict sufficient damage on the place to halt full-scale boat production for several months, perhaps longer. Himmler would be happy, perhaps ecstatic. Success might place the rank of *SS-Sturmbannführer* within Kronenhauer's reach, the German army equivalent of Major.

Kronenhauer pulled the boat up and out of the water, tied it off to one of the dozen or more rusted iron posts that dotted the concrete seawall. He took the first satchel of plastic explosives from the boat, along with a roll of detcord, and crept in darkness along the shoreline to the nearby rail line. He knew from experience that the more sensitive detonators were best kept separate from the less volatile chemical explosives and detonation cord until the last possible moment. He would have to return again to the boat later to retrieve the blasting caps.

Detonation cord — or as military types called it, detcord — was a brilliant addition to a demolition team's toolkit. It had a core of RDX bound by textile yarn and finished on the outside with a waterproof layer of plastic and wax. Such cord was perfect for use by demolition crews and in underground mines. Once the detcord was initiated, it detonated along its entire length at velocities exceeding 20,000 feet per second. This allowed a demolition team to position itself at a safe distance from the center of the explosion.

The cord itself could be initiated with any of several types of blasting caps. Initiators fell into two broad categories — electric or non-electric. Choices included an electric match or fuse head, also mercury fulminate. Kronenhauer had with him in the boat a supply of Number Ten pencil detonators, so-called because of their size, shape, and time delay. The No. 10 could be screwed into a blasting cap.

After actuation, a pencil detonator was silent in operation. It did not fizz or make a sound. What it lacked was clock-like accuracy. A pencil detonator gave little more than an approximate time-delay. A two-hour detonator, like Kronenhauer intended to use tonight, might be accurate to within plus or minus five minutes.

A further inaccuracy was introduced because of the ambient temperature. The time-delay on a pencil detonator depended on the speed of a chemical reaction. Cold temperatures slowed reaction time. Heat speeded it up.

The pencil detonator's main virtue was its small size and light weight. They were easy to carry and simple to use, the perfect combination for a covert operation.

Tonight, Captain Kronenhauer was employing the identical No. 10 Delay Switch commonly used by British SOE, the so-called timing pencil. Its key component was a brass tube with a copper section at one end. That end, the copper end, contained within it a glass vial filled with cupric chloride.

Beneath the glass vial was a spring-loaded striker. The striker was under tension and held in place by a thin metal wire. The time-delay switch was set in motion by crushing the copper section of the tube. This would break the glass vial and release the cupric chloride into the tube.

Once the chemical was released into the tube, it would begin to slowly erode the metal wire that held back the striker. When the wire eventually gave way, the spring-loaded striker would be propelled down the hollow center of the detonator tube. It would strike the percussion cap at the other end of the tube and ignite the detcord that the cap was attached to. Moments later, an explosion.

Kronenhauer set to work. There was only one rail line running into the factory yard. He could only guess at its importance. But based on the large scale of the assembly plant, the entire operation might depend on the existence of that single rail line. In fact, galvanized steel, carloads of marine engines, lumber, rivets, bolts, paint, everything needed to build any of several models of boat arrived on flatcars. At the end of the day, those same flatcars exited on that same rail line carrying finished boats. Disable this section of track and production would be crippled.

The same went for the lifting cranes. They were few in number and strategically placed. The dockside crane lowered each finished boat into the canal for its final wet-test before delivery. Once the Navy inspector signed off on it, the boat would be lifted back out of the water with the same dockside crane and placed sideways on a flatcar for shipment. Fifty-four lifts per business day. Loss of a single crane would cause a severe bottleneck.

The science of blowing up a rail line was almost as old as railroading itself. The standard rule for derailing a train car required removing a minimum twenty feet of track, a length of rail approximately equal to the fixed wheelbase of a locomotive. To shatter such a length of track required a single charge be placed directly over each wooden tie along the selected twenty feet of rail. Standard spacing between ties on most rail gauges ranged from eighteen to twenty-three inches. Do the math and that came to twelve charges, plus or minus.

To wire that many charges to a single detonator, taking into account knots and the like, required no less than twenty-four feet of detcord, often much more. Similar rules of thumb existed for all targets, depending on material, whether it be steel, concrete, or even earthen supports.

Captain Kronenhauer had a long night of work ahead of him. Working alone in the dark in an unfamiliar location made for slow, tedious progress. One hour minimum to place charges on the ties of the rail line spur. More charges at the two main loading docks. More at the base of the giant hammerhead crane.

Plus there were obstacles to overcome. Tonight thus far he had to twice dash for cover when a night watchman happened by while doing his rounds. For the moment, Kronenhauer still remained undiscovered.

Kronenhauer thought it through in his mind. Demolishing the big loading crane was an exercise in enlisting gravity as his ally. This particular type lifting crane was of the hammerhead-style, a type of crane invented by the Germans and later perfected by the British for use in their shipyards to support the construction of warships. Andrew Higgins used such cranes to load and unload barges and railcars. Back in Wilhelm Kronenhauer's Germany, his countrymen would have called them *hammerkran.*

The hammerhead was a giant, fixed-jib cantilever crane. It consisted of a steel-braced tower on which revolved a large, horizontal girder, what tradesmen called a jib or double cantilever. The forward part of the crane carried a lifting trolley. The jib extended backwards over the crane's center of gravity. This positioning served a dual purpose: to form a support for the machinery and cables and to counterbalance the weight of loads being raised or lowered. Such an arrangement also made it relatively easy to throw the crane off-balance and thus tip it over.

Simply knock out one or more of the vertical supports and over she went. *Gravity could be a bitch.*

THREE HOURS LATER

WEDNESDAY
AUGUST 12, 1942
2:30 a.m.

New Orleans

Nico Carolla had been proactive. It was in the man's blood. After all that had happened, after all the deceptions and lies, he no longer trusted anyone.

What was real and what was not? A father that was his grandfather, a brother who had never been, a mother he had never known, outsiders who could not be trusted, insiders and friends who wished him evil. Caution had now become the name of the game.

After Nico's meeting two-and-a-half days ago with the two U.S. marshals at Lafitte's Blacksmith Shop, he had doubled the number of roving guards inside the gates of the Industrial Canal and City Park Avenue plants. These were Andrew Higgins' two largest production facilities, and Nico controlled the labor force in both locations.

But in beefing up the number of roving guards, Nico had mustered every bit of spare manpower on his payroll. His roster depleted, he now had to depend on outsiders, men he barely knew and could not entirely trust. Nico hoped that after the two marshals presented their evidence to the Navy, additional manpower would be forthcoming from the Naval Air Station or the Marine Corps to cover the other plants. He had already spoken to Colonel Morgan about it.

Securing the plants was a logistic nightmare, especially along the waterfront. It had occurred to Nico that a saboteur might try to gain access to the grounds of the plants from the water. As part of his heightened security, Nico now had pairs of armed men walking the seawall every ninety minutes or so. That is how Kronenhauer's moored boat was first discovered.

"Someone is on the property," the first guard said to the second, shining his light into the beached boat. The first man's name was Alejandro.

After signing his latest production contract with the Navy, Andrew Higgins had call boxes installed at several strategic locations on the grounds and inside the main assembly building. With these call boxes in place, a roving guard might ring the main security office detailed at the front gate. Each box required a key, and each of the regular guards carried one on their person.

"Could be just some fuckin' fisherman," the second guard said. He had been drinking on the job, as he did every night. "Day shift has to chase them away all the time. Any nigger or white man with a boat and a paddle can fish these waters."

The second guard swung his light slowly from left to right in front of him. Swinging the light one way illuminated the nearest corner of Building Four twenty-five yards away. Swinging the light the other way illuminated the closest corner of Building Three even farther away. The light was weak and revealed nothing but grass wet with dew and a few tiny lizards scurrying from here to there.

The first man, Alejandro, still had his light focused on the boat. He saw now the satchel of explosives in the bottom of the boat, along with two rolls of what he knew to be detonation cord. He did not recognize the box of detonators for what they were.

"This looks bad," Alejandro said. He shone his light along the seawall, first one way, then the other.

"What looks bad?" the second man asked, not really giving a damn. The night air was hot and humid, heavy like fog. The damp air stuck to a man, made him sweat through his shirt. He was already three sheets to the wind.

"Look in the boat, you fool. Explosives." Alejandro pointed.

"Maybe our fisherman is hunting gators with sticks of dynamite," the second man said. "It has been known to happen, you know." His eyes were red, bloodshot and tired.

"And our poacher needs detonation cord to hunt alligators?" Alejandro said, reaching into the boat and pulling out a fifty-foot-long roll of detcord.

"Okay," the drunken man said. "What would you have me do?"

"Take my key. Go to the nearest call box. We need to call this in."

"You found the fucking boat, you call it in. Me? I'm going to walk further along the seawall and see what I can see."

"All you want to do is have another swig of whiskey from that bottle you're toting," Alejandro said. "I can smell the liquor on your breath from here."

"What does that make you? Sherlock Holmes?"

"Fuck you. I will call in the alarm myself. There is a call box outside Building Three. You wait here. I will be right back. Then we go looking for this fisherman together."

"Building by building? That will take all night."

"Yes, building by building. Now stay put. I will be right back."

Alejandro walked briskly away and toward the nearest call box. He fumbled in his pocket for the call key.

Kronenhauer had witnessed the entire exchange from the safety of his hiding spot behind the thick layer of rock ballast that supported the railroad tracks he had already wired to blow.

When he first saw the lantern lights down by his boat, he immediately fell prone. Now he got slowly to his feet. His placement of charges and stringing of detonation cord was not complete. Plus, he still had to run detonation cord to the charges at the base of the crane and the supports buttressing the loading dock.

But it could not be helped. He first had to deal with this pair of Guinea pigs.

The two lantern lights were moving in different directions, one along the concrete seawall in a slow leisurely manner, the other toward one of the factory buildings in a very deliberate way.

That man must be going for help, Wilhelm Kronenhauer decided.

Kronenhauer instinctively knew which of the two men he had to deal with first. He pulled his infantry knife from his belt and sprinted across the wet grass.

Twenty strides later and he was there.

At just about the last second, Alejandro heard his approach and turned. With one arm he tried to deflect the incoming knife.

But Kronenhauer had the advantages of surprise, youth, and strength. He quickly overpowered the older man and slit his throat. Warm blood shot all the way up Kronenhauer's arm. The dead man's lantern clattered to the ground.

The sound brought the second man up short. He swung his light in the direction of the sound and yelled the first man's name.

"Alejandro? Are you alright?"

Kronenhauer drew his Luger pistol and made directly for the second man's light. When he had closed the distance by half, he knelt, took careful aim and fired.

"Shit! You have shot me." The man was more than half-drunk and his brain was slow to react to the pain.

Kronenhauer fired again. This time the shot was followed by a sharp exclamation and a loud splash. Kronenhauer had hit the man square, toppling him backward, dead into the lake.

Now Kronenhauer eased his way back toward the parked boat, sticking to the shadows wherever possible. He needed those No. 10 pencil detonators, still in the boat, if he was to have any hope of successfully completing tonight's mission.

**WEDNESDAY
AUGUST 1, 1942
8:30 a.m.**

Bletchley Park, England

"I broke it! I finally broke it!"

Constance McCallister was ecstatic, more than her usual self. Liam liked this about her, when her chest rose with passion and her cheeks reddened with excitement. He would give anything to be with her again. But she would not have him.

"Good God, woman," Liam said, grabbing her hand. "You broke the code? Solved the letter anagram? That is good news indeed. Show me what you have come up with."

"Eureka Tug-Boat," she said pulling back her hand. The man was too touchy-feely for her taste.

"Come again?"

"Eureka Tug-Boat."

"I have no idea what that means," Fieldstone said, miffed that she had pulled away so quickly. "Let me see your work."

Constance handed him her notes. "The Eureka Tug-Boat Company. An American outfit. Higgins Industries. They manufacture and assemble the landing craft that every branch of the service uses, both American and British. That is the answer. It has to be."

Liam looked at the four intercepts they had already decoded. He counted the number of letters, crossed them out one by one in his mind, considered the thousands of possibilities.

BEAUT KRAUT EGO
BOA AUK TREE GUT
TAKEOUT EAR BUG
GATE OAK TUB RUE

Beneath the four intercepts, Constance had written the solution in her own hand:
EUREKA TUG BOAT
"The Higgins boats?"

Constance was beaming. She nodded her head vigorously up and down.

"Good God, woman. You have solved it! I have to call the Admiralty right away. Whitehall says the war simply cannot be won without those boats. Hundreds arrive from America in Falmouth and elsewhere each month. Andrew Higgins builds them right there in New Orleans, the place in the U.S. for a Nazi sabotage that we have suspected all along!"

WEDNESDAY
AUGUST 12, 1942
3 a.m.

New Orleans

Wilhelm Kronenhauer bent over the boat, reached up under the seat, pulled up a small, waterproof box filled with blasting caps. He had already placed the explosives on the rail ties, also on the legs of the loading dock, and the stabilization cables and support towers of the loading crane. He had killed the two roving guards, stabbed one, shot the other. He had run the many yards of detcord to a spot just beyond the seawall, the very spot he was headed for now.

Two hours remained until sunrise. As soon as he finished the job, he would jump in his Higgins boat, make a run for Industrial Canal and Lake Pontchartrain beyond. He had parked the Packard on the water's edge near the junction of Industrial Canal and the lake. From there he would make a final run west and south to the German Coast, Rudyard Pfingsten's house on Schaubhut Lane, and, hopefully, a secure way back home to Germany.

Now he heard dogs barking in the distance.

Should he be worried?

Kronenhauer's heart was beating faster.

Had someone heard the gunshot when he took out the second guard? Had someone found the dead body of the first guard beside Building Three?

Now Kronenhauer heard boats out on the water of Lake Pontchartrain, marine motors running hot and fast. More than one boat. Maybe as many as three. They were approaching shore fast.

Was he trapped?

That terrible thought crossed Captain Kronenhauer's mind now as he sprinted at top speed toward the business end of the daisy chain of detcord he had laid out earlier. His original plan had been to set the detonators, then use the time-delay to get away clean and undetected. Now he had to do something much more immediate.

Suddenly, Kronenhauer was bathed in a flood of yellow light. It was streaming in from three sources out on the open water. Three flood lamps. Three exceptionally fast, motor torpedo boats. All closing fast on the shore and on his position.

Now, from the opposite direction, the direction of Buildings Three and Four, came new sounds. Guards. Guard dogs. Loud voices. The roar of a bullhorn.

He was trapped!

"Freeze, you bastard!" the man with the bullhorn yelled.

Kronenhauer ignored the order, got down on his knees, and unpacked the box of No. 10 pencil detonators. He was out of time and out of options. Rather than take the time to carefully set the detonators according to protocol, which would have meant crushing the copper tube section and calmly walking away, he would instead dump them in a pile and pound on them with the butt of his gun.

He reasoned it out in his mind. If he struck one of the detonators with the butt of his gun, it would set off a chain reaction. The single violent impact would ignite the entire length of detonation cord.

"Freeze!" the same man yelled again. Kronenhauer could hear the approach of running men.

For a second time, Captain Kronenhauer ignored the order to stop moving. Instead, he reached down to remove his semi-automatic pistol from its holster. At about the same moment, a warning shot was fired in his direction from a spot near the water. The bullet whizzed by, just above his head.

"Last warning, you asshole!" The voice was much closer now. The three incoming boats were nearly upon him. Nico Carolla was in the closest boat, along with Luca. Vittorio was at the helm of boat number two.

Kronenhauer continued to ignore the instruction. His gun was now in his hand. He was but seconds away from striking the pile of detonators with the butt of his gun.

Almost done, he thought bravely.

That is when the second shot rang out.

Kronenhauer did not know from which direction the bullet came. All he felt was searing pain. It rocketed through his upper abdomen like a hot flame.

A fast-moving bullet packs a tremendous amount of kinetic energy. Kronenhauer fell forward onto the ground. It suddenly hurt to breathe.

"Grab him," one of the Marines said. Only two hours earlier, Nico had reached out to the naval officer he had met that day in Higgins' office, Marine Colonel Peter Morgan, the same man Martina had directed him to. "Grab him I say, and get him the hell away from those blasting caps. Take away his gun, damn it!"

"Hah, you fools!" Kronenhauer laughed, as the squad of Marines took charge. But he coughed up blood as he spoke. "If not me, then surely someone else." He then taunted them in German, calling them all fools or worse. "*Possenreißerin. Schwachkopf. Hanswurst.* You doddering American buffoons will lose the war."

"Your war is over, pussycat," Colonel Morgan said before barking out orders. "Put the Kraut bastard in a boat. Keep him under heavy guard. Get him to Charity Hospital. Hurry. I do not want to lose this son-of-a-bitch."

Three Marines hoisted Kronenhauer up, joined arms and lifted him to chest height like a manmade stretcher. As they carried him to the nearest boat, Morgan yelled after them.

"This man is a spy, a Nazi saboteur. Now he is my prisoner. Tell the surgeon at the hospital he must do everything he can to save this man's life. I want the bastard alive and well so he can stand in front of a firing squad, and I can put him down for good . . . Go, go, go!"

WEDNESDAY
AUGUST 12, 1942
7 a.m.

New Orleans

"Wounded or not, the man needs to be interrogated."

The tall, slender naval officer stood at the doorway of the hospital room peering in. His way was blocked by a large beefy nurse swaddled in a frayed white uniform. Her hands were planted firmly on her wide hips.

"Captain, do you understand even a single word the *Boche* speaks?" the nurse asked, still blocking his way. *Boche* was a derisive term used mainly by the French to describe any of the Germanic peoples. "The morphine makes him delirious. He comes to now and again, and when he does, he mutters to himself in German."

Marine Colonel Peter Morgan smiled narrowly and nodded his understanding. "I am a Colonel, not a Captain. And Nurse, I was told downstairs we might need an interpreter up here. I need to question this man the next time he regains consciousness. Do you know of anyone on your staff who is fluent in German?"

"None of the doctors, if that is what you mean. A few speak Creole. But we do have a cook downstairs in the hospital kitchen who, rumor has it, is from Berlin. I am told she came here after the last war. Maybe the old bitch can be persuaded to help translate this man's mongrel language for you."

"Instead of blocking my way into the patient's room, what say you go with one of my men down to the kitchen and bring me back that German speaking cook on the double?" Morgan signaled to a Marine standing guard in the corridor to accompany her.

Kronenhauer moaned from his bed. Ominous sounding German words oozed from his lips.

"What do you think he is saying?" the nurse asked before leaving the room.

"Hurry, woman. Go with this man. Get that translator up here pronto."

The two of them left, then the thin Navy man was joined by a second man who had just arrived. This man wore an army uniform, rank of colonel, name unknown.

"This your prisoner?" the army man asked.

"And you are?"

"Office of Strategic Services," the army man said.

"And that is what?"

"A new federal agency. Civilian cousin to military intelligence. A central intelligence agency."

"Colonel Donovan's group?"

"Yes. Your prisoner is of great interest to us."

"For the moment, he is more of a patient than a prisoner," Colonel Morgan said. "Right now, the man is pumped so full of morphine, who knows if he can even think straight, much less talk."

"We will soon see," the army man said. "Captain Kronenhauer is our only lead. We have to track this thing back to its source, back to the head of the snake."

"One snake, two heads. Hitler and Himmler."

"You know this how?" the army man said.

"I have two dead U.S. marshals, a plot to blow up a vital production facility, a Nazi collaborator, and the Sicilian mob in it up to their eyebrows. Care to share?"

"This has Waffen-SS written all over it. Did you see what was in that swamp boat, Colonel? Composition B, pencil detonators, rolls of detonation cord."

By now, the stout nurse had returned with the cook in tow, an equally large woman, though somewhat older, perhaps a little crankier. She wore flour on her apron and a scowl on her face.

"Nurse, can you wake this man?" Colonel Morgan asked impatiently.

The nurse growled at him. "He should come around any time. His last morphine shot will wear off shortly. The pain will bring him out of his stupor."

"We can use that pain to our advantage," the army man said.

"How so?"

"Refuse to give him another shot of morphine unless he cooperates."

"That is downright cruel," the nurse said, stiffening at the thought.

"And killing innocent people isn't?"

At about that moment, Kronenhauer stirred.

"Where . . . am . . . I?" he muttered in German. The cook translated.

"You have been shot," the cook answered in flawless German. "You are now in the emergency ward of Charity Hospital, New Orleans."

" . . . kessel . . . "

Kronenhauer drifted off again.

" . . . kessel . . . ring . . . "

"What is he saying now?" the army man demanded to know.

"Something about a kettle or a cauldron," the cook answered, brushing flour from her apron. "That is the closest English translation for the German word *kessel.* Also something about a ring or a circle. Does that mean anything to you?"

"We searched his belongings," Colonel Morgan said. "Found a signet ring on him, as well as a small notebook of ciphers, and a second notebook with surveillance notes, maps, drawings and the like."

The cook was stunned. "This man is some sort of *spion?* How you say in English — a spy?"

"Worse than a spy. A saboteur. A man working against our own people on our own soil. He was caught trying to blow up an important American manufacturing facility."

Now the nurse interrupted. "If this man is the enemy, why have the hospital surgeons been trying to save his life? What is he even doing in my hospital, eating our food, sleeping in one of our hospital beds? Shouldn't he be in prison?"

Colonel Peter Morgan answered. "This man is the enemy. We have been after him for some time. He may have important information. We need to interrogate him. That is why I asked you to bring the cook up here to this room to help translate. She may be able to help us get to the bottom of this, to get to the truth."

Suddenly a knock came to the door. All eyes turned in that direction. A pretty woman stood in the doorway, dark hair, dark eyes.

"May I come in?" she asked.

"And you are?" the army man asked.

"Martina Amerada." She extended her hand to the army man in a friendly manner.

"We have already met," Colonel Morgan said quietly.

"Oh, have you?" the army man from OSS said. "I guess that makes me odd man out. You are connected to the embassy?"

"Yes, you catch on delightfully fast," Martina replied sardonically. "I am here on behalf of the British Crown, intelligence services actually. My people work with your people."

"What do your people want with this Kraut?"

"Your boss sent me here to observe and to collect intell."

The army man was clearly surprised. "My boss? Colonel Donovan?"

Martina Amerada nodded.

"So you outrank me?"

"It would seem so," Martina said. "Call headquarters New York if you do not believe me. I am here to collect the proceeds of your search — the ring, the codebook, the surveillance notebook, and a satchel or strongbox filled with Eyes-Only file folders. Your Office of Strategic Services and my British Secret Service share intelligence."

"Okay lady, spill," Colonel Morgan said. "What do you know about this soldier, this Nazi soldier? Is he not the very man we have been after since before Portugal? The man you had me follow from the port that day two weeks ago?"

"Full dossier. Wilhelm Kronenhauer. Captain. Waffen-SS. Munitions expert. Skilled marksman. Extremely dangerous. Not to be underestimated. You will not get any actionable intelligence out of this man, no matter how hard you try, no matter how much you torture him. The man you should be looking for is named Kesselring, Günter Kesselring, the Field Marshal's son."

"Field Marshal?"

"Yes. Field Marshal Kesselring," Martina said. "Albert Kesselring. Günter's father. One of the highest ranking figures in the entire Nazi military chain-of-command. If we were to capture Field Marshall Kesselring's son, it would be a major coup for our side."

"Kesselring, eh? That may explain what this half-dead Kraut was muttering. He mumbled those very words: kessel and ring. We thought it was two words, not a name."

"Well, it is a name. Günter Kesselring. He is prominently mentioned in at least one of the several communiqués Bletchley Park intercepted that are related to this operation. I suspect that once we have had a chance to examine that notebook you are holding, he will be prominently mentioned in there as well. Günter Kesselring is the man you want, not this smudge." She pointed to the hospital bed.

"Any clue how to find him, this Kesselring fellow?"

"None whatsoever," she replied. "Now, if you will be so kind, Colonel. The codebooks and the ring. That is what I have come here for. And also the automobile. Please hand them all over to me and I will be on my way."

Colonel Morgan was clearly flustered, though not half as much as the army man. "And what about this man Kronenhauer? What are we supposed to do with him?"

"Not my problem," Martina answered. "Do with him as you will. He is not my prisoner and the intelligence services want nothing whatsoever to do with him or with his capture. I suggest you claim the prize for the United States Navy and call it a day. Will there be anything else, gentlemen?"

ONE MONTH LATER

SUNDAY
SEPTEMBER 13, 1942
11:30 p.m.

New Orleans

"Boys, it don't get much better than this."

The gala celebration was over, and the many guests had begun to filter home through the crowded streets of New Orleans. Thousands had gathered at the plant on Industrial Canal for the ceremony. The company and its dedicated workers were awarded the Army-Navy "E". Higgins was damn proud of the achievement. In the grade school of his youth, an "E" was considered a failing grade. But here, on this day, it stood for the very opposite. Exceptional. Exceptional production. Exceptional performance. Exceptional results. The highest commendation the military could bestow upon a private company.

"You're right, Dad." Frank raised a glass to his father. "Tonight was one of our finer moments."

"I could not agree more," Higgins said, loosening his tie and leaning back against the safety fence that ringed the loading dock. A light breeze was sweeping in off the water.

Higgins stood, now, with his four sons on the rear loading dock of the Industrial Canal facility where the presentation ceremony had taken place. He and the boys were sharing a drink and a smoke. Higgins had a glass of ripe bourbon in his hand, as he often did lately. But his hands were unsteady; he was nearly three sheets to the wind already.

"Can you believe what General Moses said?" Andrew, Jr. was talking about Marine Corps General E.P. Moses. The general had been instrumental in helping the elder Higgins develop the first LCVP as well as the more recent and much more controversial tank lighter.

"He spoke of you, Father — of us — in the most glowing terms." This was Roland, Higgins' youngest. Roland would soon resign his position at the company as superintendent of landing boat construction to enlist in the Army. "Soon, the whole country is going to know about you, Dad. The event was covered by the National Broadcasting Company. It will be like before. Your name will be in every newspaper in the land — and on every radio station."

Just hours ago, General Moses had spoken to the enthusiastic crowd from a flag-draped platform atop the flat roof of the white two-story administration building. As the packed crowd cheered, Moses told them, "I have been in the Marine Corps now forty years as an officer, and I say to you that I have never taken part in maneuvers where I thought we were landing in any craft superior to the Higgins *Eureka*s." He ended his speech by offering the thousands of workers and spectators in attendance a catchphrase he felt they could take pride in — "From the Industrial Canal to Guadalcanal." The presentation concluded with the 125-piece Higgins Company band playing a rousing rendition of "America."

Edmond Higgins now spoke up. "After the Liberty boat contract was cancelled in July, I wasn't sure we were ever going to recover from that. Steel shortage, my ass."

Edmond stared out from the loading dock onto the wide, shipping canal behind the factory. Seventy-odd finished boats of theirs were parked in the channel, boats of all sorts, Higgins steel ramp boats, motor torpedo boats, tank lighters. The lot of them would be wet-tested in the morning, run up the canal to the lake, perhaps down Bayou St. John, and then back again. A few of the faster boats would be left with McDerby for his advanced class. The rest would be hauled out of the water with a crane and loaded onto a railcar for shipment to a waiting ship, some going to the Pacific, most headed to England and some eventually to North Africa. The boats left behind with McDerby would be used by the students in his advanced boat class to complete their final examination. The class would take the boats out onto Lake Pontchartrain and — while other students "hunted" them in lightning-fast PT boats — the LCVP drivers would try to storm the beach. Later in the week, the advanced class would venture out into the open ocean and attempt a practice invasion of Fort Morgan near Mobile, Alabama.

Higgins addressed his sons. "The ceremony was very well publicized, very high profile. All those wonderful speeches. The presentation of the 'E' award. With that 'E' award in hand, things may again be looking up for us."

"How so?" Frank asked, lighting a smoke of his own.

"The Truman Committee," Higgins said.

"I don't exactly know what that is, Dad. None of us boys do."

"No, I suppose not. There has been a great deal of drama. You know how I hate drama. I have been playing most of it close to the vest. Senator Harry S. Truman. His Special Committee to Investigate the National Defense Program. They are looking for war-time corruption and inefficiency. The boys in suits and ties have waded into the fight between me and the Bureau of Ships."

"No place for a sober man to be, between a rock and a hard place," Frank quipped.

Higgins chuckled. "The Truman Committee held hearings three months ago, in early June."

"Hearings?"

"Don't act like I didn't tell you boys about those hearings, because I know that I did. The hearings focused on all the crap the Bureau has been giving us about the design and contract for the tank landing craft. Then, about five or six weeks ago the Committee forwarded their findings to Frank Knox, Secretary of the Navy. You know Knox; he has been here more than once. Knox is a fair man. The Committee report confirmed what I have been saying all along: that the Bureau of Ships is full of shit. For five long years — and for reasons known only to them — the Bureau has stubbornly clung to that unseaworthy piece-of-crap tank lighter design they came up with and rejected my much superior design."

"Come on, Dad," Roland kidded. "Don't hold back. Tell it like it really is."

"You making fun of me, boy? Senator Truman was appalled by what his committee found. They all agreed. I have been the subject of bias and prejudiced treatment, all because those eastern shipyards are in bed with the steel companies — and with the Navy brass and the politicians. The only ones who have been on my side in this fight have been the labor unions, if you can believe that."

"You have always treated your workers well. The AFL knows that," Edmond said. "Those union fellows have a lot at stake here too. They promised no work stoppages if you landed this contract."

"Yes, let's drink to that," Higgins said. By now Frank and Andrew, Jr. had wandered off to find a quiet corner to sleep it off.

Only Edmond and Roland remained at their father's side, his oldest and his youngest.

Roland asked, "So, Dad, now that this committee has made its report, do you think, at the end of the day, the politics will finally flow our way?"

"Yes, son, I do. And do you want to know why?"

Roland nodded. "I am curious, of course."

"Because in a few days, I am to meet with a professor from Yale. Secretary of the Navy is sending the professor down here."

"Shit, Pops," Edmond exclaimed. "You sure you got enough book-learning to talk to a highfalutin man like that? Professor from Yale, my ass."

"You saying I'm stupid? Not everything is book-learning."

"No, I'm not saying that at all," Edmond confessed. "You are the smartest man I know. But face facts, Father. You can't complete a sentence without tossing in a swear word or two."

"Fuck you," Higgins said with a big smile. "Hand me another smoke."

"Doc said you need to quit smoking . . . and drinking. Mom says so too."

"Yeah, like that is going to happen," Roland chimed in.

"Anyways," Higgins said. "Like I said, in a few days I am to meet with this professor. He is from Yale University. He has been sent down here by the Truman Committee. Professor Something-Or-Other Seward. The man wants a personal account of my dealings with the Navy and with the Bureau of Ships. When I file my report, it is going to be a doozy."

"You are filing a written report with the government? Our government?" Edmond asked. "You? Andrew Jackson Higgins? A written report?"

"I'm not doing it long hand, if that's what you mean. Esther takes dictation. I will be dictating it to her. She will be typing it up. But it won't be some dry recital of facts; that much I can promise you. It will be a statement from the heart, one where I pull no punches."

"Dad, you never do."

"You referring to that Irishman?" Higgins asked drunkenly. "You heard about that?"

"Dad, everyone in the plant heard about that," Roland said. "I was just a little boy when it happened. But you have told that story a thousand times over. Everyone in the city knows you had a knockdown drag-out fistfight with that big Irishman that day in your office."

Higgins laughed long and hard. "Good workmanship is my bible, you know that. I had a report that morning from my wet-test crew that boats were leaking. I drove down to the yard and sized up my caulking crew. I picked out the youngest member of the crew, a sniffling weak-kneed kid, pulled him aside and tore into him. *Who the fuck is laying down on the job?* I asked him. The boy immediately 'fessed up, said a big Irishman on the crew was the culprit. I think his name was O'Malley."

"But the man was four inches taller than you," Edmond said. "And at least twenty pounds heavier."

"Oh, yeah, he was a big fellow. But, according to custom, I invited the big man into my office for a quiet chat and closed the door."

"Quiet chat, my ass," Edmond said. "We know the rest. Hell, we *heard* the rest. Bing, bang, boom. A lot of pushing and shoving, followed by a bare knuckle fistfight. Broken furniture, a broken desk chair, one or two loose teeth. After a long while, the office door opened. You stepped out. Your hair was mussed. You said to send for an ambulance. But we were prepared. Ted Sprague, I think it was, had already ordered one. It was on standby."

"Yeah, but O'Malley got his revenge," Higgins admitted.

"I'll say."

"What happened?" Roland asked.

"You tell him, Edmond. I'm too embarrassed to say."

Edmond nodded. "The next day the Irishman's wife showed up at the factory gate. She was an immense woman, a harridan, equal in size to her husband, if not a bit larger. She charges in, stomps up the stairs to father's office, lifts up a huge umbrella, nearly breaks it over father's head, then proceeds to punch him in the face with her fist. Time to call the ambulance again, only this time for Dad."

Roland laughed hard, right along with his father.

"Labor relations have always been a struggle," Higgins said. "First the Sicilians. Then the labor unions. The Negroes. Soon the women."

"Ah, yes, the women. When is that to start?"

"Already working on it. November at the latest. We are about to announce it in the *Eureka* newsletter. George Rappleyea is writing it up for publication as we speak."

"How do you think the men on the line are going to take it? A lot of these boys are from the backwoods. Some of them barely speak English. They won't all take kindly to working beside a woman on a factory floor."

"We will have to sell it to them like anything else," Higgins said. "We have to promise these men that the women won't be taking their jobs, not forever anyway. We have to promise these men that if they or their sons get drafted into the war, that the women will be filling their positions on a temporary basis only, until the war is over. We have to promise the men that they can have their jobs back after the war."

"Can we keep all those promises, Dad?" Roland asked.

"I don't know, son. I really don't know. But can we please forget about all that and enjoy the moment?" Higgins asked, knocking back what remained of his bourbon. "For me, the high point of the night was when Admiral Henry Wiley unfurled that big red flag and everyone cheered. The 'E' stands for excellence as well, and I demand nothing less. Then, after the Admiral spoke, that big old pennant was hoisted to the top of the flagstaff by our own soldiers of the Amphibian Command. All I could think was — Boy, I love those men . . . "

THREE DAYS LATER

WEDNESDAY
SEPTEMBER 16, 1942
7 a.m.

San Diego, California

Russell Brock smiled widely as he walked out of the Navy hospital unassisted. Fresh air was a tonic.

Brock straightened his uniform, stood up straight and tall, with eyes forward and locked on the future. After five long weeks riding a bed, he could finally taste the freedom.

The shrapnel wound to Brock's chest had very nearly killed the man. He had been as close to death on that hillside as any man could be and still remain alive.

Bathed in blood and seemingly lifeless, Brock was pulled from the rubble of the explosion by his feet. Minutes later, a monk priest from the Ukraine bent down over him on the slopes of Gavutu's tallest hill and gave him the Last Rites of the Catholic Church.

But the explosion did not actually end Brock's life; it knocked him senseless, nearly stopped his heart. Minutes later, still in shock, he stirred, barely alive.

Scarcely breathing, Russell Brock was lifted by a corpsman onto a stretcher, then carried down Hill 148 by two Marines. He was given morphine and, on the beach, an IV tube was placed in his arm. Onto a Higgins boat that had been adapted as a water ambulance. Out across the reef to the USS *Solace* (AH-5), a U.S. Navy hospital ship anchored offshore. A relatively short sail to New Zealand. Two weeks later, on to San Diego.

One of the troop ships had been augmented with a surgical team. In this capacity, the modified LST was now referred to as an LSTH — Landing Ship, Tank (Hospital). During battle, the ship's normal routine was to land fresh troops on the beach like an ordinary LST, then organize a hospital on the well deck to receive wounded Marines for the return trip. On the day in question,

Russell Brock had been one of the many wounded loaded onboard the LSTH.

The well deck was located on the ship's main deck level. In this context, the term "well" had nothing at all to do with the state of a wounded Marine's health. Its use here was in an older, nautical sense of the word, a depression or recess in the main deck, a hole. The well deck was a large depression in the center of the boat at a height lower than decks either fore or aft, thus offering a measure of protection from the elements — and the enemy. A perfect location for a makeshift, temporary hospital.

Today was Brock's first day back on active duty. That wicked looking scar on his chest had earned him a Purple Heart and an elevation in rank to Corporal. As soon as today he would be assigned to a new platoon and orders cut, eventually sending him back to the Pacific.

His first stop, though, was to be in New Orleans, along with a hundred other Marines. They were to spend the next two weeks at the Higgins Boat Operators School learning how to drive, repair, and maintain an LCVP. With so many amphibious landings still to come to win this war, the Navy had not nearly enough qualified boatmen. Brock and the others were to be among many others trained to fill that need.

Even now, as Brock paused to gather himself on the steps of the Navy hospital, the battle was still raging for control of Guadalcanal, an island neighbor to Gavutu, where he had been wounded. Indeed, just yesterday the aircraft carrier USS *Wasp* had been hit and sunk by a Japanese torpedo southeast of Guadalcanal leaving, for the moment, only one Allied aircraft carrier still operating in that arena, the *Hornet.*

But that part of Russell Brock's war now lay behind him. What lay immediately ahead was for Corporal Brock to pass his physical and to collect up his orders. The physical was to take place within the hour. After that, there were plenty more Pacific islands besides Guadalcanal that needed taking, faraway places like Bougainville, Tarawa, Guam, Iwo Jima.

Brock smoothed his uniform trousers. When he touched the side seam of his trousers with his hand, his fingers brushed against something round and hard inside the pocket of his pants. The item in question had arrived two weeks earlier during mail call, a small box.

At first, Brock thought the box might be from his mother, a gift perhaps, on account of his injury. But the return address was unfamiliar. New York City. *Had his mother moved?* Last he knew she lived in New Jersey. *Did she live in the city now?*

Russell Brock had little love in his heart for his mother. But he tore open the box with expectant hope. Maybe the war had changed her. Maybe the war had changed him as well.

Hope turned to confusion. Inside the box was a letter. Also, an elegant gold ring. Large, perhaps valuable, an antique maybe. The enclosed letter was not handwritten but typed on heavy expensive paper, with an official seal pressed into it. Definitely not from his mother.

Russell Brock looked more closely at the return address label. New York City. Office of Strategic Services. *What the hell was that?*

The ring was heavy, like it might be worth something. He turned it over twice in his hand, looked again at the return address.

Office of Strategic Services, New York City. The letter was typewritten and signed by hand in ink. He could not read the signature.

The letter said the ring had been recovered as part of a murder investigation. The letter did not say how the man was killed. But it did say that the dead man was Russell's grandfather, Henry Brock. According to the OSS's records, Russell was the dead man's only known next of kin.

What the hell was the Office of Strategic Services? A branch of the military? *And how had they tracked him down?* That was unclear.

Brock thought back, back to what his mother had told him about his grandfather, back to the one time Russell had spent a few days at his grandfather's side in New Orleans. He remembered his grandfather as a drunk and a womanizer.

Brock placed the heavy ring on his finger. But it was too large for his slender fingers. The ring rolled around and slid right off, falling to the ground. That is when he picked up the ring and slipped it in the pocket of his trousers. Its former owner must have been a big man with fat fingers. *But his grandfather?*

Now, on the steps of the hospital, Brock pulled the ring from his pocket and again studied it closely. Elegant was the wrong word. An elegant ring was one a woman might wear. This was a man's ring, a heavy ring, with some sort of scrollwork on the top and sides. Russell had heard of such rings, signet rings he thought they were called, for kings and queens, influential people.

Had his grandfather been a wealthy man? No, that hardly seemed likely. His grandfather had been a gambler. His mother had complained about that. He played the ponies. Frequented red-light districts. His mother had complained about that as well. These were not the habits of a wealthy man.

Russell Brock wondered. *How had this Office of Strategic Services come to know his name?* How had they come to mail him this expensive ring? Brock could not remember. Had he listed his grandfather as next of kin on his enlistment form? Is that how they had known to send him this ring? Because he was the next of kin?

"You leaving us today, Corporal?"

"Huh?"

The sound of the civilian's voice snapped Brock back to the here and now. The voice was familiar, that of Theo Tillinghast. Brock had first met Mr. Tillinghast three weeks ago, shortly after Brock arrived here at the hospital in San Diego. They met on a day when Brock was feeling particularly sorry for himself. But as time passed and Brock recovered, he and the older man, a civilian volunteer, became fast friends.

"Yes, Mr. Tillinghast," Brock replied proudly. Tillinghast was a generation older than Brock and he hesitated to call him by his first name, Theo. "They are releasing me today."

"You going back to the war?"

"Yes sir. First, boat school. Then back to the war."

"Boat school? What does an infantryman want with boat school?"

"Marine Corps needs small boat drivers. I was picked to be one of them."

"Well then, take care of yourself, son. I don't want to see your sorry ass back in here ever again."

"You think I want to listen to any more of your silly war stories?"

"No, I suppose not. I'm glad you're back on your feet, son, and I'm glad you're about to get on with your life. It was a pleasure to have made your acquaintance. And thank you again for the return of the coin."

Brock nodded thoughtfully and the two men continued on their way, Brock towards the parking lot and a waiting bus, Tillinghast toward the hospital entrance to begin his rounds for the day.

Brock turned to say something more to his friend. But Tillinghast was already out of earshot.

Brock kicked himself for not having said something more meaningful to this man on the occasion of their final meeting. He thought back, now, to that day, three weeks ago, when he first met Theo Tillinghast, veteran of the Great War. It was one of the last days of August and the day was very, very hot, almost baking. Brock was out of bed, sitting in a chair, while the nurses changed his bedsheets. An older man approached and opened a conversation.

"What you got there, son?" the middle-aged man asked. His was a regular face at the Naval Hospital, where he came once a week to volunteer his time.

"This?" Brock was holding in his hand the Challenge Coin that Woods had given him the day he died. "It was given to me by a friend."

"May I see it?"

Brock nodded and handed it to the man. "You are Mr. Tillinghast, right?" Brock had heard the nurses address him by that name on an earlier occasion.

"Yes, Theo Tillinghast. Son, did your friend tell you what this is?"

"My friend called it a Challenge Coin. It dates back to the First World War. His uncle won it in a poker game from some guy. The guy was a pilot that got shot down behind enemy lines and used the coin to cross the border and win his freedom."

"Ah, what a small world. That guy was me. I had two pair, Jacks and Sixes; he had three of a kind."

"Oh please, old man, give me just a little break. Go peddle your bullshit story to someone else. And hand me back my coin before I have to get out of this chair and take it back." By now, the nurses had finished making his bed and moved onto the next.

"Not peddling any bullshit, son. But here's your coin back." Tillinghast handed it over and walked slowly away to assist another veteran wounded in the war and recuperating in this hospital facility.

Brock watched the man walk away and had a sudden change of heart. There seemed to be something particularly honest and sincere about the man. He couldn't quite put his finger on it.

"Mr. Tillinghast . . . Theo . . . Sir . . . please come back."

Tillinghast ignored the entreaty and kept on walking.

"Mr. Tillinghast. Please."

Tillinghast stopped; turned around. "Are we now done passing out insults?"

"Yes, sir. Sorry, sir."

"That guy in the story was me, just like I said. And this coin may very well have once belonged to me. Three of a kind still beats two pair, just like I said."

"You were a flyer in the war? My friend called you an aviator."

"Yep. 17th Aero Squadron. The 17th was a United States Army Air Service unit. It was assigned to the RAF during the First World War. Our mission was to engage and clear enemy aircraft from the skies. Also to escort recon and bombardment squadrons when they flew over enemy territory. Me and the boys of the 17th attacked enemy observation balloons and performed close air support for tactical bombing attacks of Kraut forces along the front lines. All the fliers in our unit were given one of these coins by Willoughby, the team leader. He had them made for us before we left the States."

"Were you shot down behind enemy lines, like my friend said?"

"Your friend is dead?"

"Yes. On Gavutu earlier this month. Hill 148. I was wounded there as well. That's how I ended up here."

"Walk with me, son," Tillinghast said, helping Brock to his feet. "You can't spend the rest of your life riding a hospital bed and feeling sorry for yourself."

"You think that I'm feeling sorry for myself?"

"This isn't my first day on the job, son. I know what self-pity looks like."

"Okay, maybe a little," Brock admitted. "Tell me the rest of your story."

"The 17th was the first American Aero Squadron to be sent to Canada to be trained by the British. It was also the first American squadron to be attached to a British RAF squadron and sent into combat. We flew the Sopwith Camel, much like the one etched on the obverse of this coin."

Brock studied the coin closely as they walked. The coin was badly tarnished and worn smooth in several places by years of handling. Despite the wear, the Sopwith was clearly visible on one face of the coin.

"What are these markings?" Brock pointed to a smudged blotch on the fuselage of the plane aft of the cockpit. He guessed it was a call sign or something along those lines.

"Ah yes, the dumbbell," Tillinghast said.

"Dumbbell?"

"We painted a white dumbbell on each side of the fuselage of every plane in 'C' Flight. It was how we identified each other in the sky."

"You were the dumbbells?"

"In a manner of speaking."

Brock laughed. He felt great respect for this man and for his accomplishments. Tillinghast continued.

"September 22, 1918. That was the day I was shot down, along with several others. We were in a hell of a fight. On the first patrol of the morning, fifteen Fokkers dove in on us from out of the sky-blue nowhere. We were outnumbered five to one. But we returned fire, and before long thirty aircraft, both ours and theirs were engaged in an aerial battle. We downed six of the bastards before I was shot down myself. Me — Lieutenant Theose E. Tillinghast — blasted from the sky."

"Theose?"

"Family name. I go by Theo."

"You were taken prisoner?"

"Oh yes, almost immediately. I was held prisoner in the town of Valenciennes, France, along with several other Allied officers. A couple three Americans and a Brit. One of the Americans spoke fluent German."

"But you managed to escape."

"We all did. The Krauts weren't that bright. The room they held us in was not at all secure. We cut a hole in the roof with a piece of broken sawblade we found in one corner of the room. Then the real fun began. We crawled up and out through the opening in the roof, slid down into the prison courtyard, and climbed over an adjoining wall. From there, we swam the canal bordering the prison and set out cross-country toward Holland. Thank God it was early fall. The weather was still warm. The Belgian border wasn't far away, maybe twenty miles. Brussels was further, maybe another sixty miles."

"But the story my friend told me was that you stumbled onto a French outpost; used the coin to gain safe passage. Holland wasn't part of his story."

"Well, what can I tell you? Maybe this coin doesn't belong to me after all. No French outpost in my story; just overland to Belgium. We traveled at night, slept during the day. Took us eight days on foot to cover those twenty or so miles to the Belgian frontier. After we crossed the border, we met several well-to-do Belgians who spoke English. They gave us civilian clothes and maps and moved us from house to house at night on a sort of underground railway. Eventually, we reached Brussels.

"For us, Brussels was a different world. We could move around freely on the streets. I rode a streetcar to a nearby German Aerodrome, where I took down notes on its location and defenses. The next day, I was introduced to an electrical engineer who gave me a set of wire clippers and a pair of insulated gloves. I would need both those things to get across the border into Holland."

"Your story defies imagination," Brock said.

"I haven't talked about this in years. Seeing that coin in your hand brought it all back for me. The four of us split up in Brussels. A few days later, me and another fellow reached the frontier. We cut through a closely guarded, electrified wire fence and then entered the neutral state of Holland. That was our ticket home. Rotterdam to Le Havre, then to England. We arrived in Britain only days before the war ended."

By now the two men had made a complete circuit of the hospital ward and returned to where they started, beside Brock's bed. After the long walk, Brock was tired and happy to crawl back beneath the covers.

"I want you to have this coin," Brock said, handing it to Theo that day, three weeks ago. "My friend would want you to have it."

"How can you be sure?"

"Because I know my friend. You earned it. He would want you to have it."

They shook hands that day, three weeks ago, and parted company, Theo to continue his rounds, Brock to fall asleep. Over the ensuing days, as Brock regained his strength and healed, they talked many times. Now they had met for the last time on the grounds of the hospital and parted ways for good.

It was a bittersweet moment Russell Brock would not soon forget.

TWO MONTHS LATER

SUNDAY
NOVEMBER 8, 1942
1:30 a.m.

North Africa

The men of 30 AU scrambled ashore. They had landed their boats at nearly the identical location as the French had back in 1830, when the French established a beachhead for the Invasion of Algiers more than one hundred years ago.

The men of 30 AU bolted over the gunwales and down the steel ramp of their Higgins landing craft and scrambled ashore. Their faces were blackened with soot and greasepaint, and they were heavily armed. They were behind schedule, but it took them only seconds to disembark.

The commandos first had to beach their boats, then move stealthily away from the shoreline, fifty yards inland to the nearest road. At this location, the shoreline ran southwest to northeast. The beach road ran practically parallel to the water's edge. They were to follow the beach road one-half mile southwest, where the road would turn sharply north onto the small peninsula and presque-isle of *Sidi Ferruch*. They were to gather in the clump of trees near the base of the old citadel wall, where at 0100 hours they were to rendezvous with Rygor and the other men already ashore.

Sidi Ferruch was home to the Italian navy. This is what 30 AU had trained for, to break into Italian naval headquarters and pilfer battle orders for the German and Italian fleets operating in the Mediterranean. Dicey stuff, to be sure.

In the hours and days before the commandos of 30 Assault Unit hit the beach here at *Sidi Ferruch*, they had studied the maps of the area and rehearsed their movements — terrain, landmarks, street names, natural formations. With the help of Aldo Carolla and MI6, Rygor and his crew had supplied the incursion team with detailed maps and photographs of the target area. They had enlarged the city views to one-fiftieth actual size, tacked the blowups to large bulletin boards in their training center, and studied them block by block, alley by alley, and street by street. Now they had the layout memorized and were ready to go.

The political landscape of Algeria was as complex as its physical terrain. Vichy French. Free French. French Resistance. Nazi occupiers. Pirates. Bedouin-style tribal rivalries. Italian naval officers. Sicilian *Mafiosi*.

The British commandos of 30 AU had made their way here, to this spot, under cover of darkness. They wore American uniforms, a sensible move considering how the local gendarme and Vichy French were constantly at odds with the British. The unit's assignment was quite different from that of the many thousands of British and American infantrymen about to land further east in the city of Algiers and much, much further west in Oran and Casablanca. That was a huge force. Five hundred ships, one hundred thousand men.

Operation Torch. The eventual liberation of continental Europe. It would actually begin right here, in North Africa, this day, November 8, 1942, with the amphibious landings of British and American forces in three task forces. What lay ahead were tank battles in the desert, the humiliating setbacks at Kassarine Pass, and — months down the road — the eventual surrender of German troops in Tunisia.

30 AU's role was a sideshow to the main event, which was the Eastern Task Force aimed at Algiers. The big event consisted of two brigades from the British 78th and the U.S. 34th Infantry Divisions, along with two British Commando units totaling 20,000 troops.

"You are nearly one hour late! What took you so fucking long?" Rygor demanded to know. At age forty-six he was no longer a young man. The last hour-and-a-half spent crouching in the cold shadows, braving the face of a November wind had chilled him thoroughly. Nights were long this time of year, and days short. The sun had set hours ago.

"U-boat. We had to wait at sea until it passed out of range before we could make landfall."

"HMS *Fidelity* radioed to say you might be late. But now we are one hour behind schedule and must hurry." Rygor pointed up the slope that rose steeply before them.

Italian naval headquarters were to be found at the highest point of the small peninsula, one hundred yards from where they presently stood. From this spot, it was pretty much straight uphill all the way. The incursion team had to maneuver past two encircling stone walls and two, lightly manned guard posts. The team had approximately two hours remaining in which to accomplish their mission objectives. After that, a General Alarm would likely be raised on account of the mass Allied landings just miles away in the city of Algiers, twelve miles distant overland, twenty-one by coastal highway.

"You two," Rygor said quietly, picking two men from the twenty or so assembled. "Take firecrackers, set up noisy diversion. Be sure to do it like we practiced, in clear view of outer guard post. You know the spot. We need to draw one, preferably both guards away from their station."

Rygor continued. "Snipers. I want you two men to set up there and there, just as we practiced." Rygor pointed to two locations on the high ground fifty yards away. "When fireworks draw guard far enough from post, take him out. Bing, bang, boom. Be sure your rifles are muzzled. The silencer slows bullet speed. But it keeps things rather quieter."

"Diversion coming right up," the lead commando said. "On my mark, two minutes."

Once the four men had set off to their respective locations, Rygor drew the others aside. "Security inside is light. When we get to commandant's office, do not be surprised if battle orders of fleet are sitting in plain sight right out on some desk, or perhaps in unlocked wallsafe, door open. The Italians have never been known for their — how you say? — tidiness."

Rygor continued. "Do it like we practiced. Over wall. Onto Citadel Road. Across courtyard. Up back stairs into commandant's office. Grab up fleet battle orders and whatever else you can lay hands on that looks important and can easily fit in your ruck. Lights to a minimum. Hand signals only. No talking. Fifteen minutes max. Then we are out of there. We have to get this *wywiadu* back to *Fidelity* and then on to Central Command for analysis."

"What the what?" one of the men asked. The British soldiers were sometimes lost when he tossed in random words of Polish.

"*Wywiadu.* You know what it means. *Inteligencja.* — Intelligence."

Rygor paused to allow the snipers time to get into position. "Remember, men. We cannot afford to fuck this thing up. No room for SNAFU, as the Americans say."

"Sir?"

"Situation Normal, All Fucked Up."

The men of 30 AU chuckled. "We Brits have a similar saw. TARFU."

"Yes, I am familiar." Rygor was becoming unsettled by the nervous chatter.

"Things Are Really Fucked Up."

"I like it," one of the other men said. "But I still think the Yanks have the upper hand when it comes to swearing."

"Oh?"

"FUBAR. I hear the Yanks say it all the time. FUBAR. Fucked Up Beyond All Recognition."

"The one I really like is what they say when they hazard a guess. SWAG. That's what they say. Simple Wild Ass Guess. SWAG."

"Yeah, unless it's PDOOMA. That's an answer Pulled Directly Out Of My Ass."

"Enough already," Rygor ordered. "We have no more time for this tomfoolery. After the deed is done, we are to split up into three groups coming out of citadel, just as we practiced. No SNAFU, no FUBAR, just three detachments, each with a different route of egress."

Rygor stopped, listened for any sounds around them, then continued. "If your way is blocked getting back to boats, then proceed to Rendezvous Point Two. That is Plage Moretti. Wait there twenty minutes for the rest of us. If no one shows within twenty minutes, consider us dead or captured and proceed on your own. Push east. But do it quickly. The American landings will be under way by then. It is twenty hard miles to the American beachhead. If you make it there alive and in one piece, the Americans are your ticket home. Passcode is Bright Torch. Good luck, men."

TWO WEEKS LATER

FRIDAY
NOVEMBER 20, 1942
4 p.m.

New Orleans

"You are a hero. You know that, right?"

Martina smiled as she pulled the bathrobe tighter around her shoulders. It was late November 1942, a cool wet winter in New Orleans.

Nico pulled on his underpants. "I don't see it that way. Just protecting our business interests."

"Why be so modest? People look up to you, Nico. This war is not going to end any time soon. You are a hero. The sooner you accept that fact the better. You, Aldo, Luca, all heroes."

Nico pulled on his undershirt, pushed his hair back in place. "I won't be receiving any medals from the President, if that is what you mean."

"No, probably not," Martina said, beginning to gather up her clothes. "But I do have one present for you that you might enjoy."

"Better than the one you have just given me?" he said with a wink.

"I was good, wasn't I?"

"Never better."

"Well, you might enjoy this gift as much."

"I seriously doubt that. But try me."

"It is parked outside."

"Parked?"

"Yes, on the street below. Come to the window."

Nico pulled on his trousers, went to the window, looked down on the street below. He instantly recognized it for what it was.

"How the hell did you manage that?"

"Are you absolutely certain that you want to know?"

"Yes, of course, I want to know. Why wouldn't I?"

"The U.S. Office of Strategic Services has exercised its prerogative and assumed sole jurisdiction over the Kronenhauer investigation. Everything related to the events that took place in the wee hours of August 12 at the Eureka Tug-Boat Company are now considered top-secret and classified. All physical evidence has been sequestered. There is no crime to prosecute, not in an American court anyway. Wilhelm Kronenhauer died while still in custody at the hospital. The War Department prefers this lapse in security at the Higgins boat plant not make the papers, much less become headline news. There was, however, one particular Eyes-Only file found in a strongbox in the Nazi's possession that the U.S. Navy wanted back so that it could be destroyed. The Packard is the price they had to pay me for that file and for my continued silence on the matter. Now I am handing the Packard over to you."

"Woman, you are amazing."

"I am, aren't I?"

"So, your post in Havana remains secure?"

"That man from the Ministerio de Banco Nacional?"

"Yes. What about him?"

"He won't be bothering me again."

"Do I want to know?"

"Your organization has its ways. So does mine."

"And what about us, Martina? Still business as usual?"

"Nico, the Carolla family connection is vital to the war effort. North Africa has only just begun. The Sicily campaign, when it comes, is still months down the road. The invasion of France may come sooner. Even so, for the foreseeable future, the governments of both our nations need your help more than they need another crime boss behind bars. After the war, who knows?"

"A man in my position might then wish the war to go on forever."

"No sensible man could ever wish for that."

"So long as the government is busy prosecuting the war, chasing down Mafia is a poor use of the government's resources. They will leave us alone. Plus, the war has put a hold on the deportation of my grandfather and business has never been better."

"Is that all you care about, Nico? Money?"

"No. Of course not. It was a stupid thing for me to say. I want the Nazis crushed. I want the Fascist animals to pay dearly for what they have done to my country, to my niece Josepha. I want those vicious animals to pay for all the misery they have visited upon my family and my friends."

"Yes. That is exactly what you should want."

Nico glanced again at the automobile below, then at the smart and beautiful woman standing beside him. He reached out to her.

"Martina. Thank you for every kindness you have shown me. You know I would do anything for you. You know that, right?"

"We can be lovers, Nico. But we cannot be in love. You know that, right?"

Nico refused to look her square in the eye.

"Nico, this is serious what I am saying here. You must not love me. And I can never love you, at least not in the way you imagine. You and I can never have that kind of relationship. I thought you and I were clear about this from the start."

"Do I mean nothing to you?"

"You mean everything. But we are at war, Nico, a war that is ripping apart the entire world. Empires are falling, countries are burning, millions of people are at risk of losing their lives. Every last one of us has made a pact with the Devil. Me, you, the shipbuilders, the bomb makers, the men carrying the guns, the civilians hiding in their homes, everyone. Countless acts of depravity are yet to be committed before this terrible thing is over. Mass murder. Rape. Genocide. Starvation. Disease. Pestilence. There is no place for love in this battle. It is a fight to the death, pure and simple."

"But that is so cold, Martina, colder than anything you have ever said to me in the past, colder than anything I have ever done in my entire life. — And I have done plenty."

"It is cold, Nico, the worst kind of cold. But there are only two kinds of wars in this world, existential wars and wars of necessity. Existential wars are fought with the heart. Wars of necessity are fought with the brain. An existential war is fought without thought of strategy or tactics. It is a street fight, an all-out battle for survival, no rules, odds be damned. Wars of necessity are fought with grim determination. Battle plans. Supply lines. Calculated risks. Advance planning. Training. Time tables. Boat schedules. Such wars are prosecuted not executed. Sadly, this war, this World War II, is such a war."

ACKNOWLEDGMENTS

• Dr. Robert DeGise, Ed.D., inspiration for the story, 5th Marine Division, 3rd Battalion, 26 Regiment
• John "Bud" Cunnally, Chief Electronics Technician Submarines, (SS) Retired United States Navy
• Debra Burgauer, Ph.D — wife, editor, research assistant, and lover
• John W. Brown, good neighbor and friend, Retired US Postal Service
• Linda Dollar, good friend and neighbor, avid reader
• Amanda Fallis, Archivist, New Orleans Public Library
• Heather M. Szafran, Reference Assistant, The Historic New Orleans Collection, Williams Research Center, 410 Chartres Street, New Orleans, LA 70130
• Ashley Roper, aerospace engineer and avid reader
• Bruce Harris, PT-305 Restoration Coordinator, The National WWII Museum, 945 Magazine Street, New Orleans, Louisiana, 70130
• Lynn Legner, former high school and college classmate
• Margaret Burgauer, mother and avid reader
• Mike Rucker, friend and well-known author of the "Terry the Tractor" series of books for young people
• James N. Shively, Specialist 5th Class, United States Army Security Agency
• Rev. Roman Dusanowskyj, monk priest from Nova Scotia, who taught me a great deal about the church and about life while we both traveled up the Amazon River on the *Prinsendam*
• A navy SEAL who prefers to remain unnamed.

Also, please visit this website —

http://sites.google.com/site/stevenburgauer/nazi-saboteurs-on-the-bayou

FURTHER READING & SOURCES

"The Coast Guard and the Pacific War"
Robert M. Browning, Jr.
Commandant's Bulletin insert for July 1995 issue

Life magazine
"Andrew Jackson Higgins," by Gilbert Burck
August 16, 1943, pages 100 – 112

Andrew Jackson Higgins and the Boats That Won World War II
Jerry E. Strahan
Louisiana State University Press, Baton Rouge, 1994

"Dictionary of Navy Slang"
Compiled From Various Sources

SNAFU — Sailor, Airman, and Soldier Slang of World War II
Gordon L. Rottman
2013

"New Orleans City Guide"
American Guide Series
Federal Writers' Project of the Works Progress Administration
Houghton Mifflin Company, Boston, Massachusetts
The Riverside Press, Cambridge, Massachusetts, 1938

"Let Us Die Bravely: United States Chaplains in World War II"
Jeremiah Snyder
Undergraduate Research Journal at University of Colorado at
Colorado Springs
Volume 2.1, Spring 2009

"The Negro Motorist Green Book," by Victor H. Green, an annual
guidebook for African-American roadtrippers, commonly referred to
simply as the *Green Book*, 1941

"A Pointing Finger," an undated, short memoir by PFC Robert
DeGise describing one of his many experiences in the battle by U.S.
Marines to take Iwo Jima.

"Autobiography," an undated short personal history of Dr. Robert DeGise, Ed.D. describing his upbringing, war experiences, and education.

"Scratch Built Collection, The Higgins Boat, by Dean A. Beeman http://gil-guy.com/index.html

"This site contains an introduction to a series of unique books that describe how to build a series of wooden ship models using basic tools and materials. Each text is written by and for an adult who is interested in the techniques, technologies, ships and people who make up the fabric of men and boats.

"If you're wondering about the name gil-guy, it can be found in a few obscure dictionaries. Spelled also as timenoguy, gill-guy or gilguy, the term refers to any piece of ancient and/or obsolete nautical gear found on a ship that does not have an otherwise convenient name. Or a quick way to reference a something that you otherwise can't remember, pronounce or describe. For example, a politician."

OTHER SOURCES

• Taylor's 1924 Map of New Orleans

• Greenwood Cemetery & Mausoleum

• New Orleans Street Railways map, January 1904

• Racial Slur Database — www.rsdb.org

PERSONAL INTERVIEWS

• Dr. Robert DeGise, Ed.D., inspiration for the story, 5th Marine Division, 3rd Battalion, 26 Regiment

• John "Bud" Cunnally, Chief Electronics Technician Submarines, (SS) Retired United States Navy

• Bruce Harris, PT-305 Restoration Coordinator, The National WWII Museum, 945 Magazine Street, New Orleans, Louisiana, 70130

WIKIPEDIA
entries consulted both as source materials and to verify historical accuracy

17th Aero Squadron
30 Assault Unit
A-1 Lifeboat
American Black Chamber
Arlington, Josie
Army Navy "E" Award
Battle of the Coral Sea
Battle of Tulagi and Gavutu
Bellocq, E.J.
Blasting Cap
Bletchley Park
Breaking Enigma
Brockdorff (von)
Browning M1919 machine gun
Burt, Hilma
Camp Elliott
Carolla, Sylvestro
Challenge Coins
Chevrolet Stovepipe
Code Talker
Detcord
Dieppe Raid
Emergency Carry and Lift
Enigma
Fascists vs. Mafia in Sicily
Federal Bureau of Investigations
Fleming, Ian
German Colonial Empire
German Colonization of Americas
German Nobility
Gray Marine Motor Co.
Guadalcanal Campaign
Haitian Creole
Handcrank Radio
Hero Sandwich
Higgins, Andrew Jackson
Higgins Industries

If you enjoyed this fine book, you will certainly enjoy Steven Burgauer's ***The Road to War: Duty & Drill, Courage & Capture***. Here is what others are saying about this fine book —

"Five-plus unequivocal stars to The Road to War. It's an extraordinary read that everyone should enjoy."
— October 20, 2016, Publishers Daily Reviews

"4 stars out of 5"
— October 28, 2016, "The Book Reviewers," a division of Full Media Ltd. (UK)

"Personal, inspiring & insightful. This book is precious."
— November 3, 2016, The Book Bag Reviewers (UK)

++++++++++++++++++++++++++++++++

The Road to War:
Duty & Drill, Courage & Capture

From the Author's Introduction:

When I was a boy, I lived across the lane from this man. He was different from my father. This man had a gun. He had been in the war. My father had not.

My parents were very close to this man and to his wife. The wife was at my family's house nearly every day, visiting with my mother. Her name was Dottie. His name was Bill. I called them Mr. and Mrs. Frodsham, occasionally Mr. and Mrs. F.

Bill and Dottie had two kids, both much younger than me. I was maybe fourteen at the time. When I was a bit older, I met their oldest son. His name was Dennis but he went by Buz. Dennis was married, going to college at the time, perhaps graduate school. He and his wife lived with Mr. and Mrs. Frodsham for a while. The house seemed crowded.

Sometimes, when Mr. and Mrs. F went out, I would baby-sit for the two younger kids, a boy, Christopher, and a girl, Victoria. The kids were fun, and I liked them. Apparently, my parents did too, as they soon became godparents to these kids from across the street. I wasn't sure what being a godparent meant, but it sounded important.

Fast forward now, half a decade. I am done with college, getting married. The families are still close. Vicki is a flower girl in our wedding. At rehearsal dinner, Christopher, now twelve, is sipping on a beer, slowly getting drunk. My father is playing the piano, something he loved to do. Everyone is smiling.

Now married, I moved away from home. In time, Bill and Dottie leave the area as well, move east, relocate in the Carolinas. I lived my life, lost track of theirs.

Flash forward now, three decades. I have had a career in investment brokering, retired, now teaching economics part time, writing science fiction most of the time.

Suddenly comes a question. That little girl Vicki, now a full-grown woman with children of her own, contacts me. It is the sixty-fifth anniversary of D-Day, both her parents are dead, and she has in her hand her father's memoirs recounting his experiences in World War II. She knows that I am a writer. She would like to see her father's memoirs published. Could I give her any advice how to make that dream a reality?

Next thing I know, I am deeply involved in the project. Rather than just a dry recitation of facts and events, I have written it as a "novel." I put the word in quotation marks because novels are generally fiction. This is not. This is real.

But in some sense it is fiction. To avoid making this account read like a Russian novel, filled with countless unpronounceable names and enough characters to fill a small telephone book, I have simplified matters a great deal, changing names to protect identities, eliminating characters that add little to the story, constructing others as composites of several people spliced together as one. Historical characters, such as General Eisenhower remain intact, blisters and all.

So as to not make this account an unreadable textbook, I have limited the use of maps and the like. But, inevitably, a reader may want to summon a Google map of southern England or the Normandy coast to help follow along. There are countless online sources of maps. I only mention Google, as I referred to it often.

Writing this book entailed much research. I don't know from guns or grenades. Wikipedia was an incredible aid to me in this regard.

William had a remarkable memory. Written so many years after the fact, I would say William possessed a stunning clarity in his recollection of events. I, myself, at a much younger age cannot lay claim to remembering so many details from my twenties. Even so, William had at least some of his "facts" wrong.

For instance, he reports in his text that he returned to the United States after the war onboard the U.S.S. Lafayette. He specifically mentions that the Lafayette was formerly an Italian luxury liner by the name of the Conte Grande before the United States military commandeered it to carry troops. — Not possible.

The Lafayette began life as a French-built luxury liner called the Normandie. The Normandie was seized in New York by the United States after the fall of France. It was to be converted into a high-speed troopship but caught fire and sank. It was later raised again at great expense and floated to the Brooklyn Naval Shipyard for repair but never returned to service and was later sold for scrap.

The Conte Grande, on the other hand, was indeed captured from the Italians. It did indeed become a troopship. But it was renamed the U.S.S. Monticello, not the Lafayette.

So which story is correct? I suspect William came home on the Monticello, as the Lafayette was still in a Brooklyn shipyard at the time of his return.

I found several such "problems" in Mr. Frodsham's account. In each case, I had to go with my best guess as to the actual facts. Any mistakes in this regard are entirely mine.

Thus, I call this work a "novel." It is somewhat fictionalized and somewhat improvised. William reveals very little about himself in his account. He doesn't reveal whether or not he misses home, whether he is lonely, whether he is scared. So I have tried to ferret out his feelings the best I could. Again, any mistakes in this regard are entirely mine.

But even with these admitted shortcomings, what remains is still an amazing story of youthful valor. A young man — patriotic, athletic, daring, willing to take risks — enlists in the Army to defend the country he loves so dearly. His leadership skills and acumen with guns and field artillery is quickly recognized by his superiors, and he is encouraged to become an officer.

William trains hard, leads his men into battle, makes snap decisions, is wounded, captured by the enemy, slapped into solitary confinement, sent to a prisoner-of-war camp on the Eastern Front, starved to within a few inches of his life.

Yet, he returns home after the war a hero and what does he do? — promptly enlists in the Army Reserve.

A classic American story. I think you will like it.

Respectfully,
Steven Burgauer
June 6, 2010
D-Day plus 66 years